Roots and Wings

Roots and Wings

POETRY FROM SPAIN 1900-1975

HARDIE ST. MARTIN, EDITOR

A Bilingual Anthology

Harper & Row, Publishers
New York, Hagerstown, San Francisco, London

Grateful acknowledgment is made to the authors and publishers of the poems appearing in this volume for permission to reprint their work.

SPANISH POEMS

The poems by LUIS CERNUDA appear with the permission of Ángel María Yanguas Cernuda, executor of the editorial estate of Luis Cernuda.

The poems by LEÓN FELIPE are from *Versos y oraciones de caminante, Ganaras la luz, Español del éxodo y del llanto, El payaso de las bofetadas y el pescador de caña*, all published by Finisterre Editores, Mexico, D.F.

Poems by FEDERICO GARCÍA LORCA are from *Selected Poems*, copyright 1954 by New Directions Publishing Corporation, New York, and *Obras completas*, copyright 1954 by Aguilar, S.A. de Ediciones, Madrid. Reprinted by permission of New Directions Publishing Corporation, publishers and agents for the Estate of Federico García Lorca.

The poems by MIGUEL HERNÁNDEZ appear with the permission of Josefina Manresa, vda. de Hernández.

The poems of JOSÉ LUIS HIDALGO appear with the permission of César Hidalgo Iglesias.

The poems by JUAN RAMÓN JIMÉNEZ appear with the permission of Herederos de Juan Ramón Jiménez.

The poems of ANTONIO MACHADO appear with the permission of Manual Alvarez de Lama, for the heirs of Antonio Machado.

The poems of EMILIO PRADOS appear with the permission of Carmen Balcells in representation of Jaime Salinas and Soledad Salinas.

The poems of MIGUEL DE UNAMUNO appear with the permission of Fernando de Unamuno.

Personal permission has been given by the following authors for the use of their poems reprinted here, all rights to which are reserved: RAFAEL ALBERTI, VICENTE ALEIXANDRE, CARLOS BOUSOÑO, FRANCISCO BRINES, GABRIEL CELAYA, GERARDO DIEGO, CONTINUED

FIRST EDITION

Designed by Gloria Adelson

Library of Congress Cataloging in Publication Data

Main entry under title:
Roots and wings.
    Includes bibliographical references.
    Includes index.
    1. Spanish poetry—Translations into English.
2. English poetry—Translations from Spanish.
3. Spanish poetry—20th century. I. St. Martin, Hardie.
PQ6267.E2 1976   861'.6'408   73-14293
ISBN 0-06-013976-5
ISBN 0-06-013981-1 pbk.

---

76 77 78 79 10 9 8 7 6 5 4 3 2 1

GLORIA FUERTES, JAIME GIL DE BIEDMA, ÁNGEL GONZALEZ, JORGE GUILLÉN, JOSÉ HIERRO, BLAS DE OTERO, CLAUDIO RODRÍGUEZ, LUIS ROSALES, CARLOS SAHAGÚN, JOSÉ ÁNGEL VALENTE, MANUEL VÁZQUEZ MONTALBÁN.

TRANSLATIONS

The American Poetry Review
  LEWIS HYDE: Vicente Aleixandre's "Man Doesn't Exist"
  MARK STRAND: Rafael Alberti's "The Coming Back of an Assassinated Poet"
Antaeus
  PHILIP LEVINE: Miguel Hernández's "Lullabies of the Onion"
Artes Hispánicas/Hispanic Arts
  HARDIE ST. MARTIN: José Ángel Valente's "Morning" and "The Evening Before"
Atheneum Publishers
  MARK STRAND: Rafael Alberti's "Going Back Through Color" from *The Owl's Insomnia*, translation copyright © 1973 by Mark Strand
  W. S. MERWIN: León Felipe's "Now I Am Going"; Juan Ramón Jiménez's "I Shall Run Through the Shadow"; Claudio Rodríguez's "Who Will Be My Friend Always"; Pedro Salinas's "Deaths," all from *Selected Translations, 1948–1968*, copyright © 1968 by W. S. Merwin
Beacon Press, for the following excerpts from *Selected Poems: Blas de Otero and Miguel Hernández*, copyright © 1971 by Robert Bly:
  TIMOTHY BALAND: Miguel Hernández's "To Smile with the Joyful Sadness of the Olive Tree"
  ROBERT BLY: Miguel Hernández's "I Have Plenty of Heart" and "Your Heart?—It Is a Frozen Orange"
  HARDIE ST. MARTIN: Blas de Otero's "About to Fall," "Chap. 10 Book II," "Far-Away," "Last Judgment," "The Cloister of the Shades," "The Eternal," "Censored." "Children of the Planet," "Something Like a" and "Written in Rain"; Miguel Hernández's "Each Time I Pass" and "Humming Eyelashes"
  JAMES WRIGHT: Miguel Hernández's "The Cemetery Lies Near" and "The Wounded Man"
Beacon Press, for the following excerpts from *Selected Poems: Lorca and Jiménez*, copyright © 1971 by Robert Bly:
  ROBERT BLY: Juan Ramón Jiménez's "A Remembrance Is Moving," "At First She Came to Me Pure," "Dawn Outside the City Walls," "Full Consciousness," "I Am Not I," "Intelligence, Give Me," "I Pulled on the Reins," "Oceans," "Road," "The Name Drawn from the Names" and "The Ship, Solid and Black"
Chicago Review
  WILLIAM STAFFORD with HERBERT BAIRD: Ángel González's "The Battlefield"
The Fifties
  ROBERT BLY: Antonio Machado's "From the Doorsill of a Dream They Called My Name"
Hawaii Review
  ROBERT BLY: Vicente Aleixandre's "It's Raining," "Life," "The Body and the Soul," and "The Waltz"
  LEWIS HYDE: Vicente Aleixandre's "The Old Man Is Like Moses"
Ironwood
  ROBERT BLY: Antonio Machado's "In the Fields,"
Kenyon Review
  WILLIAM STAFFORD with LILLIAN JEAN STAFFORD: Miguel de Unamuno's "It Is Night, in My Study"
Little, Brown and Company in association with The Atlantic Monthly Press
  JAMES WRIGHT: Jorge Guillén's "Nature Alive" and "I Want to Sleep," from *Cántico: A Selection by Jorge Guillén* edited by Norman Thomas di Giovanni, copyright © 1954, 1957, 1959, 1960, 1961, 1965 by Jorge Guillén and Norman Thomas di Giovanni
Malahat Review
  WILLIAM STAFFORD with HERBERT BAIRD: Vicente Aleixandre's "In Front of the Mir-

CONTINUED

ror"; Ángel González's "Summer in Slumville"; José Luis Hidalgo's "You Have to Go Down"

The Massachusetts Review
ROBERT BLY: Antonio Machado's "Memory from Childhood"

Michigan Quarterly Review
ROBERT BLY: Antonio Machado's "Clouds Ripped Open"; Miguel de Unamuno's "Throw Yourself Like Seed"

The Nation
ROBERT BLY: Antonio Machado's "For Don Francisco Giner de los Ríos"

New Directions Publishing Corporation
W. S. MERWIN: Federico García Lorca's "Gacela of an Unforseen Love"; and "Song of the Barren Orange Tree" and "The Little Mute Boy," from *The Selected Poems of Federico García Lorca*, copyright 1954 by New Directions Corporation

Poet Lore
CHARLES GUENTHER: Antonio Machado's "On the Bare Roadway" and "Tell Me if You Remember, Love"

The Seventies
ROBERT BLY: Antonio Machado's "It Doesn't Matter Now"

Translation
HARDIE ST. MARTIN: Luis Cernuda's "Impression of Exile"; Miguel de Unamuno's "The Delicately Sloping Neck"

Transpacific
TIMOTHY BALAND: Jaime Gil de Biedma's "In the Forties"

PHILIP LEVINE: Gloria Fuertes's "Birds Nest" and "Climbing"; Claudio Rodríguez's "Eugenio de Luelmo"

ROBERT MEZEY: Gabriel Celaya's "After a Native Poem from the Solomon Islands That Begins: 'Your Shameful Parts Are the White Man's Gramophone'" and "Poetry Is a Weapon Loaded with the Future"; Gloria Fuertes's "The Scrawny Women"; José Hierro's "Requiem"; Claudio Rodríguez's "Foam," "Petty Time" and "Sparrow"; Manuel Vázquez Montalbán's "Gauguin"

ROBERT MEZEY with HARDIE ST. MARTIN: Gabriel Celaya's "The Meaning of Soup" and "The Life One Leads"; Jaime Gil de Biedma's "Sad Night of October 1959"; Angel González's "Without Warning"; Carlos Sahagún's "Life in the Provinces"; José Ángel Valente's "With Plain Words"

Some material in the Introduction appeared in slightly different form in *Mosaic*, Vol. II, No. 4, Summer 1969 (University of Manitoba Press). The fragments quoted in the Introduction from Machado's foreword to the 1917 edition of *Soledades, galerías, y otras poemas* are taken from a translation by Robert Bly. All other quotations are Hardie St. Martin's translations.

Goya etching on title page courtesy of Bibliothèque Nationale, Paris.

Contents

Antonio Machado

León Felipe

Gerardo Diego

Federico García Lorca

Vicente Aleixandre

Rafael Alberti

Emilio Prados

Luis Rosales

Gabriel Celaya

Blas de Otero

Gloria Fuertes

José Luis Hidalgo

Ángel González

José Ángel Valente

Jaime Gil de Biedma

Claudio Rodríguez

Francisco Brines

EDITOR'S NOTE

The editor is grateful to the John Simon
Guggenheim Memorial Foundation for the
fellowship given him to study Spanish poetry
and to put together this anthology.

Introduction ≈∙

SEEING THE LIGHT OF THE PLANET

I

Miguel de Unamuno, Antonio Machado and Juan Ramón Jiménez, the first three poets in this anthology, blazed the paths that have led into all twentieth-century Spanish poetry. At the turn of the century, these poets found themselves at a crossroads, without clear signs ahead, and, looking back, their vision almost blocked by more than two hundred years of uninspired poetry. Azorín called this crossroads generation the Generation of '98, and in so doing, lumped together intellectuals and writers of different ages and ideas whose common denominator was their rebellious spirit and their determination to help Spain shake off her immediate past and pull herself together. Internal wrangling and corrupt and incompetent leadership in government had finally weakened her so much that the United States easily broke her will in the Spanish American War in 1898 and took her last colonies. Unamuno, Machado and Jiménez especially hated literary realism, positivism, middle-class morality, and the muddled politics of nineteenth-century Spain, and they were determined to cut all ties with the prosaic literature that surrounded them. This rupture was made easier by the arrival in Spain of the Nicaraguan poet Rubén Darío. His work was a fresh wind coming into the Spanish language. His arrival was decisive, showing the young Spaniards a way out through contemporary symbolism.

I say "young Spaniards," thinking of Machado and Jiménez, because Unamuno's ideas were not exactly young when his first book came out in 1907, and moreover, he made no bones about his thorough dislike for Darío's poetry, then at the peak of its popularity. He considered it decadent—like soda water, he said, that soon runs out of gas. In his own poems, he wanted something plainer than the frills of *modernismo*. He believed that the poet should think and feel and express himself like a man, as naturally and simply as possible.

I

In Antonio Machado's earliest poetry, there are signs that he was tempted by Darío's work, for which he expressed considerable respect. But he got his own bearings quickly and went off on a very different road, a road into his own interior landscape, saying that "I thought that the substance of poetry does not lie in the sound-value of the word, nor in its color, nor in a complex of sensations but in the deep pulse of the spirit; and this deep pulse is what the soul contributes, if it contributes anything, or what it says, if it says anything, with its own voice. . . ." He wanted to catch "some of the phrases of his inward conversations with himself, distinguishing the living voice from the dead echoes. . . ." He believed as well that the poet must stay in touch with his time, and demonstrated this belief by turning outward in his later book of poems, *Campos de Castilla*, which is among other things a bitter commentary on the provincialism of his country, which had for so long held itself in isolation from the rest of the world. But Machado always kept coming back to his intuitive poems full of sudden flashes of his own deep, mysterious world.

Juan Ramón Jiménez temperamentally was closer to Darío and stayed with his work longer, but he too started working away from him and eventually shook off what he called his "acute" *modernismo*. Like Machado, he began to cut away the rhetoric of the nineteenth century and the new rhetoric of *modernismo* until he found the simplicity he was looking for. Machado tried to write in the ordinary tone of spoken Castilian, insisting on it all his life. Jiménez, on the other hand, looked for a new language, feeling that "if you do invent words, they should be words used in the normal conversation of the spirit, so that they will not sound new to the ear." This invented language is the most valuable thing to survive from his impressionistic phase, which ended around 1916. With *Eternidades* and *Diario de un poeta recién casado* we begin to get the best Jiménez. In his search for *naked* poetry, he had absorbed symbolism and made it his own. At the same time, he had gone back through Bécquer to Góngora and other poets of Spain's Golden Age, clearing the ground for the Generation of '27. (This was one of the names given to the poets of Lorca's generation.)

In the meantime, some of the older diehards of Jiménez's generation and many of the less resourceful younger poets could not altogether resist the threadbare hand-me-downs of *modernismo*, which had become a kind of thrift shop that refused to close down. At least one poet managed to stay away from it: León Felipe was a late-comer to poetry, as was Unamuno, whom he resembles in other ways. For Felipe "A poem is a cry in the dark, a psalm," and the poet is a prophet. He attacks the modern poet, who has dropped this ancient role, and accuses him of being in league with the bishop and the politician, who are responsible for the world's agony, warning that

> Some day man will see
> the entire light of this planet
> through the window of a tear. . . .

He was not to come into his own till years later, after the Spanish Civil War, World War II and the endless man-made misery everywhere had given meaning to his terrifying prophecy.

To the brilliant cluster of young poets who dominated the 20s and the first half of the 30s, it is the poem, not the poet, that is sacred. The poet simply offers the precious thing he has discovered through hard work: the poem itself. Each of these poets would probably have applauded what Lorca said of himself: "If it's true that I'm a poet by the grace of God—or of the devil—, it's also true that I'm a poet by the grace of technique and hard work. . . ." This high esteem for the poem comes, principally, from Juan Ramón Jiménez, who was technically much more interesting than Unamuno and Machado, and whose indifference to extraliterary events appealed to the younger poets. This concentration on the interior of the poem is a part of most important European art immediately following World War I.

After the war, there was relief and the infectious feeling that something new was just around the corner to distract Europeans from the recent horrors. All the avant-garde movements of those years insisted on the autonomy of the poem and of the metaphor, which they regarded as the poem's core. Refusing to accept the old visions of what was real, these poets transformed the real to suit themselves, more often than not distorting it, for the sake of shock effect. Thus we see Gerardo Diego trying, in his creationist poems, for effects similar to those of cubist painting, piling on metaphors with no apparent logic, or simply arranging them pictorially on the page. Gerardo Diego was the only systematic Spanish creationist but some of the others, notably Lorca and Alberti, still in their formative stage, caught the irreverent and playful mood of ultraism and creationism* and were infected by the exaggerated passion for metaphor current at the time.

The new experimental writing encouraged the poets to try fresh, sometimes unusual, subjects, to loosen up their style and make their form more elastic. They took everything they could use from the avant-garde movements and, combining this with traditional materials, came up with a poetry that was surprisingly both fresh and Spanish. Each of the "poets of '27" responded in a personal way to influences they all sometimes shared, and each developed his own distinctive style. Points of contact in their poetry were the inevitable ones that exist among poets whose gifts reach maturity at approximately the same time in the same environment. In addition, there have always been two mainstreams of Spanish poetry, Andalusian and Castilian, and there is a strong difference, even in these years, between the work of poets from the south and those from Castile, in the north.

The Castilians, Pedro Salinas and Jorge Guillén, were a few years older than most of the others. When they started to publish, their styles were already so well developed and their work so objective that Ortega y Gasset's reference to "dehumanized art," only a half-truth to begin with, seemed ready-made for them, although it was applied indiscriminately to the whole group. Because of the Castilian air of reserve, other critics accused them of a lack of realism and humanity, of keeping their feelings under wraps even in love poems. Many readers were put off by this, or felt left out. Both Salinas and Guillén sometimes gave the impression that they were all alone with their thoughts and wished to remain that way. Their poems were about real things, but the poems seemed to embody some sort of distance between the poet and his audience, or even between the poet and his subject. Salinas' love poems are among the most beautiful love poems of his time, yet sometimes his

---

* Ultraism, like dada, attacked the structure of the poem. Its only connection with creationism, whose founder was the Chilean poet Vicente Huidobro, was its emphasis on metaphor. Creationism held that since there is no substitute for experience, metaphor itself has to become the experience.

feelings don't seem very strong. He often sets a distance between himself and the beloved. His love seems to grow stronger as she moves away from him. She is a real woman, but often only a step away from fading into abstraction. The cool approach of these two poets threw off the reader; yet both were trying to make their experience more immediate and accessible by suppressing distracting elements such as anecdote and description. Guillén takes the method further than Salinas, into a kind of poetic shorthand, omitting connectives and figures of speech that would slow down the poem. He relies on certain key words to carry the weight of the emotion. The effect of all this is to create a kind of transparent covering that preserves the poet's feelings; penetrating it demanded a fiercer attention than new readers were prepared to give. With time, the strangeness of these two poets, which short-sighted readers mistook for obscurity, wore off and their work has since attracted an enthusiastic readership.

None of the poets of this generation submerged themselves in poetic instinct and imagination as much as Lorca and Alberti. Both were Andalusians and they were the first poets of the group to reach a comparatively wide audience, partly because they wrote poems that passed quickly and easily into the popular tradition of ballads and songs. The ordinary people sing a wide variety of such songs in Andalusia, where it has been the favorite poetry since the time of the Arab occupation. Perhaps no other people love their popular or folk songs as much as Spaniards do; Lorca's and Alberti's audiences quickly adjusted to the spontaneity of their songs. Country singers are still singing their lyrics today, many of them having no idea where the songs came from. Alberti tells us that the first things that made his eyes light up, as a child, were "the salt of the saltflats, sails and the outspread wings of seagulls." In his early poems, there are great lyric speed and childish happiness. By contrast, in Lorca, even his earliest and shortest pieces have some of the compelling dramatic fiber of his later poems and plays. They resonate with fear and loneliness and mystery—experiences that Andalusians do not reject. The light that pulls us into them is the moonlight brooding on the giant bodies of the mountains, picking out a solitary figure in the empty landscape, or it is sunlight following long empty roads. Alberti's songs are as elegant and graceful as the dances of the south, while Lorca's note strikes deeper, resembling the rising cry and sinking moan of the *cante jondo*. Of the other three Andalusians, only Emilio Prados did much with the ballad tradition, but the poems of all of them share some of the secretiveness, the graceful phrasing, and the sensuality of the medieval Arabic-Andalusian poetry, and of the anonymous country songs.

The celebration in Madrid, in 1927, of the third centenary of Góngora's death, featuring Gongoristic poems, essays and lectures, and even a requiem Mass with catafalque, was an instance of the interior unity of this generation of poets. In the three hundred years since he had lived, Góngora had gradually become a curiosity in the history of Spanish literature. By giving him critical acclaim, the young poets were defending the mysteriousness of their own poetry and at the same time showing disrespect for a society that liked poems to reflect middle-class values. The poets seemed closer than ever now, writing poems in the forms Góngora loved. But their acts of homage also turned out to be a kind of farewell to each other. After this moment of disciplined Gongorism, poetry relaxes again and the gaps between the individual poets begin to widen. Salinas and Guillén remained loyal to symbolism, but within two or three years, the Andalusian poets were starting to find symbolism insufficient to bring up certain subterranean associations from the subconscious, and worthless as a way of facing social reality.

Explaining why he took up surrealism, Cernuda declared that it was not merely a literary fashion—it was a rebellion against society. Its revolutionary spirit appealed to the Andalusians dissatisfied with a decaying Spain. They turned to surrealism, in fact, almost at the same time the world Depression came forward, around 1929 and 1930. Surrealism had a double purpose: to probe the subconscious and the chaos there, and to attack the middle-class society's definitions of what is real. The Spanish poets used it as a weapon. It in turn allowed their imagination more free play and expanded their consciousness. These poets worked at it systematically, and they carried it in a direction different from the French, incorporating it into the already rich sensuousness of Spanish poetry. Although the Spanish poets make frequent visits to the Freudian world of dreams, they, unlike the French surrealists, had no interest in automatic writing, and they imposed their will on the structure of the poem, holding it together with strong threads of logic. They use surrealism primarily to express what is floating up from the unconscious, to put new states of mind into words and to make new associations possible.

Some of the best work of this generation leaned toward surrealism, but except for Aleixandre and Cernuda, who for a while deeply explored its possibilities, the poets in general practiced it with some reservations. Neither Alberti's *Sobre los ángeles* nor Lorca's attack on the brutality of U.S. industrialized society in *Poeta en Nueva York* is entirely surrealist. Aleixandre, by contrast, in *Espadas como labios, Pasión de la tierra, La destrucción o el amor,* and Luis Cernuda, in *Un río un amor* and *Los placeres prohibidos,* went far into it, cultivating surrealism as a means of self-discovery and to keep alive an imaginative reality opposed to scientific reality. Speaking for himself, Cernuda explains that, before it could turn into formula, he—and he could have added Aleixandre's name to his— dropped surrealism and went on to a different kind of poetry, plainer in language, more relaxed and more human.

There probably have never been in recent times so many great and distinguished poets living and working in the same place, at the same time, each one different from the others, as there were in Spain in the 20s. I can't go into all the variety of their poetry in those years nor into the later work of the poets of this generation who survived the civil war, much of it powerful. I am simply trying to indicate the general flow of Spanish poetry in this century and to give the reader a rough idea of how each generation has absorbed or refused the practices of the earlier poets and worked out its own way. This fantastic flowering of poetry in Spain was destroyed by the Fascist uprising of the mid-30s. Poets were thrown into exile or kept in silence at home. It wasn't until the middle of the 40s that poetry began to come alive once more in Spain.

2

The poets who started to write in the years immediately preceding the war took as their model the sixteenth-century poet

Garcilaso de la Vega. They put most of their poetry into tight little sonnets. Luis Rosales was considered the most important of these poets, who were called *garcilasistas*, and also the first to ease his way out into a more flexible poetry. Miguel Hernández belonged to this age group and was to become the greatest of them.

A few months before the civil war, Hernández published *El rayo que no cesa*, which brought him admiring words from older writers like Juan Ramón Jiménez and José Ortega y Gasset, the philosopher. There is a ritualistic quality in the sound and movement of these poems about love and death, and they are very moving, but the sonnet seems too intricate a form for him. Even before this book was published, Hernández, partly under the influence of Neruda and Aleixandre, was writing looser and longer poems. When the civil war came, in which he took part in the trenches against the Franco forces, the elegaic note deepened and the grief in his poems was no longer only for individual people but for Spain herself. His war books are strong and uneven. His last poems, written in various jails while he was dying of tuberculosis, are sad and tender, filled with longing for his wife and baby son.

By the end of 1939, Miguel Hernández was in prison; Unamuno, Antonio Machado and García Lorca were dead; Jiménez, León Felipe, Salinas, Guillén, Alberti, Prados and Cernuda in exile. The only poet of major importance who remained in Spain was Vicente Aleixandre, and he was not allowed to publish a book again until 1944. The *garcilasistas* returned to their old haunts. One of the later poets of the 1950s, José Agustín Goytisolo, in a poem called "Los celestiales" (The Heavenly Ones), described all the postwar poets getting together and deciding to write

> lovely poems, empty, yes, but resonant,
> like a lute filled with a melody
> that can lay our minds to sleep,
> altering them, making them calm down. . . .

Goytisolo goes on to imagine one of them later suddenly deciding that the reason the country hadn't improved was because their sweet-smelling elegies had not softened God's heart, and so "God took the place/of their old father, Garcilaso."

For three young poets, Blas de Otero, Hidalgo and Bousoño,

God was important beyond fashions of literature. In José Luis Hidalgo's *Los muertos* God stands over the poems like a shadow. Blas de Otero's early poetry is religious, embodying some terrifying upheaval that seems to have brought him close to death. He is searching for God till

> . . . Mist bleeds from my hands,
> they crashed into the steep face of rocks, into cliffs,
> they opened, turned into running sores of the infinite,
> but it was no use: You escaped.

Carlos Bousoño's religious poetry has sensuous and sometimes violent imagery also. At one point, for instance, as he calls out to God, he compares himself to a lion calling his mate, snapping at the air (invisible God) to catch and bite her passionately. His later work is calmer, but still metaphysical and far from "realistic."

In 1944 Dámaso Alonso, a member of Aleixandre's generation, whose importance had lain in his criticism till then, brought out a book of poems, *Hijos de la ira* (*Sons of Wrath*), that poured new life into Spanish poetry. One of the poems begins:

> Madrid is a city of more than a million corpses
> (according to the latest statistics) . . .

He brought into the open things that millions of Spaniards spend a great deal of time trying not to say out loud. His sprawling verse better suited his realistic themes than the old forms, and his language, sometimes prosy and coarse, had a powerful impact on the poets beginning to write in the 40s.

Alberti and Hernández had also written some very rough poetry during the war, attacking the people who stood for death. But the defeat of the Republic ended this—Alberti was in exile, Hernández in prison—until Alonso's *Sons of Wrath* sparked off a new social poetry. It became a poetry of fraternity with the poor, with suffering Spain. The aftereffects of the civil war—repression, injustice, poverty—entered the poems. The most militant poets were Victoriano Crémer and Eugenio de Nora, cofounders of a literary review, *Espadaña*, but Blas de Otero, José Hierro and Gabriel Celaya wrote the best poems. Otero began to fill the emptiness God had left in him with love for his fellow man. With *Ángel fieramente humano*, he emerged as the greatest of the protest poets. Hierro at one point said: "I'm incapable of writing without suffering, it's as if my skin were being stripped off in pieces, hurting, in order to discover what's underneath." When he talks of his private experiences, the faults of the society around him become visible, perhaps more clearly than in dogmatic poets who are not personal. His work always has a deep personal note.

3

Although most of the poets who began to write in the middle of the 1950s had respect for Celaya, Otero and Hierro, they accepted historical or critical realism with some misgivings, after a first impulse to swallow it whole. These poets had been too young for active participation in the war—the exception is a woman, Gloria Fuertes—and could look at the war and its ruins with a colder eye than their elders. This stance is particularly evident in Ángel González, José Ángel Valente, Jaime Gil de Biedma and Carlos Sahagún. In their work, the narrative, the autobiographical poem, for instance, are carryovers from their immediate seniors, and they go back again and again to the period of their childhood during or right after the Spanish Civil War; however, the attitude toward it has changed. Since they view it from a greater distance than the older group, with whom they still have in common the tendency to protest, their poetry can be more reflective and more objective about the early postwar years. The militancy of the older writers meanwhile had died down. Their work had met virtually no response at all. The country seemed more conservative than ever. Seeing this and the futility of so many things around him, Ángel González says, in "Preamble to a Silence," that there are times when there's no use speaking up. Bite your nails, tear a matchbox to shreds, spit, bang your fist into house walls but you may as well not say a thing.

> Angel,
> they call me,
> and I jump to my feet
> disciplined and stiff
> with my wings bitten off

—I mean my nails—
and I smile and hold my tongue because in the long run
I understand
how useless all words are.

This does not mean that González is giving up, it simply means let's calm down, there's no sense yelling yourself hoarse any more, when there are other important things to do—like writing well. That is something this group of poets will try to do. Valente has risked and perhaps gained more than any of the poets his age. He has tried out different styles, always intelligently though not always with the same success, and he has always taken great pains with language. The protest in his voice is low-keyed but strong, when he says,

you tell me
that words are not enough
to make us free.
I answer you
that we don't know yet
how far in time or place
a word can go,
who will pick it up, what mouth
with sufficient faith
to give it its true form.

The message is only as important as the word itself. These poets have not lost sight of their time or their place in it, but they have regained the sense of balance their immediate predecessors, with exceptions like Otero and Hierro, had lost, and they insist on the need to use language with care and precision. There was less pressure to contend with and more time for expression and structure, without the necessity to return to the formalism invalidated by Dámaso Alonso's breakthrough. And yet, in most of their work, it's clear that these young poets feel uncomfortable in their country.

An important poet of this new ironic consciousness is Jaime Gil de Biedma, whose poems outgrew their ties with social realism and gradually came to verge on the confessional. He focuses his irony on himself, already partway into middle age, dogged by an eroticism he examines with pleasure and sometimes playfully laughs off, as if it embarrassed him. Gloria Fuertes also takes herself as the target of her own humor and mockery. Resentment at Spain's condition is still there, but it is softened by a touch of humor, and there's more pity for the underdog than anger for those at the top. The dominant note in her poems is an overwhelming sense of being cut off from others. There's a self-conscious loneliness under all the humor in her last book, whose revealing title is *Sola en la sala* (Alone in the Room).

One might say a last word about Francisco Brines and Claudio Rodríguez in this connection. Brines is touched by the spiritual and physical decay he sees around him, by passing years and the shadow of death. He is a solitary taken up with himself. Claudio Rodríguez, on the other hand, is alive to the world and embraces everything around him. His gaze flows like a stream, never static, picking up "the harmonious madness of the world/in its rapid waters. . . ." Poetry is above all a way of getting close to the world, learning to know it. The morning light banked on the mountains, clouds, foam, birds, girls on their way to school, wise old men, friends, strangers and even

> Those streets
> whose prows have dug in deep, with their decrepit habit
> of lonely poverty,
> of frayed arrogance, like fingernails
> that hang on to nothing
> except an incurable rotting bone.

4

José María Castellet put together in 1970 a controversial anthology, *Nueve novísimos*, gathering nine of the most outstanding young poets who had started writing in the 1960s. Manuel Vázquez Montalbán is among them, though perhaps closer to the poets just discussed than to the other poets in Castellet's anthology. His interest in worldwide politics and economics, which is reflected in his work, and his disrespect for the society he lives in place him in the line of the older poets. Vázquez Montalbán attacks our consumer society by using against it the very thing that helped entrench it— the language of mass media, of movies, television, newspapers and magazines, advertising, etc. He sings the death of false popular myths and symbols, and the complacent reality that has been falling apart not only in Spain but here in the United States also. The other *novísimos*, especially Pedro Gimferrer, Guillermo Carnero and Félix de Azúa, keep their language artificial, and their poetry is often about literature or literary subjects, paintings, distant points in history and exotic places, as in the elegant poetry that saturated American literature in the fifties. These most recent poets were disparagingly referred to, not long after they started out, as the "Venetian school" because of their ornamentation and evocation of a baroque past; or accused of "Marienbadism" because of dreamlike situations in poems that seem to move in circles.

It is too early to tell what will happen to them. Public declarations and articles by some of these poets indicate they have been reconsidering their overemphasis on estheticism and their neglect of content and firsthand experience in their poems. There is a lot of talent among them and several have written brilliant poems. They are already moving out of a static transition, in which they were initially bogged down by their rejection of the social realism of most of the postwar poets. Work comparable in quality to some of the best of their elders' can safely be expected of them.

An anthology of foreign poetry basically has to choose between being a larger selection exclusively in English translation, or a smaller selection with the original poems present. I chose the second. I think it is important to experience the poem in Spanish; also it is possible to check the accuracy of the translation against the original. By insisting on a bilingual edition, I cut the space in half and consequently had to sacrifice some highly respected poets, among them Manuel Machado, José Moreno Villa, Manuel Altolaguirre, Leopoldo Panero, Lorenzo Gómiz and Vicente Gaos. All the poems in this book were translated by American poets and translators with whom I worked closely, and we have tried to make the poems as accurate and as natural in English as we could. A few poems originally chosen defeated their translators and were left out. What we have representing each Spanish poet are the poems of his that were best able to stand on their own feet in English.

HARDIE ST. MARTIN

ES DE NOCHE, EN MI ESTUDIO

Es de noche, en mi estudio.
Profunda soledad; oigo el latido
de mi pecho agitado
—es que se siente sólo,
y es que se siente blanco de mi mente—
y oigo a la sangre
cuyo leve susurro
llena el silencio.
Diríase que cae el hilo líquido
de la clepsidra al fondo.
Aquí, de noche, solo, este es mi estudio;
los libros callan;
mi lámpara de aceite
baña en lumbre de paz estas cuartillas,
lumbre cual de sagrario;
los libros callan;
de los poetas, pensadores, doctos,
los espíritus duermen;
y ello es como si en torno me rondase
cautelosa la muerte.
Me vuelvo a ratos para ver si acecha,
escudriño lo oscuro,
trato de descubrir entre las sombras
su sombra vaga,
pienso en la angina;
pienso en mi edad viril; de los cuarenta
pasé ha dos años.
Es una tentación dominadora
que aquí, en la soledad, es el silencio
quien me la asesta;

IT IS NIGHT, IN MY STUDY

It is night, in my study.
The deepest solitude; I hear the steady
shudder in my breast
—for it feels all alone,
and blanched by my mind—
and I hear my blood
with even murmur
fill up the silence.
You might say the thin stream
falls in the waterclock and fills the bottom.
Here, in the night, all alone, this is my study;
the books don't speak;
my oil lamp
bathes these pages in a light of peace,
light of a chapel.
The books don't speak;
of the poets, the meditators, the learned,
the spirits drowse;
and it is as if around me circled
cautious death.
I turn at times to see if it waits,
I search the dark,
I try to discern among the shadows
its thin shadow,
I think of heart failure,
think about my strong age; since my fortieth year
two more have passed.
Toward a looming temptation
here, in the solitude, the silence turns me—

el silencio y las sombras.
Y me digo: "Tal vez cuando muy pronto
vengan para anunciarme
que me espera la cena,
encuentren aquí un cuerpo
pálido y frío
—la cosa que fuí yo, éste que espera—,
como esos libros silencioso y yerto,
parada ya la sangre,
yeldándose en las venas,
el pecho silencioso
bajo la dulce luz del blando aceite,
lámpara funeraria."
Tiemblo de terminar estos renglones
que no parezcan
extraño testamento,
más bien presentimiento misterioso
del allende sombrío,
dictados por el ansia
de vida eterna.
Los terminé y aún vivo.

the silence and the shadows.
And I tell myself: "Perhaps when soon
they come to tell me
that supper awaits,
they will discover a body here
pallid and cold
—the thing that I was, this one who waits—
just like those books quiet and rigid,
the blood already stopped,
jelling in the veins,
the chest silent
under the gentle light of the soothing oil,
a funeral lamp.
I tremble to end these lines
that they do not seem
an unusual testament,
but rather a mysterious message
from the shade beyond,
lines dictated by the anxiety
of eternal life.
I finished them and yet I live on.

TRANSLATED BY WILLIAM STAFFORD
AND LILLIAN JEAN STAFFORD

¡SIÉMBRATE!

Sacude la tristeza y tu ánimo recobra,
no quieto mires de la fortuna la rueda
como gira al pasar rozando tu vereda,
que a quien quiere vivir vida es lo que le sobra.

No haces sino nutrir esa mortal zozobra
que así en las redes del morir lento te enreda,
pues vivir es obrar y lo único que queda
la obra es; echa, pues, mano a la obra.

Ve sembrándote al paso y con tu propio arado
sin volver la vista que es volverla a la muerte,
y no a lo por andar sea peso lo andado.

En los surcos lo vivo, en ti deja lo inerte,
pues la vida no pasa al paso de un nublado;
de tus obras podrás un día recojerte.

THROW YOURSELF LIKE SEED

Shake off this sadness, and recover your spirit;
sluggish you will never see the wheel of fate
that brushes your heel as it turns going by,
the man who wants to live is the man in whom life is abundant.

Now you are only giving food to that final pain
which is slowly winding you in the nets of death,
but to live is to work, and the only thing which lasts
is the work; start then, turn to the work.

Throw yourself like seed as you walk, and into your own field,
don't turn your face for that would be to turn it to death,
and do not let the past weigh down your motion.

Leave what's alive in the furrow, what's dead in yourself,
for life does not move in the same way as a group of clouds;
from your work you will be able one day to gather yourself.

TRANSLATED BY ROBERT BLY

JUNTO A LA LAGUNA DEL CRISTO, EN LA ALDEHUELA DE YELTES, UNA NOCHE DE LUNA LLENA

Noche blanca en que el agua cristalina
duerme queda en su lecho de laguna
sobre la cual redonda llena luna
que ejército de estrellas encamina

vela, y se espeja una redonda encina
en el espejo sin rizada alguna;
noche blanca en que el agua hace de cuna
de la más alta y más honda doctrina.

Es un rasgón del cielo que abrazado
tiene en sus brazos la Naturaleza;
es un rasgón del cielo que ha posado

y en el silencio de la noche reza
la oración del amante resignado
sólo al amor, que es su única riqueza.

BESIDE CHRIST'S LAKE
IN ALDEHUELA DE YELTES,
ON A NIGHT WITH A FULL MOON

White night in which the transparent water
sleeps quietly in its bed in the lake,
the round full moon is watching over it now,
and leading out an army of stars;

and a round oak sees its own image
in the mirror without any blurring—
white night in which the water becomes the cradle
of the highest and most profound thought.

The water is a piece of the sky which the green world
is holding passionately in its arms;
it is a piece of the sky which has descended

and in the silence of the night it is saying
the prayer the lover says who is resigned
to owning love, which is the only wealth he has.

TRANSLATED BY ROBERT BLY

EN UN CEMENTERIO
DE LUGAR CASTELLANO

Corral de muertos, entre pobres tapias,
hechas también de barro,
pobre corral donde la hoz no siega,
sólo una cruz, en el desierto campo
señala tu destino.

Junto a esas tapias buscan el amparo
del hostigo del cierzo las ovejas
al pasar trashumantes en rebaño,
y en ellas rompen de la vana historia,
como olas, los rumores vanos.

Como un islote en junio,
te ciñe al mar dorado
de las espigas que a la brisa ondean,
y canta sobre ti la alondra el canto
de la cosecha.

Cuando baja en la lluvia el cielo al campo
baja también sobre la santa yerba
donde la hoz no corta,
de tu rincón, ¡pobre corral de muertos!,
y sienten en sus huesos el reclamo
del riego de la vida.

Salvan tus cercas de mampuesto y barro
las aladas semillas,
o te las llevan con piedad los pájaros,
y crecen escondidas amapolas,
clavelinas, magarzas, brezos, cardos,
entre arrumbadas cruces,
no más de que las aves libres pasto.

IN A CASTILIAN GRAVEYARD

Sheep yard of the dead, between poor walls,
also made of clay,
poor yard where the scythe doesn't reap,
only a cross, in the deserted fields,
shows what you are.

Near those walls the sheep look for shelter
from the lash of the north wind
as they pass in a flock like nomads,
and the worthless noise of worthless history
breaks like surf on the walls.

Like a barren island in June,
you are surrounded by the golden sea
of grain waving in the breeze,
and above you the lark sings a song
of the harvest.

When heaven falls in rain on the fields
it also falls on the holy grass
of your corner, which the scythe doesn't cut,
poor yard of the dead!,
and in their bones they feel the call
of the life-giving waters.

The winged seeds
cross over your walls of rubble and clay,
or the merciful birds bring them to you,
and hidden poppies,
carnations, camomile, heather, and thistles
grow among the fallen crosses,
only a feeding-ground for birds.

Cavan tan sólo en tu maleza brava,
corral sagrado,
para de un alma que sufrió en el mundo
sembrar el grano;
luego, sobre esa siembra,
¡barbecho largo!

Cerca de ti el camino de los vivos,
no como tú, con tapias, no cercado,
por donde van y vienen,
ya riendo o llorando,
¡rompiendo con sus risas o sus lloros
el silencio inmortal de tu cercado!

Después que lento el sol tomó ya tierra,
y sube al cielo el páramo
a la hora del recuerdo,
al toque de oraciones y descanso,
la tosca cruz de piedra
de tus tapias de barro
queda, como guardián que nunca duerme,
de la campiña el sueño vigilando.

No hay cruz sobre la iglesia de los vivos,
en torno de la cual duerme el poblado;
la cruz, cual perro fiel, ampara el sueño
de los muertos al cielo acorralados.
¡Y desde el cielo de la noche, Cristo,
el Pastor Soberano,
con infinitos ojos centelleantes,
recuenta las ovejas del rebaño!

¡Pobre corral de muertos entre tapias
hechas del mismo barro,
sólo una cruz distingue tu destino
en la desierta soledad del campo!

Sacred sheep yard,
they only dig in your strong thicket
when a soul that suffered in the world
is buried as grain;
then, for a long time, the ground lies fallow
over this seed.

The road of the living is near you
but not like you, with your walls, not enclosed.
Along it they come and go,
sometimes laughing or weeping,
breaking the endless silence of your fold
with their laughter or their crying.

After the sun has slowly come to earth,
and the desert rises to the sky
in the hour of remembrance,
at the tolling for prayers and rest,
the rough stone cross
on your clay walls
stands like a guardian that never sleeps,
watching over the sleep of the fields.

There is no cross over the church of the living,
around which the town sleeps;
the cross, like a faithful dog, protects the sleep
of the dead, who are penned up in heaven.
And from the night sky, Christ,
the king of shepherds,
with infinite glimmering eyes,
counts the sheep of the flock again!

Poor sheep yard of the dead between walls
made of the same clay,
only a cross shows your purpose
in the solitude of the bare fields.

TRANSLATED BY DONALD HALL

Fragmento de EL CRISTO YACENTE DE SANTA CLARA (IGLESIA DE LA CRUZ) EN PALENCIA

Este Cristo español que no ha vivido,
negro como el mantillo de la tierra,
yace cual la llanura,
horizontal, tendido,
sin alma y sin espera,
con los ojos cerrados cara al cielo
avaro en lluvia y que los panes quema.
Y aun con sus negros pies de garra de águila
querer parece aprisionar la tierra.

¡O es que Dios penitente acaso quiso
para purgar de culpa su conciencia
por haber hecho al hombre, y con el hombre
la maldad y la pena,
vestido de este andrajo miserable,
gustar muerte terrena!

La piedad popular ve que las uñas
y el cabello le medran,
de la vida lo córneo, lo duro,
supersticiones secas,
lo que araña, y aquello de que se ase
la segada cabeza.

La piedad maternal de aquellas pobres
hijas de Santa Clara le cubriera
con faldillas de blanca seda y oro
las hediondas vergüenzas,
aunque el zurrón de huesos y de podre
no es ni varón ni hembra;
que este Cristo español sin sexo alguno,
más allá yace de esa diferencia
que es el trágico nudo de la historia,
pues este Cristo de mi tierra es tierra.

From THE DEAD CHRIST LYING
IN THE CHURCH OF SANTA CLARA
(CHURCH OF THE CROSS) IN PALENCIA

This Spanish Christ that hasn't lived,
black as the dung-ripened fields,
lies like an immense plain,
horizontal, packed down,
without soul, without hope,
with closed eyes, his face to the sky
that hoards its rain and scorches our bread.
And with his black feet, hooked like an eagle's,
he seems to want still to imprison the earth.

Or perhaps God, penitent,
dressed in this miserable rag,
wanted to taste the death of this world,
in order to flush his conscience of guilt
for having made man, and with man
evil and pain.

Popular superstition imagines that his nails
and hair bring in
from this life the callused, the shelled,
dry superstitions,
whatever he scratches up, whatever he binds around
his harvested head.

This motherly piety of the poor daughters
of Santa Clara has skirted
with cloth of white silk and gold
the repulsive privates,
although this pouch of bones and pus
is neither male nor female;
this Spanish Christ without sex
lies far beyond that difference
that is the tragic knot of history,
for this Christ is ground of my ground.

TRANSLATED BY PHILIP LEVINE

LA NEVADA ES SILENCIOSA

La nevada es silenciosa,
cosa lenta;
poco a poco y con blandura
reposa sobre la tierra
y cobija a la llanura.
Posa la nieve callada
blanca y leve;
la nevada no hace ruido;
cae como cae el olvido,
copo a copo.
Abriga blanda a los campos
cuando el hielo los hostiga;
con sus lampos de blancura;
cubre a todo con su capa
pura, silenciosa;
no se le escapa en el suelo
cosa alguna.
Donde cae allí se queda
leda y leve,
pues la nieve no resbala
como resbala la lluvia,
sino queda y cala.
Flores del cielo los copos,
blancos lirios de las nubes,
que en el suelo se ajan,
bajan floridos,
pero quedan pronto
derretidos;
florecen sólo en la cumbre,
sobre las montañas,
pesadumbre de la tierra,
y en sus entrañas perecen.
Nieve, blanda nieve,
la que cae tan leve
sobre la cabeza,

THE SNOWFALL IS SO SILENT

The snowfall is so silent,
so slow,
bit by bit, with delicacy
it settles down on the earth
and covers over the fields.
The silent snow comes down
white and weightless;
snowfall makes no noise,
falls as forgetting falls,
flake after flake.
It covers the fields gently
while frost attacks them
with its sudden flashes of white;
covers everything with its pure
and silent covering;
not one thing on the ground
anywhere escapes it.
And wherever it falls it stays,
content and gay,
for snow does not slip off
as rain does,
but it stays and sinks in.
The flakes are skyflowers,
pale lilies from the clouds,
that wither on earth.
They come down blossoming
but then so quickly
they are gone;
they bloom only on the peak,
above the mountains,
and make the earth feel heavier
when they die inside.
Snow, delicate snow,
that falls with such lightness
on the head,

sobre el corazón,
ven y abriga mi tristeza
la que descansa en razón.

QUÉ SILENCIO BAJO TIERRA

¡Qué silencio bajo tierra
al pie del negro ciprés!
El gemido de las olas
daba al silencio mudez,
y tiritaba la yerba,
¡qué verdura en desnudez!,
y con rocío marino
se empañaba la azulez.
La paz con sus alas muertas
cubría al mundo otra vez.
Sombras, íbanse recuerdos
derritiéndose...

CORAZÓN NEGRO CON ALAS

Corazón negro con alas
de fuego y presas a tierra,
hundido entre los trigales
que al viento de Dios se pliegan.

Amapola soñadora,
rizo de la luz, esperas
a la hoz que tus ensueños
segará en la sementera.

on the feelings,
come and cover over the sadness
that lies always in my reason.

TRANSLATED BY ROBERT BLY

HOW QUIET UNDER THE EARTH

How quiet under the earth
at the foot of the black cypress.
The moans of the waves
stopped the mouth of the silence,
the grass shivered
—all that green nakedness!—
and the blue air steamed
with spindrift.
Peace with its dead wings
covered the earth again.
Shadows, lost memories
becoming each other . . .

TRANSLATED BY PHILIP LEVINE

BLACK HEART

Black heart with wings of fire
pinned to the earth, submerged
in the wheatfields
that ripple in God's wind.

Poppy, daydreamer, ruffle
of light, you are waiting
for the sickle to come and reap
your dreams in the seedbed.

TRANSLATED BY HARDIE ST. MARTIN

LA COMBA LÁNGUIDA

La comba lánguida
del cuello de la espiga;
dóranse al sol los granos,
brúñelos la brisa
a la que cierne
su cabellera erguida.
Soñando cabecea,
soñando el lecho de la trilla,
y soñando la muela
que hace la harina,
y soñando la masa ya lluda
de pan de vida,
pan que hace mano,
y soñando la mano que echa semilla.

LEYENDO EL "JOURNAL" DE JULES RENARD

Una gota de rocío
cuajada en tela de araña,
al nacer el sol la sorbe,
¡es la eternidad que pasa!
y un diamante que a la puesta
las hebras del sol destrenza,
y en arco iris las tiñe
el momento que se queda.

THE DELICATELY SLOPING NECK

The delicately sloping neck
of the head of wheat—
the grains are turning yellow in the sun
and the light wind, in which it shakes out
its lifted hair,
is polishing them.
The head nods as it dreams,
dreaming of the thresher's bed,
of the grindstone
that makes the flour,
dreaming of the risen dough
of the bread of life,
the bread kneaded by hand,
and dreaming of the hand that casts the seed.

TRANSLATED BY HARDIE ST. MARTIN

ON READING JULES RENARD'S DIARY

A drop of dew
rounded on a spider web,
the sun drinks it as it rises—
eternity going by!
But a diamond at sundown
sorts out all the sun's threads
and colors them, making a rainbow—
the moment that does not go.

TRANSLATED BY ROBERT BLY
AND HARDIE ST. MARTIN

HE ANDADO MUCHOS CAMINOS

He andado muchos caminos,
he abierto muchas veredas;
he navegado en cien mares
y atracado en cien riberas.

En todas partes he visto
caravanas de tristeza,
soberbios y melancólicos
borrachos de sombra negra,

y pedantones al paño
que miran, callan y piensan
que saben, porque no beben
el vino de las tabernas.

Mala gente que camina
y va apestando la tierra...

Y en todas partes he visto
gentes que danzan o juegan,
cuando pueden, y laboran
sus cuatro palmos de tierra.

Nunca, si llegan a un sitio,
preguntan adónde llegan.
Cuando caminan, cabalgan
a lomos de mula vieja,

y no conocen la prisa
ni aun en los días de fiesta.

I HAVE WALKED DOWN MANY ROADS

I have walked down many roads
and opened paths through brush,
I have sailed over a hundred seas
and tied up on a hundred shores.

Everywhere I've gone I've seen
excursions of sadness,
angry and melancholy
drunkards with black shadows,

and academics in offstage clothes
who watch, say nothing, and think
they know, because they do not drink wine
in the ordinary bars.

Evil men who walk around
polluting the earth . . .

And everywhere I've been I've seen
men who dance and play,
when they can, and work
the few inches of ground they have.

If they turn up somewhere
they never ask where they are.
When they take trips, they ride
on the backs of old mules,

and they don't know how to hurry,
not even on holidays.

Donde hay vino beben vino;
donde no hay vino, agua fresca.

Son buenas gentes que viven,
laboran, pasan y sueñan,
y en un día como tantos
descansan bajo la tierra.

SOBRE LA TIERRA AMARGA

Sobre la tierra amarga,
caminos tiene el sueño
laberínticos, sendas tortuosas,
parques en flor y en sombra y en silencio;

criptas hondas, escalas sobre estrellas;
retablos de esperanzas y recuerdos.
Figurillas que pasan y sonríen
—juguetes melancólicos de viejo—;

imágenes amigas,
a la vuelta florida del sendero,
y quimeras rosadas
que hacen camino... lejos...

They drink wine, if there is some;
if not, they drink cool water.

These men are the good ones,
who live, work, walk, and dream.
And on a day no different than the rest
they lie down under the earth.

TRANSLATED BY ROBERT BLY

DAYDREAMS HAVE ENDLESSLY TURNING PATHS

Daydreams have endlessly turning
paths going over the bitter
earth, winding roads,
parks flowering, in darkness and in silence;

deep vaults, ladders against the stars;
scenes of hopes and memories.
Tiny figures that walk past and smile
—sad playthings for an old man—,

friends we think we see
at the flowery turn in the road,
and imaginary creatures
that show us roads . . . far off . . .

TRANSLATED BY ROBERT BLY

RECUERDO INFANTIL

Una tarde parda y fría
de invierno. Los colegiales
estudian. Monotonía
de lluvia tras los cristales.

Es la clase. En un cartel
se representa a Caín
fugitivo, y muerto Abel,
junto a una mancha carmín.

Con timbre sonoro y hueco
truena el maestro, un anciano
mal vestido, enjuto y seco,
que lleva un libro en la mano.

Y todo un coro infantil
va cantando la lección:
"Mil veces ciento, cien mil,
mil veces mil, un millón."

Una tarde parda y fría
de invierno. Los colegiales
estudian. Monotonía
de la lluvia en los cristales.

MEMORY FROM CHILDHOOD

A chilly and overcast afternoon
in winter. The students
are studying. Steady boredom
of raindrops across the windowpanes.

It is time for class. In a poster
Cain is shown running
away, and Abel dead,
not far from a red spot.

The teacher, with a voice husky and hollow,
is thundering. He is an old man badly dressed,
withered and dried up,
who is holding a book in his hand.

And the whole children's choir
is singing its lesson:
one thousand times one hundred is one hundred thousand,
one thousand times one thousand is one million.

A chilly and overcast afternoon
in winter. The students
are studying. Steady boredom
of raindrops across the windowpanes.

TRANSLATED BY ROBERT BLY

EN LA DESNUDA TIERRA DEL CAMINO

En la desnuda tierra del camino
la hora florida brota,
espino solitario,
del valle humilde en la revuelta umbrosa.

El salmo verdadero
de tenue voz hoy torna
al corazón, y al labio,
la palabra quebrada y temblorosa.

Mis viejos mares duermen; se apagaron
sus espumas sonoras
sobre la playa estéril. La tormenta
camina lejos en la nube torva.

Vuelve la paz al cielo;
la brisa tutelar esparce aromas
otra vez sobre el campo, y aparece,
en la bendita soledad, tu sombra.

¿MI AMOR?... ¿RECUERDAS, DIME

¿Mi amor?... ¿Recuerdas, dime,
aquellos juncos tiernos,
lánguidos y amarillos
que hay en el cauce seco?...

¿Recuerdas la amapola
que calcinó el verano,
la amapola marchita,
negro crespón del campo?...

ON THE BARE ROADWAY

On the bare roadway
the blossomed hour springs,
a lonely thorn
at the shady bend of the deep valley.

Now the true psalm
returns in a frail voice
to my heart, and to my lips
broken and trembling speech.

My old seas sleep; their noisy foam
turned to ashes
on the barren shore; the storm
travels in the grim, faraway cloud.

Peace returns to the sky;
the benevolent wind sows scents
on the meadow again, and your shadow
appears in the holy solitude.

TRANSLATED BY CHARLES GUENTHER

TELL ME IF YOU REMEMBER, LOVE

Tell me if you remember, love,
those tender, lazy
yellow reeds
that lay in the dry ditch.

Do you remember the poppy
that summer pulverized,
the withered poppy,
black crape over the prairie?

¿Te acuerdas del sol yerto
y humilde, en la mañana,
que brilla y tiembla roto
sobre una fuente helada?...

DESGARRADA LA NUBE

Desgarrada la nube; el arco iris
brillando ya en el cielo,
y en un fanal de lluvia
y sol el campo envuelto.

Desperté. ¿Quién enturbia
los mágicos cristales de mi sueño?
Mi corazón latía
atónito y disperso.

...¡El limonar florido,
el cipresal del huerto,
el prado verde, el sol, el agua, el iris ...,
¡el agua en tus cabellos!...

Y todo en la memoria se perdía
como una pompa de jabón al viento.

Do you remember the morning sun,
low and motionless,
shining and trembling, broken
on a frozen fountain?

TRANSLATED BY CHARLES GUENTHER

CLOUDS RIPPED OPEN

Clouds ripped open; a rainbow
gleaming already in the sky,
the fields entirely folded inside
the glass bowl of rain and sunlight.

I woke up. Who is clouding
the magic windowpanes of my dream?
My heart beat
astonished and upset.

The flowering lemon tree,
the cypress in rows in the garden,
the green field, the sun, the water, the rainbow!
drops of water in your hair . . . !

And it all vanished back into the memory
like a soap bubble in the wind.

TRANSLATED BY ROBERT BLY

Y ERA EL DEMONIO DE MI SUEÑO

Y era el demonio de mi sueño, el ángel
más hermoso. Brillaban
como aceros los ojos victoriosos,
y las sangrientas llamas
de su antorcha alumbraron
la honda cripta del alma.

—¿Vendrás conmigo? —No, jamás; las tumbas
y los muertos me espantan.
Pero la férrea mano
mi diestra atenazaba.

—Vendrás conmigo... Y avancé en mi sueño,
cegado por la roja luminaria.
Y en la cripta sentí sonar cadenas
y rebullir de fieras enjauladas.

DESDE EL UMBRAL DE UN SUEÑO ME LLAMARON

Desde el umbral de un sueño me llamaron...
Era la buena voz, la voz querida.

—Dime: ¿vendrás conmigo a ver el alma?...
Llegó a mi corazón una caricia.

—Contigo siempre... Y avancé en mi sueño
por una larga, escueta galería,
sintiendo el roce de la veste pura
y el palpitar suave de la mano amiga.

AND HE WAS THE EVIL SPIRIT OF MY DREAMS

And he was the evil spirit of my dreams, the most handsome
of all angels. His victorious eyes
shot fire like pieces of steel,
and the flames that fell
from his torch like blood
lit up the deep dungeon of the soul.

"Would you like to come with me?" "No, never! Tombs
and dead bodies frighten me."
But his iron hand
gripped my right hand.

"You will come with me . . ." And in my dream I walked
blinded by his red torch.
And in the dungeon I heard the sound of chains
and of beasts stirring in their cages.

TRANSLATED BY ROBERT BLY

FROM THE DOORSILL OF A
DREAM THEY CALLED MY NAME

From the doorsill of a dream they called my name . . .
It was the good voice, the voice I loved so much.

"Listen: Will you go with me to visit the soul? . . ."
A soft stroke reached up to my heart.

"With you always . . ." And in my dream I walked
down a long and solitary corridor,
aware of the touching of the pure robe
and the soft beating of blood in the hand that loved me.

TRANSLATED BY ROBERT BLY

Y NADA IMPORTA YA QUE EL VINO DE ORO

Y nada importa ya que el vino de oro
rebose de tu copa cristalina,
o el agrio zumo enturbie el puro vaso...

Tú sabes las secretas galerías
del alma, los caminos de los sueños,
y la tarde tranquila
donde van a morir... Allí te aguardan

las hadas silenciosas de la vida,
y hacia un jardín de eterna primavera
te llevarán un día.

CAMPO

La tarde está muriendo
como un hogar humilde que se apaga.

Allá, sobre los montes,
quedan algunas brasas.

Y ese árbol roto en el camino blanco
hace llorar de lástima.

¡Dos ramas en el tronco herido, y una
hoja marchita y negra en cada rama!

¿Lloras?... Entre los álamos de oro,
lejos, la sombra del amor te aguarda.

IT DOESN'T MATTER NOW

It doesn't matter now if the golden wine
is overflowing your crystal goblet,
or if the sour juice is dirtying the pure glass . . .

You know the secret corridors
of the soul, the roads that dreams take,
and the calm evening
where they go to die . . . There the good and silent spirits

of life are waiting for you,
and one day they will carry you
to a garden of eternal spring.

TRANSLATED BY ROBERT BLY

IN THE FIELDS

The evening is dying
like a simple household fire that goes out.

There, on top of the mountains,
a few coals are left.

And that tree in the white road, broken,
makes you cry with compassion.

Two branches on the torn trunk, and one
leaf, withered and black, on each branch!

Are you crying now? . . . In the golden poplars
far off, the shadow of love is waiting for you.

TRANSLATED BY ROBERT BLY

AMANECER DE OTOÑO

A Julio Romero de Torres

Una larga carretera
entre grises peñascales,
y alguna humilde pradera
donde pacen negros toros. Zarzas, malezas, jarales.

Está la tierra mojada
por las gotas del rocío,
y la alameda dorada,
hacia la curva del río.

Tras los montes de violeta
quebrado el primer albor;
a la espalda la escopeta,
entre sus galgos agudos, caminando un cazador.

AUTUMN SUNRISE

For Julio Romero de Torres

A long highway
between gray rock pinnacles
and some ordinary pastures
on which black bulls are grazing. Weeds, thorns, blackberry bushes.

The earth is still soaked
by the drops of dew
and the lombardy poplars are gold
toward the swing of the river.

Across the violet mountains
the early sunrise is breaking.
With a shotgun on his shoulder,
among his excited dogs, a hunter is walking.

TRANSLATED BY ROBERT BLY

ALLÁ, EN LAS TIERRAS ALTAS

Allá, en las tierras altas,
por donde traza el Duero
su curva de ballesta
en torno a Soria, entre plomizos cerros
y manchas de raídos encinares,
mi corazón está vagando, en sueños...

¿No ves, Leonor, los álamos del río
con sus ramajes yertos?
Mira el Moncayo azul y blanco; dame
tu mano y paseemos.
Por estos campos de la tierra mía,
bordados de olivares polvorientos,
voy caminando solo,
triste, cansado, pensativo y viejo.

NUNCA PERSEGUÍ LA GLORIA

Nunca perseguí la gloria
ni dejar en la memoria
de los hombres mi canción;
yo amo los mundos sutiles,
ingrávidos y gentiles
como pompas de jabón.
Me gusta verlos pintarse
de sol y grana, volar
bajo el cielo azul, temblar
súbitamente y quebrarse.

THERE, IN THE HIGH PART

There, in the high part of the land,
where the Duero River draws back
its crossbow
around Soria, among lead-colored hills,
and patches of worn-out oaks,
my heart is walking about, daydreaming . . .

Leonor, don't you see the river poplars
with their stiff branches?
There is Moncayo, bluish and white; give me
your hand, and let's go for a walk.
Through these fields of my country,
with their embroidery of dusty olives,
I go walking alone,
sad, tired, thoughtful and old.

TRANSLATED BY ROBERT BLY

I HAVE NEVER WANTED FAME

I have never wanted fame,
nor wanted to leave my poems
behind in the memory of men.
I love the subtle worlds,
delicate, almost without weight,
like soap bubbles.
I enjoy seeing them take the color
of sunlight and scarlet, fly
beneath the blue sky, then
suddenly quiver and break.

TRANSLATED BY ROBERT BLY

A DON FRANCISCO GINER DE LOS RÍOS

Como se fue el maestro,
la luz de esta mañana
me dijo: Van tres días
que mi hermano Francisco no trabaja.
¿Murió?... Sólo sabemos
que se nos fue por una senda clara,
diciéndonos: Hacedme
un duelo de labores y esperanzas.
Sed buenos y no más, sed lo que he sido
entre vosotros: alma.
Vivid, la vida sigue,
los muertos mueren y las sombras pasan;
lleva quien deja y vive el que ha vivido.
¡Yunques, sonad; enmudeced, campanas!

Y hacia otra luz más pura
partió el hermano de la luz del alba,
del sol de los talleres,
el viejo alegre de la vida santa.
...Oh, sí, llevad, amigos,
su cuerpo a la montaña,
a los azules montes
del ancho Guadarrama.
Allí hay barrancos hondos
de pinos verdes donde el viento canta.
Su corazón repose
bajo una encina casta,
en tierra de tomillos, donde juegan
mariposas doradas...
Allí el maestro un día
soñaba un nuevo florecer de España.

FOR DON FRANCISCO GINER DE LOS RÍOS

At the time the master disappeared
the morning light
said to me: "For three days
my brother Francisco has done nothing.
Has he died? . . ." All we know
is that he has gone off on a clear road,
telling us this: Show
your grief for me in work and hope.
Be good, forget the rest, be
what I have been among you: a soul.
Live, life moves,
the dead are dead, the shadows pass on,
the man who abandons still has, and the man who has lived lives!
Make noise, anvils; be silent, church bells!

So the brother of the morning twilight
and of the sun of hard work,
the old happy man with a holy life,
went off toward a purer light.
. . . Oh, yes, my friends, carry
his body to the mountains!
To the blue peaks
of the long Guadarrama range!
There I know deep ravines
with green pines where the wind is singing.
His heart can rest
under an ordinary oak
in the thyme fields, where the golden
butterflies are fluttering . . .
One day the master there
imagined a new blossoming of Spain.

TRANSLATED BY ROBERT BLY

*Francisco Giner de los Ríos was the founder of The Free Institution of Learning
in Madrid. During Machado's lifetime he led most of the efforts toward reform
of education in Spain.*

UNA ESPAÑA JOVEN

...Fue un tiempo de mentira, de infamia. A España toda,
la malherida España, de Carnaval vestida
nos la pusieron, pobre y escuálida y beoda,
para que no acertara la mano con la herida.

Fue ayer; éramos casi adolescentes; era
con tiempo malo, encinta de lúgubres presagios,
cuando montar quisimos en pelo una quimera,
mientras la mar dormía ahita de naufragios.

Dejamos en el puerto la sórdida galera,
y en una nave de oro nos plugo navegar
hacia los altos mares, sin aguardar ribera,
lanzando velas y anclas y gobernalle al mar.

Ya entonces, por el fondo de nuestro sueño—herencia
de un siglo que vencido sin gloria se alejaba—
un alba entrar quería; con nuestra turbulencia
la luz de las divinas ideas batallaba.

Mas cada cual el rumbo siguió de su locura;
agilitó su brazo, acreditó su brío;
dejó como un espejo bruñida su armadura
y dijo: "El hoy es malo, pero el mañana... es mío."

Y es hoy aquel mañana de ayer... Y España toda,
con sucios oropeles de Carnaval vestida
aún la tenemos: pobre y escuálida y beoda;
mas hoy de un vino malo: la sangre de su herida.

Tú, juventud más joven, si de más alta cumbre
la voluntad te llega, irás a tu aventura
despierta y transparente a la divina lumbre,
como el diamante clara, como el diamante pura.

A YOUNG SPAIN

. . . It was a time of lies and infamy. All Spain,
Spain badly wounded, dressed for the party,
was left with us, poor and weak and drunk,
for no hand will heal her wound.

It was yesterday; we were just teenagers; and she
had fallen on evil days, decked in dark omens,
when we wanted to ride a dream bareback,
while the sea slept gorged with wrecks.

We left the dirty galley in the port,
we were glad to sail away in a ship of gold
on the high seas, expecting no shore,
throwing rigging and anchors and rudders overboard.

Even then in the depth of our dream (legacy
of an age that withdrew, conquered without glory)
I wanted a dawn to enter; the light
of divine ideas fought with our disorder.

But each followed the course of his own fury;
he flexed his muscles, showed his strength;
he made his armor like a polished mirror
and said, "Today is bad but tomorrow is mine."

And today's that tomorrow of yesterday . . . And all Spain,
in her dirty spangled party dress,
is still with us: poor and weak and drunk;
but now from a bad wine: the blood of her wounds.

You, younger youth, if you ever desire
some greater height, you'll go to your adventure
clean and alive in the divine light,
clear as a diamond, pure as a diamond.

Translated by Charles Guenther

MOGUER

Anochecido, grandes nubes ahogan el pueblo.
Los faroles están tristes y soñolientos,
y la luna amarilla camina, entre agua y viento.

Viene un olor a campo mojado. Algún lucero
surje, verdoso, tras un campanario viejo.
El coche de las siete pasa... Ladran los perros...

Al salir al camino, se siente el rostro lleno
de luna fría... Sobre el blanco cementerio,
en la colina, lloran los altos pinos negros.

EL RECUERDO SE VA

El recuerdo se va
por mi memoria larga, removiendo
con finos pies las hojas secas.

—Detrás, la casa está vacía.
Delante, carreteras
que llevan a otras partes, solas,
yertas.
Y la lluvia que llora ojos y ojos,
cual si la hora eterna se quedase ciega.—

MOGUER

Dusk. Enormous clouds press down on the town.
Its streetlamps look sad and heavy-eyed
and the yellow moon walks between wind and water.

An odor of wet fields drifts in. A green star
comes out from behind an old belltower.
The seven o'clock coach goes by. . . . The dogs are barking. . . .

When I walk out to the road, I feel my face getting soaked
in cold moonlight. . . . The towering black pines cry
over the white cemetery on the hill.

TRANSLATED BY HARDIE ST. MARTIN

A REMEMBRANCE IS MOVING

A remembrance is moving
down the long memory, disturbing
the dry leaves with its delicate feet.

—Behind, the house is empty.
On ahead, highways
going on to other places, solitary highways,
stretched out.
And the rain is like weeping eyes,
as if the eternal moment were going blind.—

Aunque la casa está muda y cerrada,
yo, aunque no estoy en ella, estoy en ella.
Y... ¡adiós, tú que caminas
sin volver la cabeza!

INTELIJENCIA, DAME

¡Intelijencia, dame
el nombre exacto de las cosas!
...Que mi palabra sea
la cosa misma,
creada por mi alma nuevamente.
Que por mí vayan todos
los que no las conocen, a las cosas;
que por mí vayan todos
los que ya las olvidan, a las cosas;
que por mí vayan todos
los mismos que las aman, a las cosas...
¡Intelijencia, dame
el nombre exacto, y tuyo,
y suyo, y mío, de las cosas!

Even though the house is quiet and shut,
even though I am not in it, I am in it.
And . . . goodbye, you who are walking
without turning your head!

TRANSLATED BY ROBERT BLY

INTELLIGENCE, GIVE ME

Intelligence, give me
the exact name of things!
I want my word to be
the thing itself,
created by my soul a second time.
So that those who do not know them
can go to the things through me,
all those who have forgotten them
can go to the things through me,
all those who love them
can go to the things through me . . .
Intelligence, give me
the exact name, and your name
and theirs and mine, for things!

TRANSLATED BY ROBERT BLY

VINO, PRIMERO, PURA

Vino, primero, pura,
vestida de inocencia.
Y la amé como un niño.

Luego se fué vistiendo
de no sé qué ropajes.
Y la fuí odiando, sin saberlo.

Llegó a ser una reina,
fastuosa de tesoros...
¡Qué iracundia de yel y sin sentido!

...Mas se fué desnudando.
Y yo le sonreía.

Se quedó con la túnica
de su inocencia antigua.
Creí de nuevo en ella.

Y se quitó la túnica,
y apareció desnuda toda...
¡Oh pasión de mi vida, poesía
desnuda, mía para siempre!

AT FIRST SHE CAME TO ME PURE

At first she came to me pure,
dressed only in her innocence;
and my love was like a child's.

Then she began putting on
clothes she picked up somewhere;
and I hated her, without knowing it.

She gradually became a queen,
her jewelry was blinding . . .
What bitterness and rage!

. . . She started going back toward nakedness.
And I smiled.

Soon she was back to the single shift
of her old innocence.
I believed in her a second time.

Then she took off the cloth
and was entirely naked . . .
Naked poetry, always mine,
that I have loved my whole life!

TRANSLATED BY ROBERT BLY

¡OH TIEMPO, DAME TU SECRETO

¡Oh tiempo, dame tu secreto,
que te hace más nuevo cuanto
más envejeces!

Día tras día, tu pasado
es menos, y tu porvenir más grande,
—y tu presente
¡lo mismo siempre que el instante
de la flor del almendro!—

¡Tiempo sin huellas:
dame el secreto con que invade,
cada día, tu espíritu a tu cuerpo!

MIS PIES ¡QUÉ HONDOS EN LA TIERRA!

Mis pies ¡qué hondos en la tierra!
Mis alas ¡qué altas en el cielo!
—¡Y qué dolor
de corazón distendido!—

TIME, GIVE ME THE SECRET

Time, give me the secret
that makes you younger as
you grow older!

Day after day, your past
falls away, and your future looms ahead,
—and your present:
always the same as the instant
of the almond blossoming!

Time without footprints:
tell me how your soul
daily flows through your body!

TRANSLATED BY RALPH NELSON
AND RITA GARCÍA NELSON

MY FEET, SO DEEP IN THE EARTH

My feet, so deep in the earth!
My wings, so far into the heavens!
—And so much pain
in the heart torn between!

TRANSLATED BY RALPH NELSON
AND RITA GARCÍA NELSON

AURORA

El amanecer tiene
esa tristeza de llegar,
en tren, a una estación que no es de uno.

¡Qué agrios rumores
de un día que se sabe pasajero
—oh vida mía!

—Arriba, con el alba, llora un niño.—

COBRÉ LA RIENDA

Cobré la rienda,
di la vuelta al caballo
del alba;
me entré, blanco, en la vida.

¡Oh, cómo me miraban,
locas,
las flores de mi sueño,
levantando los brazos a la luna!

DAYBREAK

Daybreak
has that sadness of arriving
by train at a station that's not yours.

What bitter rumors
of a day that knows it is a passenger
—oh my life!

—Upstairs, at dawn, a child cries.

TRANSLATED BY RALPH NELSON
AND RITA GARCÍA NELSON

I PULLED ON THE REINS

I pulled on the reins,
I turned the horse
of the dawn,
and I came in to life, pale.

Oh how they looked at me,
the flowers of my dream,
insane,
lifting their arms to the moon!

TRANSLATED BY ROBERT BLY

SE ENTRÓ EN MI FRENTE
EL PENSAMIENTO NEGRO

Se entró en mi frente el pensamiento negro,
como un ave nictálope,
en un cuarto, de día.

—¡No sé qué hacerle para que se vaya!—

Está aquí, quieto y mudo,
sin ver las aguas ni las rosas.

CANCIÓN

Me colmó el sol del poniente
el corazón de onzas doradas.
Me levanté por la noche,
a verlas. ¡No valían nada!

De onzas de plata, la luna
de madrugada llenó mi alma.
Cerré mi puerta, en el día,
por verlas. ¡No valían nada!

A BLACK THOUGHT

A black thought came into my head
like a night-bird
in a room filled with day.

—I don't know how to chase it off!—

It's here, motionless and dumb,
blind to the water and the roses.

TRANSLATED BY RALPH NELSON
AND RITA GARCÍA NELSON

SONG

The setting sun left my heart
brimming with coins of gold.
I got up in the night
to have a look at them. Worthless!

With silver coins, the moon
of the small hours stuffed my soul.
During the day, I locked the door
to have a look at them. Worthless!

TRANSLATED BY RALPH NELSON
AND RITA GARCÍA NELSON

YO NO SOY YO

Yo no soy yo.
      Soy este
que va a mi lado sin yo verlo;
que, a veces, voy a ver,
y que, a veces, olvido.
El que calla, sereno, cuando hablo,
el que perdona, dulce, cuando odio,
el que pasea por donde no estoy,
el que quedará en pie cuando yo muera.

OH, SÍ; ROMPER LA COPA

¡Oh, sí; romper la copa
de la naturaleza con mi frente;
ganar más luz al pensamiento;
definirlo en los límites
de lo que sacia!...
      Y que me sea
el infinito que se queda fuera, como
esta calle, que el domingo
deja sola, callada y aburrida,
delante de mis ojos llameantes
a mi alma.

I AM NOT I

I am not I.
      I am this one
walking beside me whom I do not see;
whom at times I manage to visit,
and whom at other times I forget;
who remains calm and silent while I talk
and forgives, gently, when I hate,
who walks where I am not,
who will remain standing when I die.

TRANSLATED BY ROBERT BLY

YES, IF I COULD ONLY SMASH

Yes, if I could only smash
the cup of nature with my mind
and get more light for thought;
define it within the limits
of what brims over in us.
      And let it be
to my soul, this infinity that stays outside,
like this street
that Sunday has left
empty and silent and bored
in front of my burning eyes.

TRANSLATED BY RALPH NELSON
AND RITA GARCÍA NELSON

MARES

Siento que el barco mío
ha tropezado, allá en el fondo,
con algo grande.
                    ¡Y nada
sucede! Nada... Quietud... Olas...

—¿Nada sucede; o es que ha sucedido todo,
y estamos ya, tranquilos, en lo nuevo?—

RUTA

Todos duermen, abajo.
                         Arriba, alertas,
el timonel y yo.

Él, mirando la aguja, dueño de
los cuerpos, con sus llaves
echadas. Yo, los ojos
en lo infinito, guiando
los tesoros abiertos de las almas.

OCEANS

I have a feeling that my boat
has struck, down there in the depths,
against a great thing.
And nothing
happens! Nothing . . . Silence . . . Waves . . .

—Nothing happens? Or has everything happened,
and are we standing now, quietly, in the new life?

TRANSLATED BY ROBERT BLY

ROAD

They all are asleep, below.
Above, awake,
the helmsman and I.

He, watching the compass needle, lord
of the bodies, with keys turned
in the locks. I, with my eyes
toward the infinite, guiding
the open treasures of the souls.

TRANSLATED BY ROBERT BLY

EL BARCO ENTRA, OPACO Y NEGRO

El barco entra, opaco y negro,
en la negrura trasparente
del puerto inmenso.
                    Paz y frío.
                         —Los que esperan,
están aún dormidos con su sueño,
tibios en ellos, lejos todavía y yertos dentro de él,
de aquí, quizás...

¡Oh vela real nuestra, junto al sueño
de duda de los otros! ¡Seguridad, al lado
del sueño inquieto por nosotros!—
                              Paz. Silencio.
Silencio que, al romperse, con el alba,
hablará de otro modo.

DEJAD LAS PUERTAS ABIERTAS

Dejad las puertas abiertas,
esta noche, por si él
quiere, esta noche, venir,
que está muerto.
              Abierto todo,
a ver si nos parecemos
a su cuerpo; a ver si somos
algo de su alma, estando
entregadas al espacio;
a ver si el gran infinito
nos echa un poco, invadiéndonos,
de nosotros; si morimos

THE SHIP, SOLID AND BLACK

The ship, solid and black,
enters the clear blackness
of the great harbor.
              Quiet and cold.
                     —The people waiting
are still asleep, dreaming,
and warm, far away and still stretched out in this
dream, perhaps . . .

How real our watch is, beside the dream
of doubt the others had! How sure it is, compared
to their troubled dream about us!
                 Quiet. Silence.
Silence which in breaking up at dawn
will speak differently.

            TRANSLATED BY ROBERT BLY

LEAVE THE DOORS STANDING OPEN

Leave the doors standing open
tonight, the dead one
might want to come back.
              With everything open
we can see if we resemble
his body, or just a part of his soul
being handed over to space;
we can see if the great infinite
will take us over, push us out
of ourselves a little; if we die

un poco aquí; y allí, en él,
vivimos un poco.
                    ¡Abierta
toda la casa, lo mismo
que si estuviera de cuerpo
presente en la noche azul,
con nosotros como sangre,
con las estrellas por flores!

VOY A CORRER POR LA SOMBRA

Voy a correr por la sombra,
dormido, dormido, ¡a ver
si puedo alcanzarte a ti,
que has muerto sin yo saberlo!

¡Espera, espera; no corras;
espérame en el remanso,
junto al lirio que la luna
hace de luz; con el agua
que chorrea el infinito
en tu mano blanca!
                    ¡Espera;
que ya voy yo por la boca
negra de la primera nada,
del sueño hermoso y bendito,
botón en flor de la muerte!

a little bit here, and live a little
there, in him.
        The whole house open!
as if his body were there
stretched out in the blue night,
with us like our own blood,
with stars for flowers.

TRANSLATED BY RALPH NELSON

I SHALL RUN THROUGH THE SHADOW

I shall run through the shadow,
sleeping, sleeping, to see
if I can come where you are
who died, and I did not know.

Wait, wait; do not run;
wait for me in the dead water
by the lily that the moon
makes out of light; with the water
that flows from the infinite
into your white hand!
        Wait;
I have one foot already through the black
mouth of the first nothing,
of the resplendent and blessed dream,
the bud of death flowering!

TRANSLATED BY W. S. MERWIN

AURORA DE TRASMUROS

A todo se le ve la cara, blanca
—cal, pesadilla, adobe, anemia, frío—
contra el oriente. ¡Oh cerca de la vida;
oh duro de la vida! ¡Semejanza
animal en el cuerpo—raíz, escoria—
(con el alma mal puesta todavía),
y mineral y vejetal!
¡Sol yerto contra el hombre,
contra el cerdo, las coles y la tapia!
—Falsa alegría, porque estás tan solo
en la hora—se dice—, no en el alma!—

Todo el cielo tomado
por los montones humeantes, húmedos,
de los estercoleros horizontes.
Restos agrios, aquí y allá,
de la noche. Tajadas,
medio comidas, de la luna verde,
cristalitos de estrellas falsas,
papel mal arrancado, con su yeso aún fresco
de cielo azul. Los pájaros,
aún mal despiertos, en la luna cruda,
farol casi apagado.
¡Recua de seres y de cosas!
—¡Tristeza verdadera, porque estás tan solo
en el alma—se dice—, no en la hora!—

DAWN OUTSIDE THE CITY WALLS

You can see the face of everything, and it is white
—plaster, nightmare, adobe, anemia, cold—
turned to the east. Oh closeness to life!
Hardness of life! Like something
in the body that is animal—root, slag-ends—
with the soul still not set well there—
and mineral and vegetable!
Sun standing stiffly against man,
against the sow, the cabbages, the mud wall!
—False joy, because you are merely
in time, as they say, not in the soul!

The entire sky taken up
by moist and steaming heaps,
a horizon of dung piles.
Sour remains, here and there,
of the night. Slices
of the green moon, half-eaten,
crystal bits from false stars,
plaster, the paper ripped off, still faintly
sky-blue. The birds
not really awake yet, in the raw moon,
streetlight nearly out.
Mob of beings and things!
—A true sadness, because you are really deep
in the soul, as they say, not in time at all!

TRANSLATED BY ROBERT BLY

EL NOMBRE CONSEGUIDO DE LOS NOMBRES

Si yo, por ti, he creado un mundo para ti,
dios, tú tenías seguro que venir a él,
y tú has venido a él, a mí seguro,
porque mi mundo todo era mi esperanza.

Yo he acumulado mi esperanza
en lengua, en nombre hablado, en nombre escrito;
a todo yo le había puesto nombre
y tú has tomado el puesto
de toda esta nombradía.

Ahora puedo yo detener ya mi movimiento,
como la llama se detiene en ascua roja
con resplandor de aire inflamado azul,
en el ascua de mi perpetuo estar y ser;
ahora yo soy ya mi mar paralizado,
el mar que yo decía, mas no duro,
paralizado en olas de conciencia en luz
y vivas hacia arriba todas, hacia arriba.

Todos los nombres que yo puse
al universo que por ti me recreaba yo,
se me están convirtiendo en uno y en un
dios.

El dios que es siempre al fin,
el dios creado y recreado y recreado
por gracia y sin esfuerzo.
El Dios. El nombre conseguido de los nombres.

THE NAME DRAWN FROM THE NAMES

If I have created a world for you, in your place,
god, you had to come to it confident,
and you have come to it, to my refuge,
because my whole world was nothing but my hope.

I have been saving up my hope
in language, in a spoken name, a written name;
I had given a name to everything,
and you have taken the place
of all these names.

Now I can hold back my movement
inside the coal of my continual living and being,
as the flame reins itself back inside the red coal,
surrounded by air that is all blue fire;
now I am my own sea that has suddenly stopped somewhere,
the sea I used to speak of, but not heavy,
stiffened into waves of an awareness filled with light,
and all of them moving upward, upward.

All the names that I gave
to the universe that I created again for you
are now turning into one name, into one
god.

The god who, in the end, is always
the god created and re-created and re-created
through grace and never through force.
The God. The name drawn from the names.

TRANSLATED BY ROBERT BLY

CONCIENCIA PLENA

Tú me llevas, conciencia plena, deseante dios,
por todo el mundo.
                    En este mar tercero,
casi oigo tu voz; tu voz del viento
ocupante total del movimiento;
de los colores, de las luces
eternos y marinos.

Tu voz de fuego blanco
en la totalidad del agua, el barco, el cielo,
lineando las rutas con delicia,
grabándome con fúljido mi órbita segura
de cuerpo negro
con el diamante lúcido en su dentro.

FULL CONSCIOUSNESS

You are carrying me, full consciousness, god that has desires,
all through the world.
                Here, in this third sea,
I almost hear your voice: your voice, the wind,
filling entirely all movements;
eternal colors and eternal lights,
sea colors and sea lights.

Your voice of white fire
in the universe of water, the ship, the sky,
marking out the roads with delight,
engraving for me with a blazing light my firm orbit:
a black body
with the glowing diamond in its center.

TRANSLATED BY ROBERT BLY

PIE PARA EL NIÑO DE VALLECAS
DE VELÁZQUEZ

Bacía, yelmo, halo,
éste es el orden, Sancho.

De aquí no se va nadie.

Mientras esta cabeza rota
del Niño de Vallecas exista,
de aquí no se va nadie. Nadie.
Ni el místico ni el suicida.

Antes hay que deshacer este entuerto,
antes hay que resolver este enigma.
Y hay que resolverlo entre todos,
y hay que resolverlo sin cobardías,
sin huir
con unas alas de percalina
o haciendo un agujero
en la tarima.
De aquí no se va nadie. Nadie.
Ni el místico ni el suicida.

Y es inútil,
inútil toda huida
(ni por abajo
ni por arriba).
Se vuelve siempre. Siempre.
Hasta que un día (¡un buen día!)
el yelmo de Mambrino
—halo ya, no yelmo ni bacía—

CAPTION FOR "THE CHILD FROM VALLECAS" BY VELÁZQUEZ

Basin, helmet, halo,
this is the order, Sancho.

No one shall leave this place.

While this mangled head
of the Child from Vallecas exists
no one shall leave, no one.
Neither the mystic nor the suicide.

First the wrong must be undone,
first we must solve this enigma.
And we must solve it together,
and we must solve it without cringing,
without fleeing
on muslin-lined wings
or by drilling a hole
in the stage.
No one shall leave this place, no one.
Neither the mystic nor the suicide.

And it is useless,
all flight is useless
(above
or below).
We always return. Always.
Until one day (one fine day!)
when the helmet of Mambrino
—halo by then, not helmet or basin—

se acomode a las sienes de Sancho
y a las tuyas y a las mías
como pintiparado,
como hecho a la medida.
Entonces nos iremos Todos
por las bambalinas:
Tú y yo y Sancho y el Niño de Vallecas
y el místico y el suicida.

Fragmento de UN PERRO NEGRO DUERME SOBRE LA LUZ

Yo no soy nadie: un hombre
con un grito de estopa en la garganta
y una gota de asfalto en la retina.
Yo no soy nadie. Y, no obstante, estas manos
mis antenas de hormiga, han ayudado
a clavar la lanza en el costado del mundo
y detrás de la lupa de la luna
hay un ojo que me ve como a un microbio
royendo el corazón de la tierra.
Tengo ya cien mil años, y hasta ahora
no he encontrado otro mástil de más fuste
que el silencio y la sombra donde colgar mi orgullo.
Tengo ya cien mil años
y mi nombre en el cielo se escribe con lápiz.
El agua, por ejemplo, es más noble que yo.
Por eso las estrellas se duermen en el mar
y mi frente romántica es áspera y opaca.
Detrás de mi frente—escuchad esto bien—,
detrás de mi frente hay un viejo dragón:
el sapo negro que saltó de la primera charca del mundo
y está aquí, agazapado en mis sesos,
sin dejarme ver el amor y la justicia.
Yo no soy nadie.

will sit on Sancho's temples
and on mine and yours,
as if fitted to a T,
as if made to order.
Then we will all march together
out into the wings.
You, and I, and Sancho, and the Child from Vallecas
and the mystic and the suicide.

TRANSLATED BY JULIO DE LA TORRE

From A BLACK DOG IS SLEEPING
ON TOP OF THE LIGHT

I am no one: a man
with a cry stuck in his throat like pitch
and on his retina a speck of asphalt.
I am no one. And yet my hands,
these ant's antennae, helped to nail
the spear into the world's side,
and an eye is there, behind the moon's magnifying glass,
fixed on me as if I were a germ
feeding on the earth's core.
I am one hundred thousand years old, and so far
I haven't found a stronger tree stump than silence or darkness
on which to hang up my pride.
I am one hundred thousand years old
and my name is written on the sky in pencil.
And the water, for instance, is more noble than I am.
The stars sleep on the sea
because my romantic face is clouded over and rough.
Behind my face—hear this—,
there is an ancient dragon behind my face:
the black toad that hopped out of the first mud hole.
It's here, hunched inside my brain,
and will not let me look at love and justice.
I am no one.

Y no ahueco la voz para asustaros.
Siempre fue sorda mi canción.
Ahora es seca además, seca como una ley
y ahumada y rota como un film quemado
como esta hora del mundo.

Y digo secamente.
Registrad este hecho:
a aquel hombre sin piernas, del carrito,
que cruzaba una noche Wall Street,
remando en las baldosas con unos palitroques
bajo el silencio de los rascacielos solitarios,
lo he visto aquí en la plaza esta mañana
a la sombra de una palmera.

¿Más alto?... ¿Quién ha dicho más alto?
Desgarraré mi voz porque alguien no ha oído bien.
Encenderé la estopa sorda de mi grito,
reventaré mi voz, esta voz (la mía, la tuya).
Esta voz ronca que golpea vencida
en el vientre negro del mundo,
en el cóncavo barro de este cántaro obscuro,
en la curva cenicienta de todos los horizontes apagados...
Escuchad ahora bien:

Ubicua es la injusticia de los hombres...
(Polvo es el aire, polvo
de carbón apagado.)
Lo invade todo.
Lo ennegrece, lo corroe, lo afea todo
como este aliento húmedo del mar.
Y si está ahí en el viento, tumbado en la luz
ese perro negro que muerde nuestros ojos,
ese humo que infla nuestro globo,
que ciega las estrellas y que estrangula el sol,
que tizna mi sonrisa y mi garganta,
que se mete en mi sangre,

I haven't worked this hollow into my voice to scare you off.
My singing has always been dull.
What's more, it's dry now, dry as the law,
smoked up and crumbling like a burned roll of film,
like the world right now.

I speak drily.
Take this down:
the legless man who crossed Wall Street
one night, rowing his small wheel-stand
with two sticks, over the cobblestones
under the silence of the lonely skyscrapers,
I saw that man here this morning, in the square,
in the shade of the palm tree.

Louder? . . . Who said *louder*, just now?
I'm going to rip my voice to shreds because someone didn't hear me.
I'm going to set a match to the dull oakum in my cry,
I'll break open my voice, this voice (mine, yours),
this croak that's pounding, defeated,
on the black belly of the world,
on the rounded clay of this dark pitcher,
on the ash-littered curvature of all the fireless horizons . . .
Listen carefully now:

Man's injustice is everywhere . . .
(The air is dust, the dust
from cinders that have blown out.)
It seeps down into everything.
Blackens, eats up, disfigures everything
like this wet breath from the sea.
And if this black dog snapping at our eyes,
this smoke swelling up our globe,
blinding the stars and choking the sun,
smudging out my smile and my throat,
getting into my blood,
climbing into my brain

que sube a mi cerebro,
y abre y cierra la puerta de mi corazón...
mis poemas y todos los poemas del mundo
—¡oh, Poesía pura!—
tendrán una verruga violácea en la frente.

TUYA ES LA HACIENDA

Tuya es la hacienda,
la casa,
el caballo
y la pistola.
Mía es la voz antigua de la tierra.
Tú te quedas con todo
y me dejas desnudo y errante por el mundo...
mas yo te dejo mudo... ¡Mudo!
¿Y cómo vas a recoger el trigo
y a alimentar el fuego
si yo me llevo la canción?

BIOGRAFÍA, POESÍA Y DESTINO

El poeta le cuenta su vida primero a los hombres;
después, cuando los hombres se duermen, a los pájaros;
más tarde, cuando los pájaros se van, se la cuenta a los árboles...
Luego pasa el Viento y hay un murmullo de frondas.
Y esto me ha dicho el Viento:
que el pavo real levante la cola y extienda su abanico,
el poeta debe mover sólo las plumas de sus alas.

and opening and closing the door to my heart,
if it's there in the wind, sprawled on top of the light . . .
a purple wart—oh pure poetry!—
will appear on the face of my poems
and all the poems in the world.

TRANSLATED BY HARDIE ST. MARTIN

THE FARM IS YOURS

The farm is yours,
the house,
the horse,
and the pistol too.
The ancient voice of the land is mine.
You keep everything
and leave me naked and lost in the world . . .
but I leave you without a voice . . . Silent!
And how will you take in the wheat
and feed the fire
if I take the songs with me?

TRANSLATED BY HARDIE ST. MARTIN

BIOGRAPHY, POETRY, DESTINY

The poet recounts his life first to men;
then, when the men have fallen asleep, to the birds;
later, when the birds have gone, he recounts it to the trees. . . .
Presently the Wind passes and there is a murmur of leaves.
And this is what the Wind said to me:
let the peacock lift his tail and spread his fan,
the poet should move only the feathers of his wings.

Todo lo cual se puede traducir también de esta manera:
lo que cuento a los hombres está lleno de orgullo;
lo que cuento a los pájaros, de música;
lo que cuento a los árboles, de llanto.
Y todo es una canción compuesta para el Viento,
de la cual, después, este desmemoriado y único espectador
apenas podrá recordar unas palabras.
Pero estas palabras que recuerde son las que no olvidan nunca las
    piedras.

Lo que cuenta el poeta a las piedras está lleno de eternidad.
Y ésta es la canción del Destino, que tampoco olvidan las estrellas.

NO HE VENIDO A CANTAR

No he venido a cantar, podéis llevaros la guitarra.
No he venido tampoco, ni estoy aquí arreglando mi expediente para
    que me canonicen cuando muera.
He venido a mirarme la cara en las lágrimas que caminan hacia el
    mar,
por el río
y por la nube...
y en las lágrimas que se esconden
en el pozo,
en la noche
y en la sangre...

He venido a mirarme la cara en todas las lágrimas del mundo.
Y también a poner una gota de azogue, de llanto, una gota siquiera
    de mi llanto
en la gran luna de este espejo sin límites, donde me miren y se
    reconozcan los que vengan.

All of which might also be translated this way:
What I recount to men is full of pride;
what I recount to the birds, of music;
what I recount to the trees, of lamentation.
It is all of it a song composed for the Wind;
later, from this unique spectator with no memory
he will be able to recall only a few words at best.
But those words that he recalls are the ones the stones do not forget.

What the poet recounts to the stones is full of eternity.
And this is the song of Destiny, which the stars do not forget either.

TRANSLATED BY W. S. MERWIN

I HAVE NOT COME TO SING

I have not come to sing, you can put away your guitar.
I have not come either to institute proceedings to be canonized once
    I am dead.
I have come in order to look at my face in the tears running toward
    the sea
by way of the river
and by way of the cloud . . .
and in the tears which hide
in the well,
in the night,
in the blood. . . .

I have come in order to look at my face in all the tears of the world.
And also to contribute a drop of quicksilver, of lamentation, a drop,
        whatever it may amount to, of my own lamentation
to the great moon of this limitless mirror where all look and know
        themselves.

He venido a escuchar otra vez esta vieja sentencia en las tinieblas:
Ganarás el pan con el sudor de tu frente
y la luz con el dolor de tus ojos.
Tus ojos son las fuentes del llanto y de la luz.

YO NO SOY EL GRAN BUZO

A Pablo Neruda, mi viejo amigo, el Gran Buzo

Y alguien dirá mañana:
pero este poeta no bajó nunca hasta el fondo del mar,
ni escarbó en la tierra profunda de los tejones y los topos...
No visitó las galerías subterráneas
ni caminó por las fibras oscuras de la madera...
no perforó la carne ni taladró los huesos,
no llegó hasta los intestinos y las vísceras,
no se filtró por el canal de las arterias
ni navegó con la espiroqueta por la sangre hasta morder el corazón
            helado de los hombres...
Pero vió el gusano en la copa del árbol,
la nube de langostas en la torre,
las aguas lustrales rojas y estancadas,
la plegaria amarilla,
la baba verde en los belfos de los sacristanes epilépticos...
Vió el sapo en la cúpula,
la polilla en la mesa del altar,
el comején en el Arca
y el gorgojo en la mitra...
Vió el ojo torcido y guiñón del arzobispo y dijo:
la luz se está ahogando en la sombra seca del pozo
y hay que salvarla con una maroma de lágrimas.

I have come in order to hear once again that old sentence in the
      darkness:
you will earn your bread with the sweat of your brow
and your light with the sorrow of your eyes.
Your eyes are the fountain of lamentation and light.

TRANSLATED BY W. S. MERWIN

I AM NOT THE GREAT DIVER

To Pablo Neruda, my old friend, the Great Diver

And tomorrow someone will say:
But this poet never plunged to the bottom of the sea
nor dug the deep earth of badgers and moles. . . .
He left underground burrows unvisited
and failed to explore the fibers of wood.
He did not pierce through the flesh or drill into bones,
he did not reach intestines or viscerae,
he did not filter himself through the channels of arteries
or sail in the blood with the spirochete reaching and biting the cold
      heart of man. . . .
But he saw the worm on the treetop,
the storm cloud of locusts up in the tower,
the lustral waters, stagnant and red,
the yellowish prayer,
the green-colored drool on the muzzles of quivering sacristans.
He saw toads in the church domes,
moths on the altar,
termites in the Ark
and weevils on the miter. . . .
He saw the sly winking glance of the bishops and said:
Light is being drowned in the dry darkness of wells
and it must be saved by a rope of tears.

TRANSLATED BY JULIO DE LA TORRE

QUE VENGA EL POETA

Que venga el poeta.
Y me trajisteis aquí para contar las estrellas,
para bañarme en el río y para hacer dibujos en la arena.

Éste era el contrato.
Y ahora me habéis puesto a construir cepos y candados,
a cargar un fusil y a escribir en la oficina de un juzgado.

Me trajisteis aquí para cantar en unas bodas
y me habéis puesto a llorar junto a una fosa.

Y AHORA ME VOY

Y ahora me voy sin haber recibido mi legado,
sin haber habitado mi casa,
sin haber cultivado mi huerto,
sin haber sentido el beso de la siembra y de la luz.
Me voy sin haber dado mi cosecha,
sin haber encendido mi lámpara,
sin haber repartido mi pan...
Me voy sin que me hayáis entregado mi hacienda.
Me voy sin haber aprendido más que a gritar y a maldecir,
a pisar bayas y flores...
me voy sin haber visto el Amor,
con los labios amargos llenos de baba y de blasfemias,
y con los brazos rígidos y erguidos, y los puños cerrados,
        pidiendo Justicia fuera del ataúd.

LET THE POET COME

Let the poet come.
And you fetched me here to count the stars,
to bathe in the river and make sketches in the sand.

That was the contract.
And now you have set me to make pillories and padlocks,
load a gun and scribble in a magistrate's office.

You fetched me here to sing at a wedding
and you have set me to weep at a grave.

Translated by W. S. Merwin

NOW I AM GOING

And I am going without having received my inheritance,
without having lived in my house,
without having tilled my garden,
without having felt the kiss of seed time and of the light.
I am going without having yielded my harvest,
without having lit my lamp,
without having broken my bread. . . .
I am going without having been given my estate. . . .
I am going without having learned anything except how to shout and
        curse
and trample on berries and flowers. . . .
I am going without having set eyes on Love,
my bitter lips filled with slaver and blasphemies,
my arms stiff and straight, my fists clenched, demanding Justice
        outside the coffin.

Translated by W. S. Merwin

ME VOY PORQUE LA ESPIGA
Y LA AURORA NO SON MÍAS

He andado perdido por el mundo pidiendo pan y luz.
¡Y el sol es pan y luz!
¡Miradle cómo sale del horno y asciende en el alba para todos,
con su doble corona de harina y de cristal!...
¡Oh, Dios antiguo y generoso, proscrito por el hombre!
Tú ahí siempre, puntual en la espiga y en la aurora
y yo aquí hambriento y ciego, con mi grito mendigo perdido tantas
    veces en la historia:
¡Dejadme hoy el pan para ganar mañana mi sitio junto al sol!

I AM GOING BECAUSE THE EAR OF WHEAT
AND THE DAWN ARE NOT MINE

I have walked, lost, over the world, asking for bread and light.
And the sun is bread and light!
Look how he rises from the oven and ascends into the dawn for all,
with his double crown of flour and crystal! . . .
Oh ancient and generous God, proscribed by men!
You, always there, punctual in the ear of wheat and in the dawn,
and I here hungry and blind, with my beggar's cry lost so many times
    throughout history:
Let me have bread today so that I can earn my place next to the
    sun tomorrow!

TRANSLATED BY W. S. MERWIN

EL ALMA TENÍAS

El alma tenías
tan clara y abierta,
que yo nunca pude
entrarme en tu alma.
Busqué los atajos
angostos, los pasos
altos y difíciles...
A tu alma se iba
por caminos anchos.
Preparé alta escala
—soñaba altos muros
guardándote el alma—
pero el alma tuya
estaba sin guarda
de tapial ni cerca.
Te busqué la puerta
estrecha del alma,
pero no tenía,
de franca que era,
entradas tu alma.
¿En dónde empezaba?
¿Acababa, en dónde?
Me quedé por siempre
sentado en las vagas
lindes de tu alma.

SO TRANSPARENT YOUR SOUL

So transparent your
soul
so open
I could find no way in.
Searched for the sinuous
defiles the high
forbidding passes.
When wide
were the ways to it.
Brought a ladder
imagining high walls around
your soul but
no
no stockade no dirt wall guarded it.
Looked for
your soul's narrow door
but free
it had no gates. Where
did it begin?
Where end?
I was left
sitting forever on its
unmarked borders.

TRANSLATED BY W. S. MERWIN

EN LA TIERRA SECA

En la tierra seca
el alma del viento
avisos marinos me daba
con los labios trémulos
de chopos de estío.
Alientos de mar
y ansias de periplo,
quilla, proa, estela.
Circe y vellocino,
todo lo mentían
chopos sabidores
de la tierra seca.
Y una nube blanca
(una vela blanca)
en el horizonte,
con gestos de lino,
alardes de fuga
por rumbos queridos
hacía
en el mar sin viento
de aquel cielo seco
de la tierra seca
con chopos de estiío.

ON DRY LAND

On dry land
the soul of the wind
gave me messages from the sea
with the shivering lips
of summer poplars.
The ocean's breathing
and a longing to sail around the coast,
keel, prow, wake,
Circe and the golden fleece,
everything the knowing poplars
of the dry land
lied to us about.
And a white cloud
(a white sail)
on the horizon,
with gestures of canvas,
made
boasts of escape
along familiar ways
in the sea without wind
of that dry sky
of the dry land
with summer poplars.

TRANSLATED BY DONALD HALL

NO TE VEO, BIEN SÉ

No te veo, bien sé
que estás aquí, detrás
de una frágil pared
de ladrillos y cal, bien al alcance
de mi voz, si llamara.
Pero no llamaré.
Te llamaré mañana,
cuando al no verte ya,
me imagine que sigues
aquí cerca, a mi lado,
y que basta hoy la voz
que ayer no quise dar.
Mañana..., cuando estés
allá detrás de una
frágil pared de vientos,
de cielos y de años.

MUERTES

Primero te olvidé en tu voz.
Si ahora hablases aquí,
a mi lado,
preguntaría yo: "¿Quién es?"

Luego, se me olvidó de ti tu paso.
Si una sombra se esquiva
entre el viento de carne,
ya no sé si eres tú.

Te deshojaste toda lentamente,
delante de un invierno: la sonrisa,

I DON'T SEE YOU, YET I KNOW

I don't see you, yet I know
that you are here, behind
a frail wall
of bricks and mortar, within easy range
of my voice if I called you.
But I will not call you.
I will call you tomorrow
when, not seeing you any longer,
I will imagine you always
here, next to me, at my side,
and the word will be enough
which yesterday I would not give.
Tomorrow . . . when you are
there behind a
frail wall of winds,
skies, and years.

TRANSLATED BY DONALD HALL

DEATHS

The first thing I forgot was your voice.
Now if you were to
speak here at my side
I would ask, "Who is that?"

After that I forgot your footstep.
If a shadow were to gutter
in the wind of flesh
I would not be sure whether it was you.

One by one all of your leaves fell
before a winter: the smile,

la mirada, el color del traje, el número
de los zapatos.

Te deshojaste aún más:
se te cayó tu carne, tu cuerpo.
Y me quedó tu nombre, siete letras, de ti.
Y tú viviendo,
desesperadamente agonizante,
en ellas, con alma y cuerpo.
Tu esqueleto, sus trazos,
tu voz, tu risa, siete letras, ellas.
Y decirlas tu solo cuerpo ya.
Se me olvidó tu nombre.
Las siete letras andan desatadas;
no se conocen.
Pasan anuncios en tranvías; letras
se encienden en colores a la noche,
van en sobres diciendo
otros nombres.
Por allí andaras tú,
disuelta ya, deshecha e imposible.
Andarás tú, tu nombre, que eras tú,
ascendido
hasta unos cielos tontos,
en un gloria abstracta de alfabeto.

the glance, the color of your clothes, the size
of your shoes.

Even then your leaves went on falling:
your flesh fell away from you, your body.
I was left your name, seven letters of you.
And you living,
desperately dying
in them, body and soul.
Your skeleton, its shape,
your voice, your laugh, seven letters, those letters.
And repeating them was your only life, your body.
I forgot your name.
The seven letters move about, unconnected,
unknown to each other.
They form advertisements in streetcars; letters
burn at night in colors,
they travel in envelopes shaping
other names.
You're somewhere about,
all in bits, by now, dismantled and impossible.
There you are, your name, which was you,
risen
toward various stupid heavens
in an abstract alphabetical glory.

TRANSLATED BY W. S. MERWIN

LA LUZ LO MALO QUE TIENE

La luz lo malo que tiene
es que no viene de ti.
Es que viene de los soles,
de los ríos, de la oliva.
Quiero más tu oscuridad.

La alegría
no es nunca la misma mano
la que me la da. Hoy es una,
otra mañana, otra ayer.
Pero jamás es la tuya.
Por eso siempre te tomo
la pena, lo que me das.
Los besos los traen los hilos
del telégrafo, los roces
con noches densas,
los labios del porvenir.
Y vienen, de donde vienen.
Yo no me siento besar.

Y por eso no lo quiero,
ni se lo quiero deber
no sé a quién.
A ti debértelo todo
querría yo.
¡Qué hermoso el mundo, qué entero
si todo, besos y luces,
y gozo,
viniese sólo de ti!

THE TROUBLE WITH THE LIGHT

The trouble with the light
is that it doesn't
come from you. It comes
from the suns, from the rivers, from the olive tree.
I'd rather have your darkness.

Happiness—
it's never the same hand
that gives it to me. One today,
another tomorrow, another
yesterday. But it's never yours.
That's why I always take
pain, which is what you give me.
The telegraph wires
bring kisses, bring
skins pressed in the thick nights,
bring lips to the future.
And they come, from wherever.
I don't feel myself kiss.

That's why I don't want it,
don't want to feel I owe it
to I don't know who.
I wanted to owe you
everything.
How lovely the world, how complete,
if everything, kisses and lights
and delight,
came only from you!

TRANSLATED BY W. S. MERWIN

DISTÁNCIAMELA, ESPEJO

Distánciamela, espejo;
trastorna su tamaño.
A ella, que llena el mundo,
hazla menuda, mínima.
Que quepa en monosílabos,
en unos ojos;
que la puedas tener
a ella, desmesurada,
gacela, ya sujeta,
infantil, en tu marco.
Quítale esa delicia
del ardor y del bulto,
que no la sientan ya
las últimas balanzas;
déjala fría, lisa,
enterrada en tu azogue.
Desvía
su mirada; que no
me vea, que se crea
que está sola.
Que yo sepa, por fin,
cómo es cuando esté sola.
Entrégame tú de ella
lo que no me dió nunca.

Aunque así
—¡que verdad revelada!—,
aunque así, me la quites.

SET HER FAR FROM ME, MIRROR

Set her far from me, mirror.
Reverse her size.
She who fills the world,
make her little, make her almost nothing.
Let her fit into monosyllables
and any eyes at all.
So that you can hold
her enormity,
a gazelle, tame,
like a child, in your frame.
Take from her that rejoicing
in fire and fullness,
until the finest scales
can't even feel her.
Leave her cold, flat,
buried in your quicksilver.
Turn
her eyes away.
Don't let her see me, let her
think she's alone. So that I
can learn at last what she's like
when she's alone.
Give me something of her
that she herself never gave me.

Even so, even
in the revelation of her,
even so you take her from me.

TRANSLATED BY W. S. MERWIN

NO EN PALACIOS DE MÁRMOL

No en palacios de mármol,
no en meses, no, ni en cifras,
nunca pisando el suelo:
en leves mundos frágiles
hemos vivido juntos.
El tiempo se contaba
apenas por minutos:
un minuto era un siglo,
una vida, un amor.
Nos cobijaban techos,
menos que techos, nubes;
menos que nubes, cielos;
aun menos, aire, nada.
Atravesando mares
hechos de veinte lágrimas,
diez tuyas y diez mías,
llegábamos a cuentas
doradas de collar,
islas limpias, desiertas,
sin flores y sin carne;
albergue, tan menudo,
en vidrio, de un amor
que se bastaba él solo
para el querer más grande
y no pedía auxilio
a los barcos ni al tiempo.
Galerías enormes
abriendo
en los granos de arena,
descubrimos las minas
de llamas o de azares.
Y todo
colgando de aquel hilo
que sostenía, ¿quién?

NOT IN MARBLE PALACES

Not in marble palaces,
not in months, no, nor in numbers,
never treading the ground:
in frail worlds without weight
we have lived together.
Time was scarcely
reckoned in minutes:
one minute was a century,
a life, a love.
Roofs sheltered us.
Less than roofs: clouds.
Less than clouds: skies.
Still less: air, nothing.
Crossing
seas made of twenty tears,
ten of yours, ten of mine,
we came to beads
of gold,
immaculate islands, deserted,
without flowers or flesh:
so small a lodging,
and of glass, for a love
able to reach, by itself,
the greatest longing,
and that asked no help
of ships or time.
Opening
enormous galleries
in the grains of sand,
we discovered the mines
of flames or of chance.
And all
hanging from that thread
that was held—by whom?

Por eso nuestra vida
no parece vivida:
desliz, resbaladora,
ni estelas ni pisadas
dejó detrás. Si quieres
recordarla, no mires
donde se buscan siempre
las huellas y el recuerdo.
No te mires al alma,
a la sombra, a los labios.
Mírate bien la palma
de la mano, vacía.

That's why our life doesn't seem
to have been lived.
Elusive as quicksilver,
it left neither wake
nor track. If you want
to remember it, don't look
in footsteps or memory,
where people always look.
Don't look in the soul,
in the shadow, in the lips.
Look carefully in the palm
of the hand: empty.

TRANSLATED BY W. S. MERWIN

Y SI NO FUERAN LAS SOMBRAS

¿Y si no fueran las sombras
sombras? ¿Si las sombras fueran
—yo las estrecho, las beso,
me palpitan encendidas
entre los brazos—
cuerpos finos y delgados,
todos miedosos de carne?

¿Y si hubiese
otra luz en el mundo
para sacarles a ellas,
cuerpos ya de sombra, otras
sombras más últimas, sueltas
de color, de formas, libres
de sospecha de materia;
y que no se viesen ya,
y que hubiera que buscarlas
a ciegas, por entre cielos,
desdeñando ya las otras,
sin escuchar ya las voces
de esos cuerpos disfrazados
de sombras, sobre la tierra?

AND IF THE SHADOWS WEREN'T

And if the shadows weren't
shadows? If these
shadows that I clasp, kiss,
that flutter, lit,
in my arms
were slender delicate bodies
frightened of flesh?

And if there were
another light in the world
to bring them out of themselves,
bodies of shadow, other
more ultimate shadows, released
from color, from shapes, freed
from all suspicion of matter,
and they couldn't be seen,
and one had to grope for them
blindly, through the skies,
despising, by then, the others,
and heedless of the voices
of those bodies disguised
as shadows, on the earth?

TRANSLATED BY W. S. MERWIN

¿LAS OYES CÓMO PIDEN REALIDADES...?

¿Las oyes cómo piden realidades,
ellas, desmelenadas, fieras,
ellas, las sombras que los dos forjamos
en este inmenso lecho de distancias?
Cansadas ya de infinidad, de tiempo
sin medida, de anónimo, heridas
por una gran nostalgia de materia,
piden límites, días, nombres.
No pueden
vivir así ya más: están al borde
del morir de las sombras, que es la nada.
Acude, ven conmigo.
Tiende tus manos, tiéndeles tu cuerpo.
Los dos les buscaremos
un color, una fecha, un pecho, un sol.
Que descansen en ti, sé tú su carne.
Se calmará su enorme ansia errante,
mientras las estrechamos
ávidamente entre los cuerpos nuestros
donde encuentren su pasto y su reposo.
Se dormirán al fin en nuestro sueño
abrazado, abrazadas. Y así luego,
al separarnos, al nutrirnos sólo
de sombras, entre lejos,
ellas
tendrán recuerdos ya, tendrán pasado
de carne y hueso,
el tiempo que vivieron en nosotros.
Y su afanoso sueño
de sombras, otra vez, será el retorno
a esta corporeidad mortal y rosa
donde el amor inventa su infinito.

DO YOU HEAR HOW THEY BEG FOR REALITIES?

Do you hear how they beg for realities,
these with the tangled hair, these untamed ones,
these shadows that we forge together
in this immense bed of distances?
Tired by now of infinity, of time without measure,
of namelessness, wounded
by a great homesickness for matter,
they beg for limits, days, names.
No longer can they live
as they are: they stand at the brink
of the death of shadows, which is the Nothing.
Help them. Come with me.
Hold out your hands, hold out your body to them.
Together we'll look
for a color for them, a date, a breast, a sun.
Let them rest in you, be their flesh.
Their great passion for wandering will grow still
while we clasp them
avidly between our bodies
where they can find their pasture and repose.
They will sleep at last in our sleep,
embracing, embraced. So that when
we separate, to feed alone
on shadows, at a distance,
by then
they will have memories, have a past
of flesh and blood:
the time when they lived in us.
And their laborious dream
of shadows, again, will be the return
to this roseate mortal flesh
in which love invents infinity.

TRANSLATED BY W. S. MERWIN

NATURALEZA VIVA

¡Tablero de la mesa
Que, tan exactamente
Raso nivel, mantiene
Resuelto en una idea

Su plano: puro, sabio,
Mental para los ojos
Mentales! Un aplomo,
Mientras, requiere al tacto,

Que palpa y reconoce
Cómo el plano gravita
Con pesadumbre rica
De leña, tronco, bosque

De nogal. ¡El nogal
Confiado a sus nudos
Y vetas, a su mucho
Tiempo de potestad

Reconcentrada en este
Vigor inmóvil, hecho
Materia de tablero
Siempre, siempre silvestre!

NATURE ALIVE

The panel board of the table,
That smooth plane precisely
True to a hair, holds up
Its level form, sustained

By an idea: pure, exact,
The mind's image before
The mind's eyes! And yet,
Full assurance needs the touch

That explores and discovers
How the formal idea sags back
Down to the rich heaviness
Of kindling, trunk, and timber

Of walnut. The walnut wood,
Secure in its own whorls
And grains, assured of its long
Season of so much strength

Now fused into the heart
Of this quiet vigor, the stuff
Of a table board, remains
Always, always wild!

TRANSLATED BY JAMES WRIGHT

VIDA URBANA

Calles, un jardín,
Césped—y sus muertos.
Morir, no, vivir.
¡Qué urbano lo eterno!

Losa vertical,
Nombres de los otros.
La inmortalidad
Preserva su otoño.

¿Y aquella aflicción?
Nada sabe el césped
De ningún adiós.
¿Dónde está la muerte?

Hervor de ciudad
En torno a las tumbas.
Una misma paz
Se cierne difusa.

Juntos, a través
Ya de un solo olvido,
Quedan en tropel
Los muertos, los vivos.

CITY LIFE

Streets, a garden,
A plot of ground—and its corpses.
To die—no, to live.
How urbane, that eternity!

Upright, marble stone.
The names of other people.
Immortality
Preserves its aftermath.

And what about that grief?
A plot of ground knows nothing
Of partings.
Where is death?

The city seethes
All around the graves.
A similar peace
Floats far and wide.

Now joined
By a common neglect,
The living and the dead
Crowd together.

Translated by Charles Guenther

BEATO SILLÓN

¡Beato sillón! La casa
Corrobora su presencia
Con la vaga intermitencia
De su invocación en masa
A la memoria. No pasa
Nada. Los ojos no ven,
Saben. El mundo está bien
Hecho. El instante lo exalta
A marea, de tan alta,
De tan alta, sin vaivén.

ANULACIÓN DE LO PEOR

Sin luces, ya nocturna toda, bárbara,
En torno a los silencios encrespándose,
La noche con sus bestias aulladoras se yergue.

¿Una aprensión te angustia?
No temas.

Los aullidos,
El mal con sus galápagos, sus gárgolas,
Noche abajo enfángandose, cayendo,
En noche se trasfunden. La noche toda es fondo.
Espera, pues.

El sol descubrirá,
Bellísima inocente, la simple superficie.

HAPPY ARMCHAIR

Happy armchair! The house
Confirms its presence
With the vague interval
Of its total invocation
To memory. Nothing
Passes. Eyes don't see,
They perceive. The world is well
Made. The moment lifts it
Tideward, so high,
So high, without coming or going.

TRANSLATED BY CHARLES GUENTHER

WITHOUT LIGHTS

Without lights, now totally dark, fierce,
Bristling up around the silences,
Night with its howling beasts hunches up.

Does some fear torment you?
Don't be afraid.

                The howls,
Evil and its turtles, its gargoyles,
Down the night, getting mired, falling over,
Are transformed into night. All the night is depth.
Then wait.

        The sun will reveal
The harmless beauty of the plain surface.

TRANSLATED BY CHARLES GUENTHER

LA NIEVE

Lo blanco está sobre lo verde,
Y canta.
Nieve que es fina quiere
Ser alta.

Enero se alumbra con nieve, si verde,
Si blanca.
Que alumbre de día y de noche la nieve,
La nieve más clara.

¡Nieve ligera, copo blando,
Cuánto ardor en masa!
La nieve, la nieve en las manos
Y el alma.

Tan puro el ardor en lo blanco,
Tan puro, sin llama.
La nieve, la nieve hasta el canto
Se alza.

Enero se alumbra con nieve silvestre.
¡Cuánto ardor! Y canta.
La nieve hasta el canto—la nieve, la nieve—
En vuelo arrebata.

SNOW

The white is lying on top of the green
And it is singing.
Snow that is delicate wants
To be high in the air.

The lanterns of January are snow: both green
And white.
I want the snow to light up both day and night.
The snow even brighter.

Nimble snow, fluffy flake.
What fire when it gathers!
The snow, the snow in the hands,
And in the spirit.

The burning is so pure in the white.
So pure, there is no flame.
The snow, the snow lifts itself
To singing.

The lanterns of January are the snow on the trees.
Such fire! And it sings!
The snow lifted toward singing—the snow, the snow—
Ready to fly!

TRANSLATED BY ROBERT BLY

RIACHUELO CON LAVANDERAS

Los juncos flotan en el riachuelo,
Que los aguza sobre su corriente,
Balanceados como si avanzasen.

No avanzan. Allí están acompañando,
Verdeamarillos hacia el horizonte,
El rumor de una orilla laboriosa.
  En la masa del agua ya azulada
  Chascan las ropas, de creciente peso
  Bajo aquel ya raudal de un vocerío.

¡Oh riachuelo con flotantes grises
Por el verdor en curso que azulándose
También se esfuerza, todavía alegre!

Rasgueos de cepillos, dicharachos,
Ancha sobre algazara la mañana.
Acierta así la orilla, femenina.
  ¿Se vive arrodillado en las riberas?
  Inclinación forzosa de figura...
  Ese borde está ahí. ¿Tormento el mundo?

Fluvial apenas hacia un oleaje,
Chispeando, sonando, trabajando,
El riachuelo es más: hay más mañana.

STREAM WITH WASHERWOMEN

Rushes float in the stream
That stirs them on its current,
Poised as if they advanced.

They don't advance. They follow,
Green-gold, toward the horizon,
The murmur of a busy shore.
    In the mass of bluish water
    Clothes crackle with increasing weight
    Under the torrent of shouts.

Oh stream where gray tones float
By the green foliage in the current turning blue
And struggling, yet exulting!

Flourishes of brushes, sputterers of slang,
The morning wide open on their revelry.
The shore is perfect like that, feminine.
    Can life be enjoyed kneeling on the riverbanks?
    A necessary bending of the body . . .
    That shore is over there. (Is the whole world pain?)

Flowing laboriously toward the rolling sea,
Glittering, tinkling, toiling,
The stream is more: there's more morning.

                TRANSLATED BY CHARLES GUENTHER

LAS SOMBRAS

Sol. Activa persiana.
Laten sombras. —¿Quién entra?
...Huyen. Soy yo: pisadas.

(¡Oh, con palpitación
De párpado, persiana
De soledad o amor!)

Quiero lo trasparente.
También las sombras quiero,
Trasparentes y alegres.

(¡Las sombras, tan esquivas,
Soñaban con la palma
De la mano en caricia!)

¿Tal vez mi mano? Pero
No, no puede. Las sombras
Son intangibles: sueños.

THE SHADOWS

Sunlight. Rustling blinds.
Shadows knock. "Who's there?"
. . . They slip away. It's I: footsteps.

(O with a flutter
Of eyelids, window blinds
Of love or solitude!)

I like things you can see through.
I like shadows too,
Bright and frisky.

(The shadows, so elusive,
Dreamed of the palm
Of the stroking hand!)

My hand perhaps? Well,
No, it can't. The shadows
Are intangible: dreams.

TRANSLATED BY CHARLES GUENTHER

QUIERO DORMIR

Más fuerte, más claro, más puro,
Seré quien fui.
Venga la dulce invasión del olvido.
Quiero dormir.

¡Si me olvidase de mí, si fuese un árbol
Tranquilo,
Ramas que tienden silencio,
Tronco benigno!

La gran oscuridad ya maternal,
Poco a poco profunda,
Cobije este cuerpo que al alma
—Una pausa—renuncia.

Salga ya del mundo infinito,
De sus accidentes,
Y al final del reposo estrellado
Seré el que amanece.

Abandonándome a la cómplice
Barca
Llegaré por mis ondas y nieblas
Al alba.

No quiero soñar con fantasmas inútiles,
No quiero caverna.
Que el gran espacio sin luna
Me aísle y defienda.

Goce yo así de tanta armonía
Gracias a la ignorancia
De este ser tan seguro que se finge
Su nada.

I WANT TO SLEEP

I shall be still stronger.
Still clearer, purer, so let
The sweet invasion of oblivion come on.
I want sleep.

If I could forget myself, if I were only
A tranquil tree,
Branches to spread out the silence,
Trunk of mercy.

The great darkness, grown motherly,
Deepens little by little,
Brooding over this body that the soul
—After a pause—surrenders.

It may even embark from the endless world,
From its accidents,
And, scattering into stars at the last,
The soul will be daybreak.

Abandoning myself to my accomplice,
My boat,
I shall reach on my ripples and mists
Into the dawn.

I do not want to dream of useless phantoms,
I do not want a cave.
Let the huge moonless spaces
Hold me apart, and defend me.

Let me enjoy so much harmony
Thanks to the ignorance
Of this being that is so secure
It pretends to be nothing.

Noche con su tiniebla, soledad con su paz,
Todo favorece
Mi delicia de anulación
Inminente.

¡Anulación, oh paraíso
Murmurado,
Dormir, dormir y sólo ser
Y muy despacio!

Oscuréceme y bórrame,
Santo sueño,
Mientras me guarda y vela bajo su potestad
El firmamento.

Con sus gravitaciones más umbrías
Reténgame la tierra,
Húndase mi ser en mi ser:
Duerma, duerma.

Night with its darkness, solitude with its peace,
Everything favors
My delight in the emptiness
That soon will come.

Emptiness, oh paradise
Rumored about so long:
Sleeping, sleeping, growing alone
Very slowly.

Darken me, erase me,
Blessed sleep,
As I lie under a heaven that mounts
Its guard over me.

Earth, with your darker burdens,
Drag me back down,
Sink my being into my being:
Sleep, sleep.

TRANSLATED BY JAMES WRIGHT

RÍO

¡Qué serena va el agua!
Silencios unifica.
Espadas de cristal
A la deriva esquivan
—Lenta espera—sus filos...
El mar las necesita.
Pero un frescor errante
Por el río extravía
Voces enamoradas.
Piden, juran, recitan.
¡Pulso de la corriente!
¡Cómo late: delira!
Bajo las aguas cielos
Intimos se deslizan.
La corola del aire
Profundo se ilumina.
Van más enamoradas
Las voces. Van, ansían.
Yo quisiera, quisiera...
Todo el río suspira.

RIVER

How calm the water flows!
It gathers silences.
Crystal swords
Drifting past withdraw
—A lingering pause—their blades . . .
The sea needs them.
But a cool breeze wandering
By the river leads away
Lovers' voices.
They beg, make vows, recite.
The pulse of the stream!
How it throbs! Raves.
Under the water familiar
Skies slip away.
The corolla of the deep
Wind is filled with light.
The voices go away
More loving. They go away, longing.
I wish, wish . . .
The whole river sighs.

TRANSLATED BY CHARLES GUENTHER

MUERTE DE UNOS ZAPATOS

¡Se me mueren! Han vivido
Con fidelidad: cristianos
Servidores que se honran
Y disfrutan ayudando,

Complaciendo a su señor,
Un caminante cansado,
A punto de preferir
La quietud de pies y ánimo.

Saben estas suelas. Saben
De andaduras palmo a palmo,
De intemperies descarriadas
Entre barros y guijarros...

Languidece en este cuero
Triste su matiz, antaño
Con sencillez el primor
De algún día engalanado.

Todo me anuncia una ruina
Que se me escapa. Quebranto
Mortal corroe el decoro.
Huyen. ¡Espectros—zapatos!

DEATH OF A PAIR OF SHOES

They're dying on me! They've lived
Faithfully, Christian
Servants honored
And happy helping

And pleasing their master,
A tired traveler
Ready to quit
For peace of soul and foot.

These soles know. They know
Step by step long rambles
And wet days, floundering
Among slop and cobbles.

Even the color drains
From the sad skins
Which, plain as they were, livened
Some forgotten festival.

All this announces a ruin
I don't grasp. The affliction
Of living corrodes honor.
They're running. Specters! Shoes!

TRANSLATED BY PHILIP LEVINE

ÚLTIMA TIERRA EN EL DESTIERRO

El destierro terminó ya.
No es de nadie ese fondo ciego,
Que ignorando el nombre de arriba
Ni emplaza en sitio humano al muerto.
No hay país por esas honduras,
Tan remotas, del cementerio
Donde sólo nosotros somos
Melancólicos extranjeros.
Quien fue el ausente yace ahí:
Última tierra en el destierro.

LAST LAND OF EXILE

The exile is ended now.
That blind emptiness belongs to no one,
For ignoring the name above
It doesn't call the dead man to a human place.
There is no country for those remote
Depths of the graveyard
Where only we are
Sad aliens.
Who was absent lies there:
Last land of exile.

TRANSLATED BY CHARLES GUENTHER

Gerardo Diego ❧

MOVIMIENTO PERPETUO

No canta el agua en la rueda
que se murió en la alameda

La luna abre la sombrilla
camino de la alameda

La sortija   La sortija
Dame la mano   dice mi hija

El agua muerta no canta
La luna llora en mi garganta

Todos los pájaros piden limosna

En mi garganta rueda la rueda
El agua ha muerto en la alameda

El agua ha muerto   hija
La enterrarán en una sortija

PERPETUAL MOTION

The water that died on the wheel
in the public gardens no longer sings

The moon opens its parasol
on the way to these shady groves

It's a ring   a ring
Give me your hand   says my daughter

The water is dead and doesn't sing
The moon sobs in my throat

All the birds are out begging

The wheel wheeling in my throat
The water has died in the public groves

The water has died   daughter
They will bury it in a ring

TRANSLATED BY RALPH NELSON

BIOGRAFÍA INCOMPLETA

Si canta la cigarra y bajo las pestañas
hay latitudes todavía
si las cerezas callan y las nubes meditan
tiempo es ya de cantar tu biografía
oh cebra soñadora

Claveles sobre el abismo
no son tan inocentes no como tu hocico
cuando descubre por sí solo
la identidad del cielo y de una espalda desnuda
y la conducta de las vírgenes
no es menos consecuente
que tus más bellas listas a la luz del poniente

Déjame recordar
La noche que tú naciste
el cielo avergonzado se arrancaba su hedionda costra de estrellas
Mas que difícil es perseverar

Entonces sobrevino
la coalición en masa de las palomas mensajeras
y las chispas del yunque
cruzaron temerarias las fronteras
Tus cinco meses cebra
cuando tu hermoso ejemplo
imitaban las jarcias de la melancolía
Tus cinco meses seducidos
por aquel ritmo a párpados del cinema mudo
y aquel si no si no de las ruletas en flor

Adónde te llevaron
Quién fué el ángel cow-boy que te raptó
En todas partes te adivino y llamo
Mis tirantes te buscan te adoran mis pijamas

UNFINISHED LIFE STORY

If the cricket sings and I lower my eyelashes
latitudes still exist
if the cherries become silent and clouds are deep in thought
then it's time to sing your life story
oh dreamer zebra

The carnations above the cavern
are not innocent not like your pouting face
when it discovers for itself
what the sky looks like or someone's naked back
and the way virgins have of acting
goes well
with your prettiest stripes in the light of the setting sun

Let me think back
The night you were born
the blushing sky was pulling off its dirty crust of stars

But it's so hard to keep going

Then the great
confederacy of messenger pigeons took place
and the sparks struck from the anvil
flew recklessly across the border

Your five months oh zebra
when the rigging of melancholy
copied your lovely pattern
Your five months trapped
by the flicker of the silent film's eyelid
and the do I don't I of the roulette wheel in full **bloom**

Where have they taken you
Who was the cowboy angel that raped you
I think I see you everywhere and call for you to come back
My suspenders are out looking for you my pajamas adore you

Pero he aquí que de pronto cruzas entre nosotros
Un denso aroma a Egipto de seis Nilos
flota en las cercanías

Y crímenes de amor de inmenso amor
de sexo a sexo sangran generosamente
y manos multiplicadas manos rojas de asesinos
enjugan su delito
sobre las tapias que de pudor cierran los ojos

CONDICIONAL

Si cascas como un huevo
un reloj abandonado de las horas
caerá sobre tus rodillas el retrato de tu madre muerta
Si arrancas ese botón umbilical de tu chaleco
cuando nadie le observa entre las hojas
verás cerrarse uno a uno los ojos de las esponjas

Si averiguas a fuerza de contemplarlo largamente
el oleaje sin espuma de una oreja querida
se te iluminará la mitad más íntima de la vida

Si mondas esta tarde una naranja con los dedos enguantados
a la noche la luna sigilosa
paseará por la orilla del río recogiendo
anillos de viudas y proyectos
de lentos crisantemos

Si por ventura quieres
gozar del privilegio último
de los reos de muerte y de los corderillos
no olvides cercenarte tus auroras más puras
y tus uñas más fieles   No lo olvides

But suddenly you are with us
A heavy perfume like Egypt's of the six Niles
floats around us

And crimes of love of untold love
where blood gushes sex to sex
and multiplying hands murderers' red hands
wipe their crime
on the mud walls that close their eyes in shame

TRANSLATED BY RALPH NELSON

ON THESE CONDITIONS

If you take a clock from which the hours have flown
and crack it open like an egg
the photograph of your dead mother will fall onto your lap
If you tear off the umbilical button on your vest
when nobody's watching among the leaves
you'll catch the sponges one by one shutting their eyes

If by looking a long time you finally discover
the foamless waves inside an ear you love
light will be thrown on your life's most intimate side

If with your gloved fingers you peel an orange this afternoon
tonight a lonely moon
will walk along the river's edge gathering
the wedding rings of widows and the plans
of the sluggish chrysanthemums

If you ever want to enjoy
the final privileges
of prisoners sentenced to death and of baby lambs
don't forget to clip your most innocent dawns
and your most faithful fingernails   Don't forget

TRANSLATED BY RALPH NELSON

HOSTILIDAD

Sin duda está muy bien la revolución armada de las encías
contra la tiranía de los ojos en blanco
Pero yo no tomaré nunca una determinación violenta
contra los afiliados al rumor de los mares

Cuanto hoy grita y gesticula
ardor de arena nómada y de tufo a berlina
será mañana simple candor de estirpe
reverencia de sauces
o quién sabe si ángeles en celo

Mira Te cambio mi corbata por tus magníficos ojos de cólera verde
y mi pulmón izquierdo por tu manera de decir Gerardo

También como tú los poetas viejos
estrangularon ríos
sin consideración a los geólogos

Mira Mira dónde está todo
El color de los trajes que imitaba tan bien calidades de nuestra
      propia corteza
el júbilo respiratorio de los perros adheridos a nuestro sueño
el giro de los horizontes sumisos a nuestros botones de oro
el lucir y apagar de aquel gusano en el rincón querido
Y hasta el derecho de hacer rodar una corona auténtica y enorme
por fragorosas escaleras de trueno

De todo ello no queda más
que un No me olvides nunca
que un recuerdo de tren entrando y saliendo por todos los túneles del
      cerebro
que un Deme usted un cigarro caballero

HOSTILITY

Without doubt there should be an armed uprising of the gums
against the tyranny of blank eyes
But I'll never use violence
against those who are in on the seas' whispers

Everything that screams and screws up its face now
the heat of the nomad sands and the bad odor of a stagecoach
will eventually turn into the simple frankness of good breeding
into willows that curtsy
or maybe even enthusiastic angels

Look I'll swap you my necktie for your lovely angry green eyes
and my left lung for the way you pronounce Gerardo

Like you the ancient poets
used to choke rivers
without a thought for the geologists

Look Look everything is there
The color of the suits that imitated so well the good quality of our
        own rough exterior
the happy breathing of the dogs close on the heels of our dream
the spin of the horizons humbled by our gold buttons
the off-and-on glow of that worm in the corner I love
And even the right to roll a genuine enormous crown
down the thunder-clap's noisy stairway

Of all this the only thing left
is a Never forget me
is the image of a train winding in and out of all the tunnels of the
        brain
and a May I have a cigarette sir

TRANSLATED BY RALPH NELSON
AND HARDIE ST. MARTIN

AL ZARPAR

No es verdad que el cielo y su compás de espera
estén colgados del mismo modo

A la izquierda lindamos con los mares secretos
al este con una cordillera de poemas
y toda nuestra vida
entre violines y columnas de humo
transcurre contemplando
cómo juegan al corro los pastores del Atica
y en reverencias de mitología
se ordenan y estrechocan las cerámicas

A veces todo está quieto
El paisaje olvidado permanece
la esquiva zapatilla arde sin tregua
y en un clavel de indiferencia
el termómetro hostil se endurece

Qué silbido de conciencia qué flemón de hemisferio
cómo todas las teclas coagulan
su vocación de lágrimas
y es cada una un oscilante fleco
de mensaje de luna

Cómo en el interior de cada hilo itinerario
se constituye el hueso
y el promontorio del jorobado
cómo suena a piano de cola

El mareo que antaño prendía tantas frentes
se refugia en el honesto vientre de la consola

A bordo sólo queda
un perro desempedrado de ladrillos
y un grumete de viento

De deciros adiós llegó el momento

SETTING SAIL

It's not true that the sky and its way of holding out
are hung with the same perspective

On the left we are flanked by secret seas
on the east by a mountain range of poems
and our entire life
among violins and pillars of smoke
is spent watching
how the shepherds of Attica form circles to play
and how with mythological curtsies
ceramics line up and crash against each other

Sometimes everything is hushed
The countryside remains forgotten
the bashful slipper burns and burns
and the hostile thermometer stiffens
into a carnation of indifference

What ringing of good faith inflames the hemisphere
it's as if in their calling to come to tears
all the piano keys coagulate
and each key is the whispering fringe
of a message from the moon

As if bone were thickening the center
of each wayfaring thread
and the hump of the hunchback
gives off the sound of a concert piano

The seasickness that years ago flushed so many faces
looks for safety in the dresser's honest belly

The only things left on board
are a dog of torn-out bricks
and the wind for cabin boy

It's time to say goodbye

TRANSLATED BY RALPH NELSON

UNA A UNA DESMONTÉ LAS PIEZAS DE TU ALMA

Una a una desmonté las piezas de tu alma.
Vi cómo era por dentro:
sus suaves coyunturas,
la resistencia esbelta de sus trazos.
Te aprendí palmo a palmo.
Pero perdí el secreto
de componerte.
Sé de tu alma menos que tú misma,
y el juguete difícil
es ya insoluble enigma.

SIEMPRE ABIERTOS TUS OJOS

Siempre abiertos tus ojos
(muchas veces se dijo) como un faro.
Pero la luz que exhalan
no derrama su chorro en los naufragios.
Enjuto, aunque desnudo,
voy derivando orillas de tu radio.
Soy yo el que giro
como un satélite imantado.
Y dime. Esta luz mía—tuya—que devuelvo,
¿a qué te sabe muerta en tu regazo?
¿Puede aumentar tu lumbre
este selenio resplandor lejano?

I STRIPPED YOUR SOUL DOWN

I stripped your soul down, part after part.
I saw what it was like inside:
its tender bone-hinges,
the slim resistance of its lines.
I came to know you, inch by inch.
But then I lost the secret,
how to put you back together.
I know even less about your soul than you do,
and the complicated pastime has turned
into something I don't know how to solve.

TRANSLATED BY HARDIE ST. MARTIN

YOUR EYES ARE ALWAYS OPEN

Your eyes are always open
(it's been said and said) like a lighthouse.
But the light they throw off
doesn't cast its beam on wrecked ships.
Lean-boned and naked,
I drift along the coastline of your body.
I am the one who circles
attracted like a magnetized moon.
Tell me. This light that I return, your light,
how does it taste dead there in your lap?
Can this distant moonlight
add anything to the light of your body?

TRANSLATED BY RALPH NELSON

JULIO CAMPAL

Íbamos once amigos a tu entierro.
Y tus veintiocho letras de alfabeto,
tus letras, Julio, sueltas,
tan voluntariamente encadenadas.

Lanzad letras al aire, como dados:
siempre caerá un poema.
Sembrad huesos descabalados
en esta o en la otra
o en la de más allá parcela:
siempre se reunirán hasta el completo
esqueleto.

Tu Mar del Plata o tierra natural,
Julio Campal.
Veintiocho letras velan tu secreto.

JULIO CAMPAL

We were walking to your funeral, eleven friends.
And the twenty-eight letters of your alphabet,
your letters, Julio, all set free
that were once so gladly bound together.

Throw letters into the air, like dice:
always a poem turns up.
Sow the scattered fragments of bone
in this or that
or in the remotest grave:
they will be made whole again, down
to the least fingerbone.

Your Mar del Plata or native land,
Julio Campal.
Twenty-eight letters hiding your secret.

TRANSLATED BY ROBERT MEZEY

LAS SEIS CUERDAS

La guitarra,
hace llorar a los sueños.
El sollozo de las almas
perdidas,
se escapa por su boca
redonda.
Y como la tarántula
teje una gran estrella
para cazar suspiros,
que flotan en su negro
aljibe de madera.

THE SIX STRINGS

The guitar
makes dreams cry.
The crying of lost
souls
escapes from its round
mouth.
And like the tarantula
it weaves a huge star
to catch sighs
that float on its black
wooden tank.

Translated by Donald Hall

MALAGUEÑA

La muerte
entra y sale
de la taberna.

Pasan caballos negros
y gente siniestra
por los hondos caminos
de la guitarra.

Y hay un olor a sal
y a sangre de hembra,
en los nardos febriles
de la marina.

La muerte
entra y sale,
y sale y entra
la muerte
de la taberna.

MALAGUEÑA

Death
is entering and leaving
the tavern.

Black horses and dark
people are riding
over the deep roads
of the guitar.

There is an odor of salt
and female blood
in the warm spice plants
near the sea.

Death
is coming in and leaving
the tavern,
death
leaving and coming in.

TRANSLATED BY ROBERT BLY

AGOSTO

Agosto.
Contraponientes
de melocotón y azúcar,
y el sol dentro de la tarde,
como el hueso en una fruta.

La panocha guarda intacta
su risa amarilla y dura.

Agosto.
Los niños comen
pan moreno y rica luna.

EL NIÑO MUDO

El niño buscaba su voz.
(La tenía el rey de los grillos.)
En una gota de agua
buscaba su voz el niño.

No la quiero para hablar;
me haré con ella un anillo
que llevará mi silencio
en su dedo pequeñito.

En una gota de agua
buscaba su voz el niño.

(La voz cautiva, a lo lejos,
se ponía un traje de grillo.)

AUGUST

August.
The opposing
of peach and sugar,
and the sun inside the afternoon
like the stone in the fruit.

The ear of corn keeps
its laughter intact, yellow and firm.

August.
The little boys eat
brown bread and delicious moon.

TRANSLATED BY JAMES WRIGHT

THE LITTLE MUTE BOY

The little boy was looking for his voice.
(The king of the crickets had it.)
In a drop of water
the little boy was looking for his voice.

I do not want it for speaking with;
I will make a ring of it
that my silence may wear
on its little finger.

In a drop of water
the little boy was looking for his voice.

(The captive voice, far away,
put on a cricket's clothes.)

TRANSLATED BY W. S. MERWIN

CANCIÓN DEL NARANJO SECO

Leñador.
Córtame la sombra.
Líbrame del suplicio
de verme sin toronjas.

¿Por qué nací entre espejos?
El día me da vueltas,
y la noche me copia
en todas sus estrellas.

Quiero vivir sin verme.
Y hormigas y vilanos,
soñaré que son mis
hojas y mis pájaros.

Leñador.
Córtame la sombra.
Líbrame del suplicio
de verme sin toronjas.

REYERTA

A Rafael Méndez

En la mitad del barranco
las navajas de Albacete,
bellas de sangre contraria,
relucen como los peces.
Una dura luz de naipe
recorta en el agrio verde,
caballos enfurecidos

SONG OF THE BARREN ORANGE TREE

Woodcutter.
Cut my shadow from me.
Free me from the torment
of seeing myself without fruit.

Why was I born among mirrors?
The day walks in circles around me,
and the night copies me
in all its stars.

I want to live without seeing myself.
And I will dream that ants
and thistleburrs are my
leaves and my birds.

Woodcutter.
Cut my shadow from me.
Free me from the torment
of seeing myself without fruit.

TRANSLATED BY W. S. MERWIN

QUARREL

To Rafael Méndez

In the middle of the canyon
the switchblades of Albacete,
prettied with a foreman's blood,
scatter and shine like fish.
A hard light like a playing card
carves out of the bitter green
the horses driven to a madness

y perfiles de jinetes.
En la copa de un olivo
lloran dos viejas mujeres.
El toro de la reyerta
se sube por las paredes.
Ángeles negros traían
pañuelos y agua de nieve.
Ángeles con grandes alas
de navajas de Albacete.
Juan Antonio el de Montilla
rueda muerto la pendiente,
su cuerpo lleno de lirios
y una granada en las sienes.
Ahora monta cruz de fuego,
carretera de la muerte.

El juez, con guardia civil,
por los olivares viene.
Sangre resbalada gime
muda canción de serpiente.
Señores guardias civiles:
aquí pasó lo de siempre.
Han muerto cuatro romanos
y cinco cartagineses.

La tarde loca de higueras
y de rumores calientes
cae desmayada en los muslos
heridos de los jinetes.
Y ángeles negros volaban
por el aire del poniente.
Ángeles de largas trenzas
y corazones de aceite.

and the edged profiles of the horsemen.
In the shelter of an olive
two old women do their weeping.
The wild bull of this quarrel
is breaking through the barrier.
Black angels came bearing
bandages and snow water.
Angels with gigantic wings
of the switchblades of Albacete.
Juan Antonio, the one from Montilla,
rolls murdered down the slope,
his body overflowed with lilies,
and a pomegranate on his temple.
He mounts now his cross of fire
on the wide highway of his death.

The judge, with the gentlemen of the posse,
arrives through the olive grove.
Shed blood cries out,
a serpent's wordless song.
Honored gentlemen of the posse:
here happened what always happens.
Four Romans have been murdered
and five Carthaginians.

The afternoon crazed with fig trees
and aseethe with whisperings
falls collapsed on the mangled
thighbones of the horseback riders.
And black angels have been flying
through the winds from out the west.
Angels with flowing braids
and hearts bearing soothing oil.

TRANSLATED BY WILLIAM STAFFORD
AND HERBERT BAIRD

CIUDAD SIN SUEÑO

(Nocturno del Brooklyn Bridge)

No duerme nadie por el cielo. Nadie, nadie.
No duerme nadie.
Las criaturas de la luna huelen y rondan sus cabañas.
Vendrán las iguanas vivas a morder a los hombres que no sueñan
y el que huye con el corazón roto encontrará por las esquinas
al increible cocodrilo quieto bajo la tierna protesta de los astros.

No duerme nadie por el mundo. Nadie, nadie.
No duerme nadie.
Hay un muerto en el cementerio más lejano
que se queja tres años
porque tiene un paisaje seco en la rodilla;
y el niño que enterraron esta mañana lloraba tanto
que hubo necesidad de llamar a los perros para que callase.

No es sueño la vida. ¡Alerta! ¡Alerta! ¡Alerta!
Nos caemos por las escaleras para comer la tierra húmeda
o subimos al filo de la nieve con el coro de las dalias muertas.
Pero no hay olvido, ni sueño;
carne viva. Los besos atan las bocas
en una maraña de venas recientes
y al que le duele su dolor le dolerá sin descanso
y al que teme la muerte la llevará sobre sus hombros.

Un día
los caballos vivirán en las tabernas
y las hormigas furiosas
atacarán los cielos amarillos que se refugian en los ojos de las vacas.

CITY THAT DOES NOT SLEEP

(Nightsong of Brooklyn Bridge)

In the sky there is nobody asleep. Nobody, nobody.
Nobody is asleep.
The creatures of the moon sniff and prowl about their cabins.
The living iguanas will come to bite the men who do not dream,
and the man who rushes out with his spirit broken will meet on the
   street corner
the unbelievable alligator quiet beneath the tender protest of the
   stars.

Nobody is asleep on earth. Nobody, nobody.
Nobody is asleep.
In the graveyard far off there is a corpse
who has moaned for three years
because of a dry countryside on his knee;
and that boy they buried this morning cried so much
it was necessary to call out the dogs to keep him quiet.

Life is not a dream. Careful! Careful! Careful!
We fall down the stairs in order to eat the moist earth
or we climb to the knife-edge of the snow with the voices of the dead
   dahlias.
But forgetfulness does not exist, dreams do not exist;
flesh exists. Kisses tie our mouths
in a thicket of new veins,
and whoever his pain pains will feel that pain forever
and whoever is afraid of death will carry it on his shoulders.

One day
the horses will live in the saloons
and the enraged ants
will throw themselves on the yellow skies that take refuge in the
   eyes of cows.

Otro día
veremos la resurrección de las mariposas disecadas
y aun andando por un paisaje de esponjas grises y barcos mudos
veremos brillar nuestro anillo y manar rosas de nuestra lengua.
¡Alerta! ¡Alerta! ¡Alerta!
A los que guardan todavía huellas de zarpa y aguacero,
a aquel muchacho que llora porque no sabe la invención del puente
o aquel muerto que ya no tiene más que la cabeza y un zapato,
hay que llevarlos al muro donde iguanas y sierpes esperan,
donde espera la dentadura del oso,
donde espera la mano momificada del niño
y la piel del camello se eriza con un violento escalofrío azul.

No duerme nadie por el cielo. Nadie, nadie.
No duerme nadie.
Pero si alguien cierra los ojos,
¡azotadlo, hijos míos, azotadlo!
Haya un panorama de ojos abiertos
y amargas llagas encendidas.
No duerme nadie por el mundo. Nadie, nadie.
Ya lo he dicho.
No duerme nadie.
Pero si alguien tiene por la noche exceso de musgo en las sienes,
abrid los escotillos para que vea bajo la luna
las copas falsas, el veneno y la calavera de los teatros.

Another day
we will watch the preserved butterflies rise from the dead
and still walking through a country of gray sponges and silent boats
we will watch our ring flash and roses spring from our tongue.
Careful! Be careful! Be careful!
The men who still have marks of the claw and the thunderstorm,
and that boy who cries because he has never heard of the invention
        of the bridge,
or that dead man who possesses now only his head and a shoe,
we must carry them to the wall where the iguanas and the snakes
        are waiting,
where the bear's teeth are waiting,
where the mummified hand of the boy is waiting,
and the hair of the camel stands on end with a violent blue shudder.

Nobody is sleeping in the sky. Nobody, nobody.
Nobody is sleeping.
If someone does close his eyes,
a whip, boys, a whip!
Let there be a landscape of open eyes
and bitter wounds on fire.
No one is sleeping in this world. No one, no one.
I have said it before.

No one is sleeping.
But if someone grows too much moss on his temples during the
        night,
open the stage trapdoors so he can see in the moonlight
the lying goblets, and the poison, and the skull of the theaters.

TRANSLATED BY ROBERT BLY

NEW YORK

Oficina y denuncia

A Fernando Vela

Debajo de las multiplicaciones
hay una gota de sangre de pato;
debajo de las divisiones
hay una gota de sangre de marinero;
debajo de las sumas, un río de sangre tierna.
Un río que viene cantando
por los dormitorios de los arrabales,
y es plata, cemento o brisa
en el alba mentida de New York.
Existen las montañas. Lo sé.
Y los anteojos para la sabiduría.
Lo sé. Pero yo no he venido a ver el cielo.
Yo he venido para ver la turbia sangre.
La sangre que lleva las máquinas a las cataratas
y el espíritu a la lengua de la cobra.
Todos los días se matan en New York
cuatro millones de patos,
cinco millones de cerdos,
dos mil palomas para el gusto de los agonizantes,
un millón de vacas,
un millón de corderos
y dos millones de gallos,
que dejan los cielos hechos añicos.
Más vale sollozar afilando la navaja
o asesinar a los perros
en las alucinantes cacerías,
que resistir en la madrugada
los interminables trenes de leche,
los interminables trenes de sangre
y los trenes de rosas maniatadas
por los comerciantes de perfumes.

NEW YORK

(*Office and Attack*)

For Fernando Vela

Beneath all the statistics
there is a drop of duck's blood.
Beneath all the columns
there is a drop of sailor's blood.
Beneath all the totals, a river of warm blood.
A river that goes singing
past the bedrooms of the suburbs,
and the river is silver, cement, or wind
in the lying daybreak of New York.
The mountains exist, I know that.
And the lenses ground for wisdom,
I know that. But I have not come to see the sky.
I have come to see the stormy blood,
the blood that sweeps the machines to the waterfalls,
and the spirit on to the cobra's tongue.
Every day they kill in New York
ducks, four million,
pigs, five million,
pigeons, two thousand, for the enjoyment of dying men,
cows, one million,
lambs, one million,
roosters, two million
who turn the sky to small splinters.
You may as well sob filing a razor blade
or assassinate dogs
in the hallucinating foxhunts,
as try to stop in the dawnlight
the endless trains carrying milk,
the endless trains carrying blood,
and the trains carrying roses put in chains
by those in the field of perfume.

Los patos y las palomas,
y los cerdos y los corderos
ponen sus gotas de sangre
debajo de las multiplicaciones,
y los terribles alaridos de las vacas estrujadas
llenan de dolor el valle
donde el Hudson se emborracha con aceite.
Yo denuncio a toda la gente
que ignora la otra mitad,
la mitad irredimible
que levanta sus montes de cemento
donde laten los corazones
de los animalitos que se olvidan
y donde caeremos todos
en la última fiesta de los taladros.
Os escupo en la cara.
La otra mitad me escucha
devorando, orinando, volando, en su pureza
como los niños de las porterías
que llevan frágiles palitos
a los huecos donde se oxidan
las antenas de los insectos.
No es el infierno, es la calle.
No es la muerte, es la tienda de frutas.
Hay un mundo de ríos quebrados
y distancias inasibles
en la patita de ese gato
quebrada por el automóvil,
y yo oigo el canto de la lombriz
en el corazón de muchas niñas.
Óxido, fermento, tierra estremecida.
Tierra tú mismo que nadas
por los números de la oficina.
¿Qué voy a hacer? ¿Ordenar los paisajes?
¿Ordenar los amores que luego son fotografías,
que luego son pedazos de madera
y bocanadas de sangre?

The ducks and the pigeons
and the hogs and the lambs
lay their drops of blood down
underneath all the statistics;
and the terrible bawling of the packed-in cattle
fills the valley with suffering
where the Hudson is getting drunk on its oil.
I attack all those persons
who know nothing of the other half,
the half who cannot be saved,
who raise their cement mountains
in which the hearts of the small
animals no one thinks of are beating,
and from which we will all fall
during the final holiday of the drills.
I spit in your face.
The other half hears me,
as they go on eating, urinating, flying in their purity
like the children of the janitors
who carry delicate sticks
to the holes where the antennas
of the insects are rusting.
This is not hell, it is a street.
This is not death, it is a fruit stand.
There is a whole world of crushed rivers
and unachievable distances
in the paw of the cat
crushed by a car,
and I hear the song of the worm
in the heart of so many girls.
Rust, rotting, trembling earth.
And you are earth, swimming
through the figures of the office.
What shall I do, set my landscapes in order?
Set in place the lovers who will afterwards be photographs,
who will be bits of wood
and mouthfuls of blood?

San Ignacio de Loyola
asesinó un pequeño conejo
y todavía sus labios gimen
por las torres de las iglesias.
No, no, no, no; yo denuncio.
Yo denuncio la conjura
de estas desiertas oficinas
que no radian las agonías,
que borran los programas de la selva,
y me ofrezco a ser comido
por las vacas estrujadas
cuando sus gritos llenan el valle
donde el Hudson se emborracha con aceite.

St. Ignatius of Loyola
murdered a small rabbit
and its lips moan still
high on the church steeples.
No, I won't; I attack,
I attack the conspiring
of these empty offices
that will not broadcast the sufferings,
that rub out the plans of the forest,
and I offer myself to be eaten
by the packed-in cattle
when their mooing fills the valley
where the Hudson is getting drunk on its oil.

TRANSLATED BY ROBERT BLY

CUERPO PRESENTE

La piedra es una frente donde los sueños gimen
sin tener agua curva ni cipreses helados.
La piedra es una espalda para llevar al tiempo
con árboles de lágrimas y cintas y planetas.

Yo he visto lluvias grises correr hacia las olas
levantando sus tiernos brazos acribillados,
para no ser cazadas por la piedra tendida
que desata sus miembros sin empapar la sangre.

Porque la piedra coge simientes y nublados,
esqueletos de alondras y lobos de penumbra;
pero no da sonidos, ni cristales, ni fuego,
sino plazas y plazas y otras plazas sin muros.

Ya está sobre la piedra Ignacio el bien nacido.
Ya se acabó; ¿qué pasa? Contemplad su figura:
la muerte le ha cubierto de pálidos azufres
y le ha puesto cabeza de oscuro minotauro.

Ya se acabó. La lluvia penetra por su boca.
El aire como loco deja su pecho hundido,
y el Amor, empapado con lágrimas de nieve,
se calienta en la cumbre de las ganaderías.

¿Qué dicen? Un silencio con hedores reposa.
Estamos con un cuerpo presente que se esfuma,
con una forma clara que tuvo ruiseñores
y la vemos llenarse de agujeros sin fondo.

¿Quién arruga el sudario? ¡No es verdad lo que dice!
Aquí no canta nadie, ni llora en el rincón,
ni pica las espuelas, ni espanta la serpiente:
aquí no quiero más que los ojos redondos
para ver ese cuerpo sin posible descanso.

THE LAID-OUT BODY

This stone is a forehead where dreams groan
for lack of winding water and frozen cypresses.
This stone is a shoulder for carrying time away
with trees of tears and ribbons and planets.

I have seen gray rains running toward the sea
holding up tender riddled arms
to get away from the stone lying here
which tears limbs off but doesn't soak up the blood.

For this stone hooks into seeds and clouds,
skeletons of larks, wolves of the twilight:
yet makes no cry, no crystals, no flames,
only bullrings, bullrings, more bullrings without walls.

Ignacio the well-born is lying on stone.
It's all over now. What's happening? Look at him:
Death has spread pale sulphur on his face
and put the head of a dark minotaur upon him.

It's all over now. The rain seeps in through his mouth.
The air, as though gone crazy, flies out of his broken chest,
and love, soaked through with snowy tears,
tries to get warm on the heights of the ranches.

What are they saying? A stenching silence settles down.
We are here, before this body about to disappear,
this pure shape that once held nightingales,
we watch it being gored full of bottomless holes.

Who rumples the shroud? It's not true what he says!
Here no one is to sing, no one is to wail in a corner,
or dig his spurs in, or frighten the snake:
here I want only eyes wide open
to gaze on this body without ever resting.

Yo quiero ver aquí los hombres de voz dura.
Los que doman caballos y dominan los ríos:
los hombres que les suena el esqueleto y cantan
con una boca llena de sol y pedernales.

Aquí quiero yo verlos. Delante de la piedra.
Delante de este cuerpo con las riendas quebradas.
Yo quiero que me enseñen dónde está la salida
para este capitán atado por la muerte.

Yo quiero que me enseñen un llanto como un río
que tenga dulces nieblas y profundas orillas,
para llevar el cuerpo de Ignacio y que se pierda
sin escuchar el doble resuello de los toros.

Que se pierda en la plaza redonda de la luna
que finge cuando niña doliente res inmóvil;
que se pierda en la noche sin canto de los peces
y en la maleza blanca del humo congelado.

No quiero que le tapen la cara con pañuelos
para que se acostumbre con la muerte que le lleva.
Vete, Ignacio: No sientas el caliente bramido.
Duerme, vuela, reposa: ¡También se muere el mar!

(Fragmento de Llanto por Ignacio
Sánchez Mejías)

I want to see here those men of ringing voice.
Those men who break stallions and master rivers:
men whose skeletons make themselves heard and who sing
with mouths full of sunlight and flints.

This is where I want to see them. Facing the stone.
Facing this body whose reins have been broken.
I want them to show me if there is some way out
for this captain death has tied down.

I want them to teach me to weep like a river,
one with gentle mists and banks that are so tall
I could bear Ignacio's body away on it silently,
out of earshot of the double snorts of the bulls.

Let him go off into the round bullring of the moon
who has, when she is new, the horns of a sad, quiet bull;
let him go off into the night where fish stop singing
and into the white thickets of frozen smoke.

I do not want them to put handkerchiefs over his face
to help him get used to the death he carries.
Go, Ignacio: leave behind the hot bellowing.
Sleep, soar, rest: even the sea dies.

(*From* Lament for Ignacio Sánchez Mejías)

TRANSLATED BY GALWAY KINNELL

GACELA DEL AMOR IMPREVISTO

Nadie comprendía el perfume
de la oscura magnolia de tu vientre.
Nadie sabía que martirizabas
un colibrí de amor entre los dientes.

Mil caballitos persas se dormían
en la plaza con luna de tu frente,
mientras que yo enlazaba cuatro noches
tu cintura, enemiga de la nieve.

Entre yeso y jazmines, tu mirada
era un pálido ramo de simientes.
Yo busqué, para darte, por mi pecho
las letras de marfil que dicen *siempre*,

siempre, siempre: jardín de mi agonía,
tu cuerpo fugitivo para siempre,
la sangre de tus venas en mi boca,
tu boca ya sin luz para mi muerte.

GACELA OF UNFORESEEN LOVE

No one understood the perfume
of the dark magnolia of your womb.
No one knew that you tormented
a hummingbird of love between your teeth.

A thousand Persian ponies fell asleep
in the moonlit plaza of your forehead,
while through four nights I embraced
your waist, enemy of the snow.

Between plaster and jasmines, your glance
was a pale branch of seeds.
I sought in my heart to give you
the ivory letters that say *always*,

always, always: garden of my agony,
your body elusive always,
the blood of your veins in my mouth,
your mouth already lightless for my death.

TRANSLATED BY W. S. MERWIN

CERRADA

Campo desnudo. Sola
la noche inerme. El viento
insinúa latidos
sordos contra sus lienzos.

La sombra a plomo ciñe,
fría, sobre tu seno
su seda grave, negra,
cerrada. Queda opreso

el bulto así en materia
de noche, insigne, quieto
sobre el límpido plano
retrasado del cielo.

Hay estrellas fallidas.
Pulidos goznes. Hielos
flotan a la deriva
en lo alto. Fríos lentos.

Una sombra que pasa,
sobre el contorno serio
y mudo bate, adusta,
su látigo secreto.

Flagelación. Corales
de sangre o luz o fuego
bajo el cendal se auguran,
vetean, ceden luego.

CLOSED

Bare earth. The defenseless
night alone. The wind
insinuates deaf throbbings
against its draperies.

The shadow of lead,
cold, wraps your breast
in its heavy silk, black,
closed. So the mass

is pressed down by the material
of night, famous, quiet,
over the limpid
late plain of night.

There are bankrupt stars.
Polished hinges. Ice
drifts along
in the heights. Slow streams of cold.

A shadow passing
over the mute grave contour
lashes, austere,
its secret whip.

Flagellation. Corals
of blood or light or fire
are divined under the gauze,
grow mottled, then give way.

O carne o luz de carne,
profunda. Vive el viento
porque anticipa ráfagas,
cruces, pausas, silencios.

EL VALS

Eres hermosa como la piedra,
oh difunta;
oh viva, oh viva, eres dichosa como la nave.
Esta orquesta que agita
mis cuidados como una negligencia,
como un elegante biendecir de buen tono,
ignora el vello de los pubis,
ignora la risa que sale del esternón como una gran batuta.

Unas olas de afrecho,
un poco de serrín en los ojos,
o si acaso en las sienes,
o acaso adornando las cabelleras;
unas faldas largas hechas de colas de cocodrilos;
unas lenguas o unas sonrisas hechas con caparazones de cangrejos.
Todo lo que está suficientemente visto
no puede sorprender a nadie.

Las damas aguardan su momento sentadas sobre una lágrima,
disimulando la humedad a fuerza de abanico insistente.
Y los caballeros abandonados de sus traseros
quieren atraer todas las miradas a la fuerza hacia sus bigotes.

Pero el vals ha llegado.
Es una playa sin ondas,

Either flesh or the light of flesh,
deep. The wind lives
because it looks forward to gusts,
cross-currents, pauses, silences.

TRANSLATED BY W. S. MERWIN

THE WALTZ

You are beautiful as a stone,
oh my dead woman!
Oh my living, living woman, you are happy as a ship!
This orchestra which stirs up
my worries like a thoughtlessness,
like an elegant witticism in a fashionable drawl,
knows nothing of the down on the secret mound,
knows nothing of the laugh which rises from the breastbone like an
        immense baton.

A few waves made of bran,
a bit of sawdust in the eyes,
or perhaps even on the temples
or perhaps decorating the women's hair.
Trailing skirts made of alligator tails,
some tongues or smiles made of the shells of crabs.
All those things that have been seen so often
can take no one by surprise.

The ladies wait for their moment seated upon a tear,
keeping their dampness hidden with a stubborn fan,
and the gentlemen, abandoned by the women's buttocks,
try to draw all looks toward their mustaches.

But the waltz is here.
It is a beach with no waves,

es un entrechocar de conchas, de tacones, de espumas o de dentaduras
  postizas.
Es todo lo revuelto que arriba.

Pechos exuberantes en bandeja en los brazos,
dulces tartas caídas sobre los hombros llorosos,
una languidez que revierte,
un beso sorprendido en el instante que se hacía "cabello de angel,"
un dulce "sí" de cristal pintado verde.

Un polvillo de azúcar sobre las frentes
da una blancura cándida a las palabras limadas,
y las manos se acortan más redondeadas que nunca,
mientras fruncen los vestidos hechos de esparto querido.

Las cabezas son nubes, la música es una larga goma,
las colas de plomo casi vuelan, y el estrépito
se ha convertido en los corazones en oleadas de sangre,
en un licor, si blanco, que sabe a memoria o a cita.

Adiós, adiós, esmeralda, amatista o misterio;
adiós, como una bola enorme ha llegado el instante,
el preciso momento de la desnudez cabeza abajo,
cuando los vellos van a pinchar los labios obscenos que saben.
Es el instante, el momento de decir la palabra que estalla,
el momento en que los vestidos se convertirán en aves,
las ventanas en gritos,
las luces en ¡socorro!
y ese beso que estaba (en el rincón) entre dos bocas
se convertirá en una espina
que dispensará la muerte diciendo:
Yo os amo.

it is a clashing together of seashells, heels, foam, and false teeth.
It is the churned up things arriving.

Exultant breasts on the serving tray of arms,
sweet cakes fallen on the weeping shoulders,
a languorousness that comes over you again,
a kiss taken by surprise just as it turns into cotton candy,
a sweet "yes" of glass painted green.

Powdered sugar on the foreheads
gives a simple whiteness to the polished words
and the hands grow short, and rounder than ever
and wrinkle up the dresses as though they were sweet esparto grass.

The heads are clouds, the music is a long piece of rubber,
the tails made of lead almost fly, and the noise
has turned into waves of blood inside the heart,
and into a white liqueur that tastes of memories or a rendezvous.

Goodbye, goodbye, emerald, amethyst, secret,
goodbye, the instant has arrived like an enormous ball,
the precise moment of nakedness head down
when the downy hair begins to penetrate the obscene lips that know.

It is the instant, the moment of pronouncing the word that explodes,
the moment in which the dresses will turn into birds,
the windows into cries,
the lights into "help!",
and the kiss that was over there (in the corner) between two mouths
will be changed into a fishbone
that will distribute death saying:
I love you.

TRANSLATED BY ROBERT BLY

VIDA

Un pájaro de papel en el pecho
dice que el tiempo de los besos no ha llegado;
vivir, vivir, el sol cruje invisible,
besos o pájaros, tarde o pronto o nunca.
Para morir basta un ruidillo,
el de otro corazón al callarse,
o ese regazo ajeno que en la tierra
es un navío dorado para los pelos rubios.
Cabeza dolorida, sienes de oro, sol que va a ponerse;
aquí en la sombra sueño con un río,
juncos de verde sangre que ahora nace,
sueño apoyado en ti calor o vida.

NO EXISTE EL HOMBRE

Sólo la luna sospecha la verdad.
Y es que no existe el hombre.

La luna tantea por los llanos, atraviesa los ríos,
penetra por los bosques.
Modela las aún tibias montañas.
Encuentra el calor de las ciudades erguidas.
Fragua una sombra, mata una oscura esquina,
inunda de fulgurantes rosas
el misterio de las cuevas donde no huele a nada.

La luna pasa, sabe, canta, avanza y avanza sin descanso.
Un mar no es un lecho donde el cuerpo de un hombre puede tenderse
    a solas.
Un mar no es un sudario para una muerte lúcida.

LIFE

A paper bird I have in my chest
tells me the time for kisses has not yet come.
To live! To live! . . . no one sees the sun crackle,
kisses or birds, late or on time or never.
A tiny noise is enough to kill you,
the noise of some other heart falling silent,
or that far-off lap which on this earth
is a gold ship where the blond hair sails!
Head full of pain, gold temples, sun dying.
I keep dreaming of a river in this darkness,
reeds full of green blood just being born,
warmth or life, I dream leaning on you.

TRANSLATED BY ROBERT BLY

MAN DOESN'T EXIST

Only the moon suspects the truth.
And it's that man doesn't exist.

The moon feels its way over the fields and crosses the rivers,
it probes into the woods.
It gives a shape to the still warm mountains.
It runs into the heat from built-up cities.
It forms a shadow and kills a dark corner,
and its flashing roses flood
the mystery of the caves where there is no odor.

The moon chants a tune and understands and moves and goes on and
    on without stopping.
An ocean isn't a bed where a man's body can stretch out all alone.
An ocean isn't a shroud to cover a shining death.

La luna sigue, cala, ahonda, raya las profundas arenas.
Mueve fantástica los verdes rumores aplacados.
Un cadáver en pie un instante se mece,
duda, ya avanza, verde queda inmóvil.
La luna miente sus brazos rotos,
su imponente mirada donde unos peces anidan.
Enciende las ciudades hundidas donde todavía se pueden oír
(qué dulces) las campanas vívidas;
donde las ondas postreras aún repercuten sobre los pechos neutros,
sobre los pechos blandos que algún pulpo ha adorado.

Pero la luna es pura y seca siempre.
Sale de un mar que es una caja siempre,
que es un bloque con límites que nadie, nadie estrecha,
que no es una piedra sobre un monte irradiando.

Sale y persigue lo que fuera los huesos,
lo que fuera las venas de un hombre,
lo que fuera su sangre sonada, su melodiosa cárcel,
su cintura visible que a la vida divide,
o su cabeza ligera sobre un aire hacia oriente.

Pero el hombre no existe.
Nunca ha existido, nunca.
Pero el hombre no vive, como no vive el día.
Pero la luna inventa sus metales furiosos.

The moon keeps going, it scratches and soaks and sinks into the
    packed sand.
It gives the calm green murmurs an incredible motion.
A corpse stands up and sways for a moment,
he wavers and then goes on. He stops, green and still.
The moon alters his broken arms,
his stern gaze where some fish are nestling.
The moon sets fire to the sunken cities where you can still hear
(how pleasing!) the clear bells;
where the last ripples still echo over the neuter breasts,
over the soft breasts that some octopus has worshipped.

But the moon is always pure and dry.
It comes from an ocean that's always a container,
that's a block of stone whose limits no one, no one can cut down,
an ocean that isn't a rock glowing on top of a mountain.

The moon comes out and chases what used to be a man's bones,
what used to be his blood vessels,
what used to be his sonorous blood, his prison full of songs,
his visible waist that divides life,
or his light head going east on the wind.

But man doesn't exist.
He has never existed, never.
But man doesn't live, as the day doesn't live.
But the moon invents his furious metals.

TRANSLATED BY LEWIS HYDE

EL CUERPO Y EL ALMA

Pero es más triste todavía, mucho más triste.
Triste como la rama que deja caer su fruto para nadie.
Más triste, más. Como ese vaho
que de la tierra exhala después la pulpa muerta.
Como esa mano que del cuerpo tendido
se eleva y quiere solamente acariciar las luces,
la sonrisa doliente, la noche aterciopelada y muda.
Luz de la noche sobre el cuerpo tendido sin alma.
Alma fuera, alma fuera del cuerpo, planeando
tan delicadamente sobre la triste forma abandonada.
Alma de niebla dulce, suspendida
sobre su ayer amante, cuerpo inerme
que pálido se enfría con las nocturnas horas
y queda quieto, solo, dulcemente vacío.

Alma de amor que vela y se separa
vacilando, y al fin se aleja tiernamente fría.

THE BODY AND THE SOUL

But it is sadder than that, much, much sadder.
Sad as a branch letting its fruit fall for no one.
Sadder, much sadder. Like the mist
the dead fruit breathes out from the earth.
Like this hand that rises from the corpse lying in state
and merely wants to touch the lamps,
the grieving smile, the night speechless and velvet.
Luminous night above the corpse stretched out without its soul.
The soul outside, soul outside the body, swooping
with such delicacy over the shape sad and abandoned.
Soul of soft mist, held floating
above its former lover, the defenseless and pale
body, which grows colder as the night goes on,
it remains silent, alone, empty in a gentle way.

Soul of love that watches and hesitates
to free itself, but finally leaves, gentle and cold.

TRANSLATED BY ROBERT BLY

EL VIEJO Y EL SOL

Había vivido mucho.

Se apoyaba allí, viejo, en un tronco, en un gruesísimo tronco, muchas
   tardes cuando el sol caía.

Yo pasaba por allí a aquellas horas y me detenía a observarle.

Era viejo y tenía la faz arrugada, apagados, más que tristes, los
   ojos.

Se apoyaba en el tronco, y el sol se le acercaba primero, le mordía
   suavemente los pies

y allí se quedaba unos momentos como acurrucado.

Después ascendía e iba sumergiéndole, anegándole,

tirando suavemente de él, unificándole en su dulce luz.

¡Oh el viejo vivir, el viejo quedar, cómo se desleía!

Toda la quemazón, la historia de la tristeza, el resto de las arrugas,
   la miseria de la piel roída,

¡cómo iba lentamente limándose, deshaciéndose!

Como una roca que en el torrente devastador se va dulcemente
   desmoronando,

rindiéndose a un amor sonorísimo,

así, en aquel silencio, el viejo se iba lentamente anulando, lentamente
   entregando.

Y yo veía el poderoso sol lentamente morderle con mucho amor y
   adormirle

para así poco a poco tomarle, para así poquito a poco disolverle en
   su luz,

como una madre que a su niño suavísimamente en su seno lo
   reinstalase.

Yo pasaba y lo veía. Pero a veces no veía sino un sutilísimo resto.
   Apenas un levísimo encaje del ser.

Lo que quedaba después que el viejo amoroso, el viejo dulce, había
   pasado ya a ser la luz

y despaciosísimamente era arrastrado en los rayos postreros del sol,

como tantas otras invisibles cosas del mundo.

THE OLD MAN AND THE SUN

He had lived a long time.
There he leaned, the old man, against a tree trunk, against an
    enormous tree trunk, many afternoons as the sun was setting.
I passed there at that hour and paused to watch him.
He was old and his face was wrinkled, with the eyes faded and
    inexpressibly sad.
He leaned against the trunk and the sun came up to him first and
    gently nibbled his feet
and there it stayed for a few moments as though huddled up.
Then it climbed and went on immersing him, flooding him,
drawing him gently, mingling him in its soft light.
Oh the old living, the old enduring, how it dissolved!
All the smarting, the history of sadness, the wrinkles that were left,
    the wretchedness of the fretted skin,
how they wore away slowly, and were undone!
Like a rock that the smashing torrent wears down little by little,
giving itself up to a thunderous love,
so in the silence the old man was slowly effaced, slowly surrendered.
And I saw the powerful sun slowly eat him away with great love
    and put him to sleep
to swallow him down that way, little by little, to dissolve him a
    little at a time that way in its light
like a mother who very gently settles her baby again at her breast.

I passed there and I saw it. But at times I saw nothing but the
    frailest of remnants. The faintest tracery of being, hardly
    there.
What was left when the loving old man, the honeyed old man, had
    already turned into light
and was slowly drawn off in the last rays of the sun
like so many other invisible things of the world.

TRANSLATED BY W. S. MERWIN

ANTE EL ESPEJO

Como un fantasma que de pronto se asoma
y entre las cortinas silenciosas adelanta su rostro y nos mira,
y parece que mudamente nos dijera...

Así tú ahora, mientras sentada ante el vidrio elevas tus brazos,
componiendo el cabello que, sin brillo, organizas.
Desde tu espalda te he mirado en el espejo.
Cansado rostro, cansadas facciones silenciosas
que parecen haberse levantado tristísimas como después de un largo
        esfuerzo que hubiese durado el quedar de los años.
Como un cuerpo que un momento se distendiese
después de haber sufrido el peso de la larguísima vida,
y un instante se mirase en el espejo y allí se reconociera...,

así te he visto a ti, cansada mía, vivida mía,
que día a día has ido llevando todo el peso de tu vivir.
A ti, que sonriente y ligera me mirabas cada mañana como reciente,
        como si la vida de los dos empezase.
Despertabas, y la luz entraba por la ventana, y me mirabas
y no sé qué sería, pero todos los días amanecías joven y dulce.
Y hoy mismo, esta mañana misma, me has mirado riente,
serena y leve, asomándote y haciéndome la mañana graciosamente
        desconocida.
Todos los días nuevos eran el único día. Y todos
los días sin fatigarte tenías tersa la piel, sorprendidos los ojos,
fresca la boca neuva y mojada de algún rocío la voz que
        se levantaba.

Y ahora te miro. De pronto a tu espalda te he mirado.
Qué larga mirada has echado sobre el espejo donde te haces.

IN FRONT OF THE MIRROR

Like a ghost that suddenly confronts us
and through the silent curtains raises its face to stare,
and appears mutely to speak . . .

So you now seated before the glass raise your arms,
putting up the lusterless hair you are arranging.
From behind I have stared at you in the mirror.
Tired face, tired silent features
which appear to have arisen so sadly, as if after effort that lasted all
        the long years.
Like a figure that for a moment extends itself forth
after enduring the weight of long-suffering life
and glimpses itself in the mirror and there recognizes itself . . . ,

so I have seen you, my tired one, my lifelong one,
who day by day have carried all the weight of your life.
Even you, who smiling and lightsome used to look at me every
        morning brand new, as if both of our lives were beginning.
You would wake up, and the light from the window would be coming
        in, and you would look at me
and I don't know how but you started each day young and sweet.
And even today, this very morning, you looked at me laughing,
serene and lively, looking out and offering me the morning delight-
        fully unknown.
Every new day was the one day. And all
those untiring days your skin held smooth, your eyes surprised,
your cool mouth stayed fresh and moistened with dew the voice
        that was getting up.

And now I'm watching you. Suddenly from behind I have seen you.
What a long look you've given the mirror where you make yourself
        up.

Allí no estabas. Y una sola mujer fatigada, cansada como por una
   larga vigilia que durase toda la vida,
se ha mirado al espejo y allí se ha reconocido.

COMO MOISÉS ES EL VIEJO

Como Moisés en lo alto del monte.

Cada hombre puede ser aquél
y mover la palabra y alzar los brazos
y sentir como barre la luz, de su rostro,
el polvo viejo de los caminos.

Porque allí está la puesta.
Mira hacia atrás: el alba.
Adelante: más sombras. ¡Y apuntaban las luces!
Y él agita los brazos y proclama la vida,
desde su muerte a solas.

Porque como Moisés, muere.
No con las tablas vanas y el punzón, y el rayo en las alturas,
sino rotos los textos en la tierra, ardidos
los cabellos, quemados los oídos por las palabras terribles,
y aún aliento en los ojos, y en el pulmón la llama,
y en la boca la luz.

Para morir basta un ocaso.
Una porción de sombra en la raya del horizonte.
Un hormiguear de juventudes, esperanzas, voces.
Y allá la sucesión, la tierra: el límite.
Lo que verán los otros.

You were not there. And a woman all by herself, tired, wearied as
      by a long vigil lasting her whole life
has looked at herself in the mirror and there recognized herself.

TRANSLATED BY WILLIAM STAFFORD
AND HERBERT BAIRD

THE OLD MAN IS LIKE MOSES

Like Moses on top of the mountain.

Every man can be like that
and deliver the word and lift up his arms
and feel how the light sweeps
the old road dust off his face.

Because the sunset is over there.
Looking behind him: the dawn.
In front: the growing shadows. And the lights began to shine!
And he swings his arms and speaks for the living
from inside his death, all alone.

Because like Moses, he dies.
Not with the useless tablets and the chisel and the lightning up in the
      mountains
but with the words broken on the ground, his hair
on fire, his ears singed by the terrifying words.
And the breath is still in his eyes and the spark in his lungs
and his mouth full of light.

A sunset will do for death.
A serving of shadow on the edge of the horizon.
A swarming of youth and hope and voices.
And in that place the generations to come, the earth: the border.
The thing the others will see.

TRANSLATED BY LEWIS HYDE

LLUEVE

En esta tarde llueve, y llueve pura tu imagen. En mi recuerdo el día
      se abre. Entraste.
No oigo. La memoria me da tu imagen sólo.
Sólo tu beso o lluvia cae en recuerdo.
Llueve tu voz, y llueve el beso triste,
el beso hondo,
beso mojado en lluvia. El labio es húmedo.
Húmedo de recuerdo el beso llora
desde unos cielos grises
delicados.
Llueve tu amor mojando mi memoria,
y cae y cae. El beso
al hondo cae. Y gris aún cae
la lluvia.

IT'S RAINING

This evening it's raining, and my picture of you is raining. The day
      falls open in my memory. You walked in.
I can't hear. Memory gives me nothing but your picture.
There only your kiss or the rain is falling.
Your voice is raining, your sad kiss is raining,
the deep kiss,
the kiss soaked with rain. Lips are moist.
Moist with its memories the kiss weeps
from some delicate
gray heavens.
Rain falls from your love, dampening my memory,
keeps on falling. The kiss
falls far down. The gray rain
goes on falling.

TRANSLATED BY ROBERT BLY

Rafael Alberti ✌

SI MI VOZ MURIERA EN TIERRA

Si mi voz muriera en tierra,
llevadla al nivel del mar
y dejadla en la ribera.

Llevadla al nivel del mar
y nombradla capitana
de un blanco bajel de guerra.

¡Oh mi voz condecorada
con la insignia marinera:
sobre el corazón un ancla
y sobre el ancla una estrella
y sobre la estrella el viento
y sobre el viento la vela!

IF MY VOICE DIES WHILE ON LAND

If my voice dies while on land,
carry it down to the sea
and leave it on the sand.

Carry it down to the sea
and appoint it a captain
of a white sloop of war.

Oh my voice, decorated
with the emblem of the sailor:
over the heart an anchor
and over the anchor a star,
and over the star the wind,
and over the wind the sail!

TRANSLATED BY ROBERT BLY

DESAHUCIO

Ángeles malos o buenos,
que no sé,
te arrojaron en mi alma.

Sola,
sin muebles y sin alcobas,
deshabitada.

De rondón, el viento hiere
las paredes,
las más finas, vítreas láminas.

Humedad. Cadenas. Gritos.
Ráfagas.

Te pregunto:
¿cuándo abandonas la casa,
dime,
que ángeles malos, crueles,
quieren de nuevo alquilarla?

Dímelo.

EVICTION

Angels bad or good,
I don't know which,
hurled you into my soul.

Lonely,
with no furniture and no bedrooms,
uninhabited.

All around, the wind bruises
the walls,
the even finer sheets of glass.

Dampness. Chains. Cries.
Gusts of wind.

I ask you:
tell me,
when are you leaving the house?
Cruel, evil angels
want to rent it again.

Tell me.

TRANSLATED BY RACHEL BENSON

EL ÁNGEL BUENO

Un año, ya dormido,
alguien que no esperaba
se paró en mi ventana.

—¡Levántate! Y mis ojos
vieron plumas y espadas.

Atrás, montes y mares,
nubes, picos y alas,
los ocasos, las albas.

—¡Mírala ahí! Su sueño,
pendiente de la nada.

—¡Oh anhelo, fijo mármol,
fija luz, fijas aguas
movibles de mi alma!

Alguien dijo: ¡Levántate!
Y me encontré en tu estancia.

THE GOOD ANGEL

One year, as I was sleeping,
someone I wasn't expecting
stopped at my window.

"Wake up!" And my eyes
saw plumes and swords.

Behind, mountains and seas,
clouds, beaks and wings,
sunsets, dawns.

"Look at her there! Her dream
hanging from nothing."

"O longing, firm marble,
steady light, steadfast moving
waters of my soul."

Someone said: Wake up!
And I found myself in your room.

TRANSLATED BY JOHN HAINES

EL ÁNGEL DE ARENA

Seriamente, en tus ojos era la mar dos niños que me espiaban,
temerosos de lazos y palabras duras.
Dos niños de la noche, terribles, expulsados del cielo,
cuya infancia era un robo de barcos y un crimen de soles y de lunas.
Duérmete. Ciérralos.

Vi que el mar verdadero era un muchacho que saltaba desnudo,
invitándome a un plato de estrellas y a un reposo de algas.
¡Sí, sí! Ya mi vida iba a ser, ya lo era, litoral desprendido.
Pero tú, despertando, me hundiste en tus ojos.

LOS SOLDADOS SE DUERMEN

Contémplalos.
          Dormidos, con un aire de aldea,
de animales tiernísimos, duros y acostumbrados
a que de pronto el sueño les coja donde sea,
como a los incansables perros de los ganados.

Sobre una pesadumbre parecida a un paisaje
batido por pezuñas y osamentas rendidas,
mordiéndoles el lento son de un mismo rodaje,
solas y ausentes ruedan las pupilas dormidas.

Duermen, sí, con las manos, que son puños, abiertas,
un instante olvidadas del reciente ejercicio
de dejar las contrarias vidas turbias desiertas.
...Mas también los fusiles descansan de su oficio.

THE ANGEL OF SAND

I'm serious. In your eyes the sea was two children, spying on me,
fearful of snares and hard words.
Two terrible children of the night, expelled from the sky,
whose infancy was a plunder of ships and a crime of suns and moons.
Sleep. Close them.

I saw that the real sea was a boy leaping naked,
inviting me to a dish of stars and a sleep of seaweed.
Yes, yes! Now my life was going to be, now was, a detached shore.
But you, awaking, sank me in your eyes.

TRANSLATED BY RACHEL BENSON

THE SOLDIERS SLEEP

Look at them.
Asleep, with a country village air,
like very young animals, hardened, used
to having sleep overtake them suddenly, no matter where,
as it does the tireless sheepdogs.

Distant and lonely, their sleeping pupils roll
over a grief that is like a landscape
beaten down by cloven hoofs and defeated skeletons,
the slow sound of similar wheels gnawing at them.

They sleep with their fists opened for once,
the recent drill forgotten;
they quit for an instant their adverse, muddy, empty existences.
. . . But the guns, too, are resting from their duties.

TRANSLATED BY RACHEL BENSON

AL SOL DE LA GUERRA

Viejo y barbudo sol, buen sol soldado
de veterana luz, y en la trinchera;
obstinado español, tan obstinado
en que el toro de España no se muera.
Tú le enciendes los cuernos, tú le afilas
de rayos las agujas,
tú para que dibuje lo dibujas.

Viejo sol patriota, héroe sol sobre el lomo
de fiera tan humana y sobrehumana:
tuerce el tiro que busque su derrota,
rompe o derrite el vértigo del plomo
que la intente acabar vertida en grana.
Éntrale en sus pulmones tu resuello,
aún más inexpugnables y ofensivos
hazle la frente, la pasión, el cuello
y sus generadores distintivos.

Sol entrañable, viejo voluntario
de los primeros días;
sol marítimo, agrario,
de la muerte en la ola
o en las tierras baldías,
España, con su toro, no está sola.
Tú, ciego combatiente,
lo haces temblar del cuerno hasta la cola
y, entre escarbada luz, hundiendo en miedo,
en sangre, en polvo, a la extranjera gente,
barrer de sombra el invadido ruedo.

TO THE SUN OF THE WAR

Old and bearded sun, good soldier sun
in the trenches, of veteran light;
hard-headed Spaniard, determined
that the bull of Spain shall not die.
You kindle his horns, whet
the points on your rays,
you draw him on, outline
the course that he must trace.

Old patriot sun,
hero sun astride the loins
of a beast so human and more than human:
deflect the shot that seeks his downfall,
shatter or melt the dizzy fall of lead
that would finish him in a flow of scarlet seeds.
Let your breath enter his lungs,
and make his forehead, heart, neck,
the genitals that are his badge,
even more impregnable and belligerent.

Good-hearted sun, old volunteer
from the first days;
sailor sun, farmer sun,
whether death advances in the waves
or in the untilled lands,
Spain, with her bull, is not alone.
You, blind combatant,
you make him quiver from head to tail,
and, in the pawed-up light, submerging the foreigners
in fear, in blood, in dust, you make him
sweep with shadow the invaded bull ring.

TRANSLATED BY RACHEL BENSON

AMPARO

A Arturo Mom

Amparo.
Vine a tu mar de trigos y caballos.

Tu mar dulce tenía
sabor de plata, amargo,
de plata, sin saberlo, en agonía.

Te vi en el puerto, Amparo.
Hermosa de luz, contra los barcos.

Te vi, tú me veías.
Morena del silencio,
de la palabra ya de tierra, fría.

De la otra mar de sangre,
llegué a tu mar llorando.
Hermosa de la gracia,
clavel de altura, Amparo.

Te oí, tú no me oías.
Morena del reposo,
hermosa del descanso.

Mírame aquí cantando,
por ti, a lágrima viva.
Morena de lo ido,
hermosa de las luces ya perdidas.

Amparo.
Vine a tu mar de trigos y caballos.
(Adonde tú querías.)

AMPARO

To Arturo Mom

Amparo.
I came to your sea of wheat and horses.

Your sweet sea
tasted of silver, bitter,
of silver in unknowing agony.

I saw you in the harbor, Amparo.
Beautiful woman of light, against a background of ships.

I saw you, you saw me.
Dark woman of silence,
of the word now grounded, cold.

From the other sea of blood,
I reached your sea weeping.
Beautiful woman of grace,
a tall carnation, Amparo.

I heard you, you did not hear me.
Dark woman of serenity,
beautiful one of rest.

See me here, singing
for you with sharpest grief.
Dark woman of all that has gone,
beautiful one of lights now lost.

Amparo.
I came to your sea of wheat and horses.
(To where you desired.)

TRANSLATED BY RACHEL BENSON

REMONTANDO LOS RÍOS

1

Para ti, niña Aitana,
remontando los ríos,
este ramo de agua.

De agua dulce, ramito,
que no de agua salada.

Agua de azúcar, ramo,
ramito, que no amarga.

Remontando los ríos...

2

Cierro los ojos...
              Pasan
los ríos por mi cara.

Los ojos...
            Son los ríos...
Son los ojos...
               ¿Quién canta,
quién se ríe, quién grita,
quién llora?
            Se desatan
los ríos...
           De mis ojos
vuela, alegre, una barca.

(Adiós, ramo, ramito.
Para ti toda el agua.)

Remontando los ríos...

GOING UP THE RIVERS

1

For you, Aitana child,
this bough of water,
going up the rivers.

Of sweet water, little twig,
not brackish water.

Sugar water, bough,
little twig, not bitter.

Going up the rivers . . .

2

I close my eyes . . .
               The rivers
pass over my face.

My eyes . . .
            are the rivers . . .
are eyes . . .
            Who is singing,
who is laughing, who crying out,
who weeping?
            The rivers
break loose . . .
            From my eyes
a gay ship sets sail.

(Farewell, bough, twig.
All the water is for you.)

Going up the rivers . . .

3

Hay ríos que son toros:
toros azules, granas,
tristes toros de barro,
toros verdes de algas.

Por los toros azules
el viento se hace largas
colgaduras de sauce;
relumbre, por los granas;
por los de barro, sombra,
y por los verdes, agua.

(Sube y baja, ramito,
por los verdes de agua.)

Remontando los ríos...

4

...Y así como son toros,
los hay que son rizadas
ovejas, que son tiernos
corderos que resbalan
hacia los grandes ríos
sus diminutas aguas.

Por los ríos ovejas,
el viento se hace alas
clarísimas de arcángeles,
vilanos de la lana.

(Adiós, ramo florido
de vilanos de lana.)

Remontando los ríos...

3

There are rivers that are bulls:
blue bulls, scarlet,
sad muddy bulls,
bulls green with weeds.

For the blue bulls
the wind makes itself into long
trappings of willow;
glitter for the scarlet;
shadow for the muddy ones;
and for the green bulls, water.

(Rise and fall, little branch,
along the green ones of water.)

Going up the rivers . . .

4

. . . And just as some are bulls,
there are those that are curly
sheep, are tender lambs
who slide their diminutive waters
toward the big rivers.

Along the sheep rivers,
the wind becomes
fine, shining archangel wings,
bits of thistledown from the wool.

(Farewell, flowering branch
of woolen thistledown.)

Going up the rivers . . .

5

Ríos caballos, ríos
de colas levantadas,
ríos ciegos, a tumbos,
heridos por las ramas.

¿Quién los doma, ramito?
Mi ramo, ¿quién los para?

¡A la doma del río!
¡A la doma del agua!

(Duerme en caballo dulce...
Ya no galopa el agua.)

Remontando los ríos...

5

Horse rivers, rivers
with tails upraised,
blind rivers, plunging,
lashed by branches.

Who breaks them in, little branch?
Who holds them back, my bough?

To the taming of the river!
To the taming of the water!

(Sleep on a gentle horse . . .
The river gallops no more.)

Going up the rivers . . .

TRANSLATED BY RACHEL BENSON

EL APARECIDO

Se me aparece blanco en la mañana.
Me mira y largamente pensativo
se va girando en torno de la casa.

Luego, en el bosque, me lo encuentro verde.
Me mira, las orejas levantadas.
Suena el aire del mar. Lo aspira y lento
se va girando en torno de la casa.

Rojo, se me aparece por la tarde,
perdido en las arenas de la playa.
Arden las olas, las contempla y triste
se va girando en torno de la casa.

Se me aparece negro por la noche,
altas las crines, fija la mirada.
Sube la luna. Le relincha y solo
se va girando en torno de la casa.

THE GHOST

He seems white to me in the morning.
Watching me thoughtfully for a long time,
he goes circling around the house.

Then in the forest I find him green.
He watches me with his ears cocked.
The sea wind sounds. He breathes it and slowly
goes circling around the house.

At evening he seems red to me,
lost in the sand on the shore.
The waves burn. He studies them and sadly
goes circling around the house.

He seems black to me at night,
mane flying high, gaze fixed.
The moon rises. He whinnies at it and, all alone,
goes circling around the house.

TRANSLATED BY CHARLES GUENTHER

RETORNOS A TRAVÉS DE LOS COLORES

Esta tarde te alivian los colores: el verde,
aparecido niño grácil de primavera,
el claro mar del cielo que cambia en los cristales
el ala sonreída de un añil mensajero.

Te hacen viajar el blanco tembloroso y erguido
que abren las margaritas contra la enredadera,
el marfil de los senos nacientes del magnolio,
el albo de las calas de pie sobre el estanque.

Piensas en los colores lejanos de otros días:
aquel azul dormido de espalda en los esteros,
el áureo de las piedras derribadas al borde
de los dientes antiguos de su mar endiosado.

Escuchas en el rosa del rosal el caído
de los lazos tronchados tras el balcón del arpa,
y en el negro fulgente de las sombras, el lustre
del sombrero difunto de los altos abuelos.

No pierdas los colores que te juegan caminos
esta tarde en tu breve jardín murado. Mira.
Aquí están. Tú los tocas. Son los mismos colores
que en tu corazón viven ya un poco despintados.

GOING BACK THROUGH COLOR

Colors calm you this afternoon: green
shows up like a child of spring,
in the windows a clear sea of sky changes
the smiling wing of a blue homing pigeon.

The trembling and proud whites
that daisies open against the vines make you go back
and so does the ivory of the magnolia's budding breasts,
and the snow-white of calla lilies standing over the pond.

You think of the distant colors of other days:
that blue asleep on its back on the marshes,
the gold of stones fallen beside
the ancient teeth of the sea they worship.

In the pink of the rosebush you listen for the pink falling
from the roses torn up behind the balcony of the harp,
and in the bright black of shadows, you see the luster
of the dead hats of tall grandfathers.

Don't lose the colors that open paths for you
in your small walled garden this afternoon. Look.
Here they are. Touch them. They are the same colors
that live in your heart, a little faded now.

TRANSLATED BY MARK STRAND

RETORNOS DE UN POETA ASESINADO

Has vuelto a mí más viejo y triste en la dormida
luz de un sueño tranquilo de marzo, polvorientas
de un gris inesperado las sienes, y aquel bronce
de olivo que tu mágica juventud sostenía,
surcado por el signo de los años, lo mismo
que si la vida aquella que en vida no tuviste
la hubieras paso a paso ya vivido en la muerte.

Yo no sé qué has querido decirme en esta noche
con tu desprevenida visita, el fino traje
de alpaca luminosa, como recién cortado,
la corbata amarilla y el sufrido cabello
al aire, igual que entonces
por aquellos jardines de estudiantiles chopos
y calientes adelfas.

Tal vez hayas pensado—quiero explicarme ahora
ya en las claras afueras del sueño—que debías
llegar primero a mí desde esas subterráneas
raíces o escondidos manantiales en donde
desesperadamente penan tus huesos.
                                        Dime,
confiésame, confiésame
si en el abrazo mudo que me has dado, en el tierno
ademán de ofrecerme una silla, en la simple
manera de sentarte junto a mí, de mirarme,
sonreír y en silencio, sin ninguna palabra,
dime si no has querido significar con eso
que, a pesar de las mínimas batallas que reñimos,
sigues unido a mí más que nunca en la muerte
por las veces que acaso
no lo estuvimos—¡ay, perdóname!—en la vida.

Si no es así, retorna nuevamente en el sueño
de otra noche a decírmelo.

THE COMING BACK OF AN ASSASSINATED POET

You have come back to me older and sadder in the drowsy
light of a quiet dream in March, your dusty temples
disarmingly gray, and that olive
bronze you had in your magical youth,
furrowed by the passing of years, just as if
you lived out slowly in death
the life you never had while you were alive.

I do not know what you wanted to tell me tonight
with your unexpected visit, the fine alpaca
suit, looking like new, the yellow tie,
and your carefully combed hair
suffering the wind the same as when
you walked through those gardens of poplars
and hot oleanders of our school days.

Maybe you thought—I want to explain myself
now that I stand outside the dream—that you
had to come first to me from those buried
roots or hidden springs where
your bones despair.
                    Tell me,
tell me,
if in the mute embrace you have given me,
in the tender gesture of offering me a chair, in the simple
manner of sitting near me, of looking at me,
smiling and in silence, without a single word,
tell me if you did not mean
that in spite of our minor disagreements,
you remain joined to me more than ever in death
for the times perhaps
we were not—oh, forgive me!—in life.

If this is not true, come back again in a dream
some other night to tell me so.

TRANSLATED BY MARK STRAND

CANCIÓN

Quisiera cantar: ser flor
de mi pueblo.

Que me paciera una vaca
de mi pueblo.

Que me llevara en la oreja
un labriego de mi pueblo.

Que me escuchara la luna
de mi pueblo.

Que me mojaran los mares
y los ríos de mi pueblo.

Que me cortara una niña
de mi pueblo.

Que me enterrara la tierra
del corazón de mi pueblo.

Porque, ya ves, estoy solo,
sin mi pueblo.
(Aunque no estoy sin mi pueblo.)

SONG

I want to sing: to be a flower
in my village.

A cow of my village
to graze over me.

A peasant of my village
to wear me in his ear.

The moon of my village
to hear me.

The rivers and seas
of my village to drench me.

A girl from my village
to pick me.

The earth of the heart
of my village to bury me.

For, you see, I'm alone
without my village.
(Though not without my people.)

TRANSLATED BY CHARLES GUENTHER
AND HARDIE ST. MARTIN

MILLARES 1965

En Roma o en París,
Nueva York, Buenos Aires, Madrid, Calcuta, El Cairo...
en tantísimas partes todavía,
hay arpilleras rotas,
destrozados zapatos adheridos al hueso,
muñones, restos duros,
basuras calcinadas,
hoyas profundas, secos
mundos de preteridos oxidados,
de coagulada sangre,
piel humana roída como lava difunta,
rugosidades trágicas, signos que acusan, gritan,
aunque no tengan boca,
callados alaridos que lastiman
tanto como el silencio.
¿De dónde estos escombros,
estos mancos derrumbes,
agujeros en trance de aún ser más agrandados,
lentas tiras de tramas desgarradas,
cuajados amasijos, polvaredas de tiza,
rojos lacre, de dónde?
¿Qué va a saltar de aquí, qué a suceder,
qué a reventar de estos violentos espantajos,
qué a tumbar esta ciega, andrajosa corambre
cuando rompa sus hilos, haga morder de súbito
sus abiertas costuras, ilumine sus negros,
sus minios y sus calcios de un resplandor rasante,
capaz de hacer parir la más nueva hermosura?
Ah, pero mientras tanto,
un "No toquéis, peligro de muerte" acecha oculto
bajo tanta zurcida realidad desflecada.
Guardad, guardad la mano,
no avancéis ningún dedo los pulidos de uñas.
Ratas, no os atreváis por estos albañales.

MILLARES 1965

In Rome or in Paris,
New York, Buenos Aires, Madrid, Calcutta, Cairo . . .
in so many places right now there are
gunny sacks in shreds,
pieces of shoe stuck to the bone,
amputated stumps, stiff human leftovers,
trash reduced to ashes,
yawning holes, dried up
worlds of rusty things that have been overlooked,
of coagulated blood,
human skin gnawed through like dead lava,
tragic shriveled skin, signs that accuse, cry out
even when they have no mouth,
choked back howls that are just as painful
as the silence.
Where did all this start, these wrecks,
these maimed human ruins,
these holes that are being ripped even wider,
slow rags of twisted silk with slashed threads,
caked lumps of something like dough, flying clouds of chalky clay,
sealing-wax reds, where?
What will come flying out of all this, what will happen,
what will break loose from these desperate scarecrows,
what will pull down this blind, seedy bundle of pelts
when it bursts its fibers, when it makes its open seams
suddenly start biting, when it lets the light in on its black colors,
its iron ochers, its stark whites with their sweeping glare
that can breathe life into a new kind of loveliness?
But, ah, in the meantime
a HANDS OFF. DANGER OF DEATH is lying unseen
under all this patched-up reality with its frayed strings.
Keep, keep your hands off,
don't even stick out one finger, you with your polished nails.
Rats, don't try to come into these sewers.

Lívidos de la usura, pálidos de la nada,
atrás, atrás, ni un paso por aquí, ni el intento
de arriesgar una huella, ni el indicio de un ojo.
Corre un temblor eléctrico capaz de fulminaros
y una luz y una luz y una luz subterránea
que está amasando el rostro de tan tristes derribos.

Back, back! You are sallow-faced from usury,
white-faced with emptiness, don't come a step closer,
don't even risk a footprint or a signal with your eye.
An electric charge runs through here that can blast you to kingdom
come,
and a light also, a light, a hidden light
kneading the faces of these sad human ruins.

TRANSLATED BY HARDIE ST. MARTIN

CERRÉ MI PUERTA AL MUNDO

Cerré mi puerta al mundo;
se me perdió la carne por el sueño...
Me quedé interno, mágico, invisible,
desnudo como un ciego.

Lleno hasta el mismo borde de mis ojos
me iluminé por dentro.

Trémulo, transparente,
me quedé sobre el viento,
igual que un vaso limpio
de agua pura,
como un ángel de vidrio
en un espejo.

I LOCKED THE WORLD OUT

I locked the world out,
my body lost its way in a dream. . . .
I stayed in, fantastic, invisible,
naked like a blind man.

Brimming at the edges of my eyes,
shot through with light.

Trembling, shining through,
I rested on top of the wind
like a clean tumbler
of settled water,
like a glass angel
in a mirror.

Translated by Hardie St. Martin

RECUERDO

Desvanecida, ahogada,
tu cabeza flotando,
resbaló por tus hombros
hasta entrar en mis brazos.

Como un papel mi sangre
se escapó por el viento.
Desmayado, en mis manos
se derramó tu cuerpo.

De perfil, por sus aguas,
medio hundido en el río
de mis pulsos, tu rostro
navegó por tu olvido...

Como un barco, mi carne
flotaba por la música.
El silencio, en mi espalda
clavó sus largas plumas...

Deshojó su corola
la rosa de la estancia.
Libre del mundo, el sueño
me colgó por sus alas.

SOMETHING REMEMBERED

Lifeless, floating, drowned,
your head slid down past
your shoulder
till it came into my arms.

My blood escaped into the wind
like a sheet of paper.
Your body dropped
into my hands, drained out.

Half sinking in the river
of my pulse, your profile
sailed in its waters looking
for your lost memory. . . .

My own body drifted like a ship
through the music.
The silence dug its feathers
into my back. . . .

The rose in the room
shed its petals.
Shaking off the world, sleep
slung me over its wings.

TRANSLATED BY HARDIE ST. MARTIN

EL SILENCIO, DESNUDO

El silencio, desnudo
como una luz sin cuerpo,
al buscarte en mis ojos,
entero se hundió en ellos.

Por salvarte, mi sangre
quiso sacarte al sueño.
El silencio, al notarlo,
metiéndose en tu cuerpo,
te iluminó la carne
igual que un cristal hueco.

LIKE A NAKED LIGHT

Like a naked light
without body, the silence
came looking for you in my eyes
and sank down into them.

My blood wanted to pull you
aboard a dream, to save your life,
but seeing this,
the silence got down into your body
and flooded it with light,
like a piece of hollow glass.

TRANSLATED BY HARDIE ST. MARTIN

CANCIÓN

Puente de mi soledad:
con las aguas de mi muerte
tus ojos se calmarán.

Tengo mi cuerpo tan lleno
de lo que falta a mi vida,
que hasta la muerte, vencida,
busca por él su consuelo.

Por eso, para morir,
tendré que echarme hacia dentro
las anclas de mi vivir.

Y llevo un mundo a mi lado
igual que un traje vacío
y otro mundo en mí guardado
que es por el mundo que vivo.

Por eso, para vivir,
tendré que echarme hacia dentro
las anclas de mi morir.

Puente de mi soledad:
por los ojos de mi muerte
tus aguas van hacia el mar,
al mar del que no se vuelve.

SONG

Bridge of my solitude:
with the waters of my death
your eyes will grow calm.

I have a body so full
of all that is lacking in my life
that even death, the loser,
searches all through it for consolation.

Therefore, in order to die,
I'll have to cast into myself
the anchors of my living.

And I carry a world by my side
like an empty suit of clothes
and another world put away inside me
which is the world I live for.

Therefore, in order to live,
I'll have to cast into myself
the anchors of my dying.

Bridge of my solitude:
through the eyes of my death
your waters run down to the sea,
to the sea from which there is no coming back.

TRANSLATED BY ROBERT MEZEY

CANCIÓN DE DESPEDIDA

Vengo de la sombra. Mira
la blancura de mis huesos
levantándome sin carne
frente a la luz de tu pecho.
Tú, nada comprendes. Mira
cómo me aprietan tus besos
y, sin temor, iluminan
los límites de mi cuerpo.
Tus labios me están cercando
y sobre mi piel abiertos
quedan arriba, en mis bordes,
cerrándome, como un cielo.
Yo te miro desde abajo,
pero no sé si estoy ciego
o sin recuerdo, ni olvido,
renazco bajo tus besos.
Como una piedra en un pozo
voy hundido, en el espectro
altísimo de mi llanto,
sin dolor y sin consuelo.
Y vivo tan escondido
al fondo de mi esqueleto
que, apenas mi corazón
reconozco en mis deseos.
Tú, nada entiendes... Un mundo
rueda por mi sangre, muerto...
Míralo al fondo de mí,
como un guijarro que el tiempo
fuera arrastrando en su cauce
al hondo mar de lo eterno.
Nada me preguntes. Ciñe
mi cintura a tu universo...
Vengo de la sombra... Escucha
los ecos de mi silencio.

SONG OF TAKING LEAVE

I come from shadows. Look
at the whiteness of my bones
raising me up without flesh
in the light of your breasts.
You understand nothing. Look
how your kisses crush me,
how recklessly they light up
the boundaries of my body.
Your lips surround me
and just above my skin
they float open at my edges,
enclosing me like a heaven.
I watch you from below,
but I don't know whether I am blind
or without memory or even
the lack of memory—
I am born again under your kisses.
Like a stone in a pool
I am lost in the transparent
ghost of my tears,
without grief, without joy.
And I live so concealed
at the bottom of my skeleton
that I scarcely recognize
my heart in my desires.
And you, you understand nothing. . . . A world
turns through my blood, a dead world. . . .
Look at it in my depths,
like a pebble time
was washing along its bed
into the open sea of the eternal.
You must not ask me anything. Fasten
my waist to your universe. . . .
I come from shadows. . . . Listen
to the echoes of my silence.

TRANSLATED BY ROBERT MEZEY

CUANDO ERA PRIMAVERA

Cuando era primavera en España:
frente al mar, los espejos
rompían sus barandillas
y el jazmín agrandaba
su diminuta estrella,
hasta cumplir el límite
de su aroma en la noche...
¡Cuando era primavera!

Cuando era primavera en España:
junto a la orilla de los ríos,
las grandes mariposas de la luna
fecundaban los cuerpos desnudos
de las muchachas
y los nardos crecían silenciosos
dentro del corazón,
hasta taparnos la garganta...
¡Cuando era primavera!

Cuando era primavera en España:
todas las playas convergían en un anillo
y el mar soñaba entonces,
como el ojo de un pez sobre la arena,
frente a un cielo más limpio
que la paz de una nave, sin viento, en su pupila.
¡Cuando era primavera!

Cuando era primavera en España:
los olivos temblaban
adormecidos bajo la sangre azul del día,
mientras que el sol rodaba
desde la piel tan limpia de los toros,
al terrón en barbecho
recién movido por la lengua caliente de la azada.
¡Cuando era primavera!

WHEN IT WAS SPRING

When it was spring in Spain:
facing the sea, the mirrors
shattered the balustrades
and the jasmine spread out
its miniature star
until it reached the limits
of its fragrance in the night. . . .
When it was spring!

When it was spring in Spain:
down by the banks of rivers,
the great lunar butterflies
seeded the nude bodies
of girls
and spikenard grew silently
in our hearts
till we were choking on it. . . .
When it was spring!

When it was spring in Spain:
the beaches all came together in a ring
and the sea dreamed then,
like the eye of a fish on the sand,
under a sky cleaner than
the peace of a ship, becalmed, in its pupil.
When it was spring!

When it was spring in Spain:
the olives trembled
half asleep under the azure blood of the day,
while the sun rolled
off the gleaming hides of the bulls
down to lumps of fallow earth
just turned over by the hot tongue of the hoe.
When it was spring!

Cuando era primavera en España:
los cerezos en flor
se clavaban de un golpe contra el sueño
y los labios crecían,
como la espuma en celo de una aurora,
hasta dejarnos nuestro cuerpo a su espalda,
igual que el agua humilde
de un arroyo que empieza...
¡Cuando era primavera!

Cuando era primavera en España:
todos los hombres desnudaban su muerte
y se tendían confiados, juntos, sobre la tierra,
hasta olvidarse el tiempo
y el corazón tan débil por el que ardían...
¡Cuando era primavera!

Cuando era primavera en España:
yo buscaba en el cielo,
yo buscaba
las huellas tan antiguas
de mis primeras lágrimas
y todas las estrellas levantaban mi cuerpo
siempre tendido en una misma arena,
al igual que el perfume, tan lento,
nocturno, de las magnolias...
¡Cuando era primavera!

Pero, ¡ay!, tan sólo
cuando era primavera en España.
¡Solamente en España,
antes, cuando era primavera!

When it was spring in Spain:
the blossoming cherry trees
pinned themselves all at once to the floor of sleep
and the lips grew,
like the foam hungering at dawn,
till they left our bodies behind,
like the mild water
of a stream just bubbling up. . . .
When it was spring!

When it was spring in Spain:
all the men stripped off their deaths
and stretched out peacefully together on the ground,
till they forgot about time
and the faint heart for which they were burning. . . .
When it was spring!

When it was spring in Spain:
I searched the sky,
I searched
for the ancient prints
of my first tears,
and all the stars lifted my body
sprawled as always in the same sand,
just like the heavy perfume
of magnolias at night. . . .
When it was spring!

But, oh! only then,
when it was spring in Spain.
Only in Spain,
then, when it was spring!

TRANSLATED BY ROBERT MEZEY

VUELVO AL CIELO MIS OJOS

Vuelvo al cielo mis ojos...
—Las nubes se han perdido—.
Un blanco acorde suena
sobre el cielo sin nubes.
Un sitio. Un cuerpo nuevo.
Una eterna armonía...

(Bajo el azul misterio
que vivieron las nubes,
un diminuto sol
comienza por sus llamas...)

¡Cruje el tiempo!
          (Los huecos
contemplados, se prenden...
El sol invade el sitio
de las nubes.)
          Ya en alba!

(Contemplo a Dios?...)
                ¡Escucho
a su espejo en mi alma!

I LOOK INTO THE SKY

I look into the sky . . .
—The clouds have slipped off—
A white chord rings out
across the cloudless sky.
Somewhere. A new body.
An eternal harmony . . .

(Under the mysterious blue
where the clouds lived
a minute sun
starts through its flames . . .)

Time creaks.
           (The contemplated hollows
catch fire . . .
The sun invades the cloud-site.)
                    It is dawn!

(Am I looking at God . . . ?)
                  I listen
to His mirror in my soul!

TRANSLATED BY
MARIA ISABEL CHIPMAN PRADOS

REMORDIMIENTO EN TRAJE DE NOCHE

Un hombre gris avanza por la calle de niebla;
No lo sospecha nadie. Es un cuerpo vacío;
Vacío como pampa, como mar, como viento,
Desiertos tan amargos bajo un cielo implacable.

Es el tiempo pasado, y sus alas ahora
Entre la sombra encuentran una pálida fuerza;
Es el remordimiento, que de noche, dudando,
En secreto aproxima su sombra descuidada.

No estrechéis esa mano. La yedra altivamente
Ascenderá cubriendo los troncos del invierno.
Invisible en la calma el hombre gris camina.
¿No sentís a los muertos? Mas la tierra está sorda.

REMORSE DRESSED UP AS NIGHT

A gray man comes down the foggy street:
No one would guess it's he. He's just a vacant body,
Vacant as sea, wind, the prairie grass—
Such bitter wastelands beneath a stony sky.

He embodies time past, and in the dark now
His wings collide with something stark and pale.
It is remorse. With deep misgiving
He brings his neglected shadow up close at night.

Don't shake that hand. Lordly vines
Will climb up to cover tree trunks of winter.
The gray man moves along unseen in the stillness.
Don't you hear the dead? But the earth itself is deaf.

TRANSLATED BY TIMOTHY BALAND

NO DECÍA PALABRAS

No decía palabras,
Acercaba tan sólo un cuerpo interrogante,
Porque ignoraba que el deseo es una pregunta
Cuya respuesta no existe,
Un hoja cuya rama no existe,
Un mundo cuyo cielo no existe.

La angustia se abre paso entre los huesos,
Remonta por las venas
Hasta abrirse en la piel,
Surtidores de sueño
Hechos carne en interrogación vuelta a las nubes.

Un roce al paso,
Una mirada fugaz entre las sombras,
Bastan para que el cuerpo se abra en dos,
Ávido de recibir en sí mismo
Otro cuerpo que sueñe;
Mitad y mitad, sueño y sueño, carne y carne,
Iguales en figura, iguales en amor, iguales en deseo.

Aunque sólo sea una esperanza,
Porque el deseo es una pregunta cuya respuesta nadie sabe.

SPEAKING OTHER THAN WITH WORDS

He was speaking other than with words,
He just kept coming closer, his body questioning,
Because he didn't realize desire is a question
For which there is no answer,
Desire is a leaf without its twig,
A world without its heavens.

Despair opens a passage for itself between the bones,
It winds upward through the veins,
Until it unfolds in the skin,
Fountains of the dream
Become a questioning body turned toward the clouds.

That they brush up against each other as they pass,
Catching each other's eyes an instant in the shadows,
Is enough to divide in two
The body yearning to draw inside itself
Another dreaming body:
One half and the other, dream on dream, body upon body,
The same in shape, in love, in what they desire.

And yet desire is no more than a hope,
Because it is a question no one can answer.

TRANSLATED BY TIMOTHY BALAND

DE QUÉ PAÍS

De qué país eres tú,
Dormido entre realidades como bocas sedientas,
Vida de sueños azuzados,
Y ese duelo que exhibes por la avenida de los monumentos,
Donde dioses y diosas olvidados
Levantan brazos inexistentes o miradas marmóreas.

La vieja hilaba en su jardín ceniciento;
Tapias, pantanos, aullidos de crepúsculo,
Hiedras, batistas, allá se endurecían,
Mirando aquellas ruedas fugitivas
Hacia las cuales levantaba la arcilla un puño amenazante.

El país es un nombre;
Es igual que tú, recién nacido, vengas
Al norte, al sur, a la niebla, a las luces;
Tu destino será escuchar lo que digan
Las sombras inclinadas sobre la cuna.

Una mano dará el poder de sonrisa,
Otra dará las rencorosas lágrimas,
Otra el puñal experimentado,
Otra el deseo que se corrompe, formando bajo la vida
La charca de cosas pálidas,
Donde surgen serpientes, nenúfares, insectos, maldades,
Corrompiendo los labios, lo más puro.

No podrás pues besar con inocencia,
Ni vivir aquellas realidades que te gritan con lengua
        inagotable.
Deja, deja, harapiento de estrellas;
Muérete bien a tiempo.

FROM WHAT COUNTRY

From what country are you,
Asleep among everyday things with their thirsty mouths,
Life bitten by dreams,
And that grief you bear without shame down the avenue of
      monuments
Where forgotten gods and goddesses
Lift arms that are not there and looks of marble.

The old woman was spinning in her garden of ashes;
Mud walls, quagmires, howls at dusk,
Ivies, and cambrics, stiffened there,
As they watched those flying wheels
Toward which the clay raised a threatening fist.

The country is a name;
Nothing will change if you, born just now, come
To the north, to the south, to the mist, to the lights;
Your destiny will be to listen to what
The shadows leaning over your crib have to say.

One hand will give you the power of smiling,
Another will give you spiteful tears,
Another the knife of experience,
Another the desire that turns inward, forming the pool
Of wasted things under your life,
Where snakes, waterlilies, insects, guilty thoughts, break
      the surface,
Corrupting your lips, the purest thing you have.

Then you won't be able to kiss with innocence
Nor give life to the realities that cry out to you with tireless
      tongue.
Stop, stop, you who are ragged with stars,
Die while you still have time.

TRANSLATED BY JOHN HAINES

NIÑO TRAS UN CRISTAL

Al caer la tarde, absorto
Tras el cristal, el niño mira
Llover. La luz que se ha encendido
En un farol contrasta
La lluvia blanca con el aire oscuro.

La habitación a solas
Le envuelve tibiamente,
Y el visillo, velando
Sobre el cristal, como una nube,
Le susurra lunar encantamiento.

El colegio se aleja. Es ahora
La tregua, con el libro
De historias y de estampas
Bajo la lámpara, la noche,
El sueño, las horas sin medida.

Vive en el seno de su fuerza tierna,
Todavía sin deseo, sin memoria,
El niño, y sin presagio
Que afuera el tiempo aguarda
Con la vida, al acecho.

En su sombra la perla ya se forma.

BOY BEHIND A WINDOW

As evening comes down, the boy
Buried in thought behind the glass
Watches it rain. The glow from a burning
Streetlamp makes the white rain
Stand out against the darkened air.

The room he has to himself
Wraps him in its warmth
And the thin curtain, guarding
The window like a cloud, whispers to him
That the moon has things under a spell.

School fades from his mind. This is
A break for him, with the book
Full of stories and pictures
Under the study lamp, the night,
Sleep, hours that weigh nothing.

The boy is living in the heart
Of his small power, with no desires
So far, no memories, never suspecting
That time waits out there,
With life, ready to spring.

The pearl is taking form in his shadow.

TRANSLATED BY HARDIE ST. MARTIN

A LARRA
CON UNAS VIOLETAS
(1837–1937)

Aún se queja su alma vagamente,
El oscuro vacío de su vida.
Mas no pueden pesar sobre esa sombra
Algunas violetas,
Y es grato así dejarlas,
Frescas entre la niebla,
Con la alegría de una menuda cosa pura
Que rescatara aquel dolor antiguo.

Quien habla ya a los muertos,
Mudo le hallan los que viven.
Y en este otro silencio, donde el miedo impera,
Recoger esas flores una a una
Breve consuelo ha sido entre los días
Cuya huella sangrienta llevan las espaldas
Por el odio cargadas con una piedra inútil.

Si la muerte apacigua
Tu boca amarga de Dios insatisfecha,
Acepta un don tan leve, sombra sentimental,
En esa paz que bajo tierra te esperaba,
Brotando en hierba, viento y luz silvestres,
El fiel y último encanto de estar solo.

Curado de la vida, por una vez sonríe,
Pálido rostro de pasión y de hastío.
Mira las calles viejas por donde fuiste errante,
El farol azulado que te guiara, carne yerta,
Al regresar del baile o del sucio periódico,
Y las fuentes de mármol entre palmas:
Aguas y hojas, bálsamo del triste.

TO LARRA
WITH SOME VIOLETS
(1837–1937)

Even now his soul, the dark emptiness
Of his life, dimly complains.
But a few violets can't weigh too heavily
On that shadow
And it's pleasant to leave them,
Fresh in the mist,
With their gaiety of a tiny pure thing
That redeems that ancient grief.

The living do not hear anybody
Who speaks to the dead.
And in this other silence, where terror rules,
Picking these flowers one after another
Has been a brief solace among days
Whose bloodstained prints ride on the shoulders
Sagged down by hatred with a useless stone.

If death hushes
Your mouth, bitter and dissatisfied with God,
Take this light gift, sensitive shadow,
Into the peace that was waiting for you
Under the earth,
Growing as grass, wind, uncultivated light,
The faithful and last pleasure of being alone.

Cured of life, smile once,
Face, white with passion and disgust.
Look at the old streets you strolled down,
The bluish streetlamp that lighted your way, lifeless flesh,
As you returned from the dance or the filthy newspaper,
And the marble fountains among the palms:
Waters and leaves, the sad man's healing.

La tierra ha sido medida por los hombres,
Con sus casas estrechas y matrimonios sórdidos,
Su venenosa opinión pública y sus revoluciones
Más crueles e injustas que las leyes,
Como inmenso bostezo demoníaco;
No hay sitio en ella para el hombre solo,
Hijo desnudo y deslumbrante del divino pensamiento.

Y nuestra gran madrastra, mírala hoy deshecha,
Miserable y aún bella entre las tumbas grises
De los que como tú, nacidos en su estepa,
Vieron mientras vivían morirse la esperanza,
Y gritaron entonces, sumidos por tinieblas,
A hermanos irrisorios que jamás escucharon.

Escribir en España no es llorar, es morir,
Porque muere la inspiración envuelta en humo,
Cuando no va su llama libre en pos del aire.
Así, cuando el amor, el tierno monstruo rubio,
Volvió contra ti mismo tantas ternuras vanas,
Tu mano abrió de un tiro, roja y vasta, la muerte.

Libre y tranquilo quedaste en fin un día,
Aunque tu voz sin ti abrió un dejo indeleble.
Es breve la palabra como el canto de un pájaro,
Mas un claro jirón puede prenderse en ella
De embriaguez, pasión, belleza fugitivas,
Y subir, ángel vigía que atestigua del hombre,
Allá hasta la región celeste e impasible.

The earth has been measured by men,
With their narrow houses and sordid marriages,
Their poisonous public opinion and their revolutions
More cruel and unjust than the laws,
Like the devil's enormous yawn;
There is no room on it for the solitary man,
Naked and radiant child of divine thought.

And look at our great stepmother now, torn apart,
Wretched and still beautiful among the gray tombstones
Of those who, born like you on the high flatlands,
Saw hope die in their lifetime
And were buried by darkness and cried out
To their derisive brothers who would not listen.

To write in Spain is not to weep, it is to die,
Because inspiration dies, wrapped up in smoke,
When its free flame does not go out searching for air.
So when love, the tender blond monster,
Turned back on you so many futile tender feelings,
Your hand smashed death open, red and vast, with one bullet.

One day at last you were left free and at peace,
Though, without you, your voice left an indelible accent.
The word is as brief as bird song
But a clear banner upon it can catch fire
With fugitive rapture, passion, loveliness,
And soar, a watchful angel that bears witness for men,
All the way to some heaven, a peaceful place.

TRANSLATED BY JAMES WRIGHT

Mariano José de Larra (1809–1837) was a journalist whose articles were deeply critical of his time. His preoccupation with his country anticipates the attitude of writers like Unamuno and Machado, who respected his work. Cernuda picks up and carries further Larra's words about the writer's plight in Spain: "To write in Spain is to weep."

IMPRESIÓN DE DESTIERRO

Fue la pasada primavera,
Hace ahora casi un año,
En un salón del viejo Temple, en Londres,
Con viejos muebles. Las ventanas daban,
Tras edificios viejos, a lo lejos,
Entre la hierba el gris relámpago del río.
Todo era gris y estaba fatigado
Igual que el iris de una perla enferma.

Eran señores viejos, viejas damas,
En los sombreros plumas polvorientas;
Un susurro de voces allá por los rincones,
Junto a mesas con tulipanes amarillos,
Retratos de familia y teteras vacías.
La sombra que caía
Con un olor a gato,
Despertaba ruidos en cocinas.

Un hombre silencioso estaba
Cerca de mí. Veía
La sombra de su largo perfil algunas veces
Asomarse abstraído al borde de la taza,
Con la misma fatiga
Del muerto que volviera
Desde la tumba a una fiesta mundana.

En los labios de alguno,
Allá por los rincones
Donde los viejos juntos susurraban,
Densa como una lágrima cayendo,
Brotó de pronto una palabra: España.
Un cansancio sin nombre
Rodaba en mi cabeza.
Encendieron las luces. Nos marchamos.

IMPRESSION OF EXILE

It was last spring,
Almost a year now,
In a shabbily furnished sitting room
In London's Old Temple. Its windows opened
On the river's gray streak of lightning
In the grass, out beyond some old buildings.
Everything was gray and worn out
Like the iris of a sick pearl.

Old men, old ladies with dusty
Feathers on their hats were there:
A rustle of voices over in the corner
At tables with yellow tulips,
Family portraits and empty teapots.
The evening shadows came down
With a smell like a cat's
And stirred up noises in kitchens.

Next to me there was
A silent man. I watched
The shadow of his drawn-out profile peer
Over the rim of his cup, from time to time,
Absentmindedly,
With the tired air
Of a dead man who had just come back
From the grave to a lively party.

Over in the corner
Where the old people huddled, whispering,
A word broke from someone's lips
Without warning,
Like a top-heavy teardrop falling off: Spain.
A weariness there is no word for
Lumbered around in my head.
They turned the lights on. We left.

Tras largas escaleras casi a oscuras
Me hallé luego en la calle,
Y a mi lado, al volverme,
Vi otra vez a aquel hombre silencioso,
Que habló indistinto algo
Con acento extranjero,
Un acento de niño en voz envejecida.

Andando me seguía
Como si fuera solo bajo un peso invisible,
Arrastrando la losa de su tumba;
Mas luego se detuvo.
"¿España?", dijo. "Un nombre.
España ha muerto." Había
Una súbita esquina en la calleja.
Le vi borrarse entre la sombra húmeda.

After long stairways almost in the dark
I found myself in the street.
I turned around and there, close to me,
I saw the quiet man again.
He said something hard to make out,
In a foreign accent,
A child's accent in an old man's voice.

He walked behind me
As if he were walking alone, shouldering a weight I
     couldn't see,
Dragging his gravestone.
And then he stopped.
"Spain?" he said. "A name.
Spain is dead." There was
A sudden turn in the lane.
I watched him fade into the damp evening shadows.

Translated by Hardie St. Martin

CEMENTERIO EN LA CIUDAD

Tras de la reja abierta entre los muros,
La tierra negra sin árboles ni hierba,
Con bancos de madera donde allá a la tarde
Se sientan silenciosos unos viejos.
En torno están las casas, cerca hay tiendas,
Calles por las que juegan niños, y los trenes
Pasan al lado de las tumbas. Es un barrio pobre.

Como remiendos de las fachadas grises,
Cuelgan en las ventanas trapos húmedos de lluvia.
Borradas están ya las inscripciones
De las losas con muertos de dos siglos,
Sin amigos que les olviden, muertos
Clandestinos. Mas cuando el sol despierta,
Porque el sol brilla algunos días hacia junio,
En lo hondo algo deben sentir los huesos viejos.

Ni una hoja ni un pájaro. La piedra nada más. La tierra.
¿Es el infierno así? Hay dolor sin olvido,
Con ruido y miseria, frío largo y sin esperanza.
Aquí no existe el sueño silencioso
De la muerte, que todavía la vida
Se agita entre estas tumbas, como una prostituta
Prosigue su negocio bajo la noche inmóvil.

Cuando la sombra cae desde el cielo nublado
Y el humo de las fábricas se aquieta
En polvo gris, vienen de la taberna voces,
Y luego un tren que pasa
Agita largos ecos como bronce iracundo.
No es el juicio aún, muertos anónimos.
Sosegaos, dormid; dormid si es que podéis.
Acaso Dios también se olvida de vosotros.

CEMETERY IN THE CITY

Beyond the iron gates set into the walls,
Black earth only, with no trees or grass,
But wooden benches, on which some old men
Sit at dusk saying nothing.
Buildings surround the cemetery, small grocery shops,
Streets with playing children, trains
Pull by near the graves. The district is run down.

The rain-soaked rags hang from the windows
Like patches on the gray building-fronts.
The inscriptions are already gone
From the stones of the bodies dead two centuries,
Having no friends to forget them, dead
In secrecy. Yet when the sun wakes,
For the sun does shine a few days in June,
The ancient bones should feel something down there in
      the earth.

No leaves, no birds. Only the stone. Earth.
Is hell like this? Here suffering is never forgotten.
Noise and misery, chill abundant and hopeless.
The dead do not find their sweet and silent sleep
In this place, where life continues
Constantly among the graves, as a whore
Pushes on with her trade under the calm stars.

When the night falls from the overcast heavens,
And the smoke from the factories dies down
As gray dust, out of the bars nearby come voices,
And soon a train that stirs up as it goes by
Long echoes like a church bell full of rage.
It is not the Last Judgment yet, you dead with no names.
Rest now, sleep; if you are able to, sleep.
It's possible God has forgotten you too.

TRANSLATED BY ROBERT BLY

TU CORAZÓN, UNA NARANJA HELADA

Tu corazón, una naranja helada
con un dentro sin luz de dulce miera
y una porosa vista de oro: un fuera
venturas prometiendo a la mirada.

Mi corazón, una febril granada
de agrupado rubor y abierta cera,
que sus tiernos collares te ofreciera
con una obstinación enamorada.

¡Ay, qué acontecimiento de quebranto
ir a tu corazón y hallar un hielo
de irreductible y pavorosa nieve!

Por los alrededores de mi llanto
un pañuelo sediento va de vuelo
con la esperanza de que en él lo abreve.

YOUR HEART?—IT IS A FROZEN ORANGE

Your heart?—it is a frozen orange,
inside it has juniper oil but no light
and a porous look like gold: an outside
promising joys to the man who looks.

My heart is a fiery pomegranate,
its scarlets clustered, and its wax opened,
which could offer you its tender beads
with the stubbornness of a man in love.

Yes, what an experience of sorrow it is
to go to your heart and find a frost
made of primitive and terrifying snow!

A thirsty handkerchief flies through the air
along the shores of my weeping,
hoping that it can drink in my tears.

Translated by Robert Bly

ME SOBRA EL CORAZÓN

Hoy estoy sin saber yo no sé como,
hoy estoy para penas solamente,
hoy no tengo amistad,
hoy sólo tengo ansias
de arrancarme de cuajo el corazón
y ponerlo debajo de un zapato.

Hoy reverdece aquella espina seca,
hoy es día de llantos en mi reino,
hoy descarga en mi pecho el desaliento
plomo desalentado.

No puedo con mi estrella.
Y me busco la muerte por las manos
mirando con cariño las navajas,
y recuerdo aquel hacha compañera,
y pienso en los más altos campanarios
para un salto mortal serenamente.

Si no fuera ¿por qué?... no sé por qué,
mi corazón escribiría una postrera carta,
una carta que llevo allí metida,
haría un tintero de mi corazón,
una fuente de sílabas, de adioses y regalos,
y *ahí te quedas*, al mundo le diría.

Yo nací en mala luna.
Tengo la pena de una sola pena
que vale más que toda la alegría.

Un amor me ha dejado con los brazos caídos
y no puedo tenderlos hacia más.
¿No véis mi boca qué desengañada,
qué inconformes mis ojos?

I HAVE PLENTY OF HEART

Today I am, I don't know how,
today all I am ready for is suffering,
today I have no friends,
today the only things I have is the desire
to rip out my heart by the roots
and stick it underneath a shoe.

Today that dry thorn is growing strong again,
today is the day of crying in my kingdom,
depression unloads today in my chest
a depressed heavy metal.

Today my destiny is too much for me.
And I'm looking for death down by my hands,
looking at knives with affection,
and I remember that friendly ax,
and all I think about is the tallest steeples
and making a fatal leap serenely.

If it weren't for . . . I don't know what,
my heart would write a suicide note,
a note I carry hidden there,
I would make an inkwell out of my heart,
a fountain of syllables, and goodbyes and gifts,
and *you stay here* I'd say to the world.

I was born under a rotten star.
My grief is that I have only one grief
and it weighs more than all the joys together.

A love affair has left me with my arms hanging down
and I can't lift them any more.
Don't you see how disillusioned my mouth is?
How unsatisfied my eyes are?

Cuanto más me contemplo más me aflijo:
cortar este dolor ¿con qué tijeras?

Ayer, mañana, hoy
padeciendo por todo
mi corazón, pecera melancólica,
penal de ruiseñores moribundos.

Me sobra corazón.

Hoy descorazonarme,
yo el más corazonado de los hombres,
y por el más, también el más amargo.

No sé por qué, no sé por qué ni cómo
me perdono la vida cada día.

The more I look inward the more I mourn!
Cut off this pain?—who has the scissors?

Yesterday, tomorrow, today
suffering for everything,
my heart is a sad goldfish bowl,
a pen of dying nightingales.

I have plenty of heart.

Today to rip out my heart,
I who have a bigger heart than anyone,
and having that, I am the bitterest also.

I don't know why, I don't know how or why
I let my life keep on going every day.

TRANSLATED BY ROBERT BLY

EL HERIDO

Para el muro de un
hospital de sangre

I

Por los campos luchados se extienden los heridos.
Y de aquella extensión de cuerpos luchadores
salta un trigal de chorros calientes, extendidos
en roncos surtidores.

La sangre llueve siempre boca arriba, hacia el cielo.
Y las heridas suenan, igual que caracolas,
cuando hay en las heridas celeridad de vuelo,
esencia de las olas.

La sangre huele a mar, sabe a mar y a bodega.
La bodega del mar, del vino bravo, estalla
allí donde el herido palpitante se anega,
y florece y se halla.

Herido estoy, miradme: necesito más vidas.
La que contengo es poca para el gran cometido
de sangre que quisiera perder por las heridas.
Decid quién no fué herido.

Mi vida es una herida de juventud dichosa.
¡Ay de quien no esté herido, de quien jamás se siente
herido por la vida, ni en la vida reposa
herido alegremente!

Si hasta a los hospitales se va con alegría,
se convierten en huertos de heridas entreabiertas,
de adelfos florecidos ante la cirujía
de ensangrentadas puertas.

THE WOUNDED MAN

*For the wall of a
blood hospital*

I

The wounded stretch out across the battlefields.
And from that stretched field of bodies that fight
a wheatfield of warm fountains springs up and spreads
    out
into streams with husky voices.

Blood always rains upward toward the sky.
And the wounds lie there making sounds like seashells,
if inside the wounds there is the swiftness of flight,
essence of waves.

Blood smells like the sea, and tastes like the sea, and
    the wine cellar.
The wine cellar of the sea, of rough wine, breaks open
where the wounded man drowns, shuddering,
and he flowers and finds himself where he is.

I am wounded, look at me: I need more lives.
The one I have is too small for the consignment
of blood I want to lose through wounds.
Tell me who has not been wounded.

My life is a wound with a happy childhood.
Pity the man who is not wounded, who doesn't feel
wounded by life, and never sleeps in life,
joyfully wounded.

If a man goes toward the hospitals joyfully,
they change into gardens of half-opened wounds,
of flowering oleanders in front of surgery
with its blood-stained doors.

2

Para la libertad sangro, lucho, pervivo.
Para la libertad, mis ojos y mis manos,
como un árbol carnal, generoso y cautivo,
doy a los cirujanos.

Para la libertad siento más corazones
que arenas en mi pecho: dan espumas mis venas,
y entro en los hospitales, y entro en los algodones
como en las azucenas.

Para la libertad me desprendo a balazos
de los que han revolcado su estatua por el lodo.
Y me desprendo a golpes de mis pies, de mis brazos,
de mi casa, de todo.

Porque donde unas cuencas vacías amanezcan,
ella pondrá dos piedras de futura mirada
y hará que nuevos brazos y nuevas piernas crezcan
en la carne talada.

Retoñarán aladas de savia sin otoño
reliquias de mi cuerpo que pierdo en cada herida.
Porque soy como el árbol talado, que retoño:
porque aún tengo la vida.

2

Thinking of freedom I bleed, fight, manage to live on.
Thinking of freedom, like a tree of blood
generous and imprisoned, I give my eyes and hands
to the surgeons.

Thinking of freedom I feel more hearts than grains of
        sand
in my chest: my veins give up foam,
and I enter the hospitals and I enter the rolls of gauze
as if they were lilies.

Thinking of freedom I break loose in battle
from those who have rolled her statue through the mud.
And I break loose from my feet, from my arms,
from my house, from everything.

Because where some empty eye-pits dawn,
she will place two stones that see into the future
and cause new arms and new legs to grow
in the lopped flesh.

Bits of my body I lose in every wound
will sprout once more, sap-filled, autumnless wings.
Because I am like the lopped tree, and I sprout again:
because I still have my life.

TRANSLATED BY JAMES WRIGHT

RUMOROSAS PESTAÑAS

Rumorosas pestañas
de los cañaverales.
Cayendo sobre el sueño
del hombre hasta dejarle
el pecho apaciguado
y la cabeza suave.

Ahogad la voz del arma,
que no despierte y salte
con el cuchillo de odio
que entre sus dientes late.

Así, dormido, el hombre
toda la tierra vale.

CADA VEZ QUE PASO

Cada vez que paso
bajo tu ventana,
me azota el aroma
que aún flota en tu casa.

Cada vez que paso
junto al cementerio
me arrastra la fuerza
que aún sopla en tus huesos.

HUMMING EYELASHES

Humming eyelashes
of the canefields.
Falling on man's sleepiness
until his breast
is eased
and his head light.

Choke the gun's voice.
Don't make him wake up and pounce
with hatred's knife
throbbing between his teeth.

So, sleeping, a man
is worth the whole world.

TRANSLATED BY HARDIE ST. MARTIN

EACH TIME I PASS

Each time I pass
under your window
I am struck by the fragrance
that still floats through your house.

Each time I pass
the cemetery
I am pulled back by the strength
that still breathes inside your bones.

TRANSLATED BY HARDIE ST. MARTIN

EL CEMENTERIO ESTÁ CERCA

El cementerio está cerca
de donde tú y yo dormimos,
entre nopales azules,
pitas azules y niños
que gritan vívidamente
si un muerto nubla el camino.

De aquí al cementerio, todo
es azul, dorado, límpido.
Cuatro pasos y los muertos.
Cuatro pasos y los vivos.

Límpido, azul y dorado,
se hace allí remoto el hijo.

THE CEMETERY LIES NEAR

The cemetery lies near
where you and I are sleeping,
among blue prickly pear,
blue century plants and children
who cry out with such life
if a dead body throws its shadow on the road.

From here to the cemetery, everything
is blue, golden, clear.
Four steps and the dead.
Four steps and the living.

Clear, blue and golden,
my son, there, seems far away.

TRANSLATED BY JAMES WRIGHT

SONREÍR CON LA ALEGRE TRISTEZA DEL OLIVO

Sonreír con la alegre tristeza del olivo,
esperar, no cansarse de esperar la alegría.
Sonriamos, doremos la luz de cada día
en esta alegre y triste vanidad de ser vivo.

Me siento cada día más leve y más cautivo
en toda esta sonrisa tan clara y tan sombría.
Cruzan las tempestades sobre tu boca fría
como sobre la mía que aún es un soplo estivo.

Una sonrisa se alza sobre el abismo: crece
como un abismo trémulo, pero batiente en alas.
Una sonrisa eleva calientemente el vuelo.

Diurna, firme, arriba, no baja, no anochece.
Todo lo desafías, amor: todo lo escalas.
Con sonrisa te fuiste de la tierra y el cielo.

TO SMILE WITH THE JOYFUL
SADNESS OF THE OLIVE TREE

To smile with the joyful sadness of the olive tree.
To wait and never stop waiting for joy.
Let us smile, let us make the light every day gold
in this sad and joyful hopelessness of being alive.

Every day I feel myself more able to fly, and more caught up
in this smile, so clear, so full of darkness.
The storms that make their way past your cold mouth
also move past mine; it is a brief summer wind.

A smile rises over the final emptiness: it swells
like an emptiness that quivers, still fluttering its wings.
A smile breaks warmly into flight.

Ordinary, steady, it does not fall, it does not darken.
You defy everything, love: you climb over it all.
With your smile you parted from both heaven and earth.

TRANSLATED BY TIMOTHY BALAND

NANAS DE LA CEBOLLA

*(Dedicadas a su hijo, a raíz de recibir una
carta de su mujer, en la que decía que no
comía más que pan y cebolla.)*

La cebolla es escarcha
cerrada y pobre.
Escarcha de tus días
y de mis noches.
Hambre y cebolla,
hielo negro y escarcha
grande y redonda.

En la cuna del hambre
mi niño estaba.
Con sangre de cebolla
se amamantaba.
Pero tu sangre,
escarchada de azúcar,
cebolla y hambre.

Una mujer morena
resuelta en luna
se derrama hilo a hilo
sobre la cuna.
Ríete, niño,
que te tragas la luna
cuando es preciso.

Alondra de mi casa,
ríete mucho.
Es tu risa en los ojos
la luz del mundo.
Ríete tanto
que mi alma al oírte
bata el espacio.

LULLABIES OF THE ONION

*Dedicated to his son, after receiving a letter
from his wife saying that all she had to eat
was bread and onion*

The onion is frost
shut in and poor.
Frost of your days
and of my nights.
Hunger and onion,
black ice and frost
large and round.

My little boy was
in hunger's cradle.
He suckled on
onion blood.
But your blood is
frosted with sugar,
onion and hunger.

A dark woman dissolved
into moonlight
spills, thread by thread,
over the cradle.
Laugh, child,
you can drink moonlight
if you have to.

Lark of my house,
laugh freely.
Your laughter in your eyes
is the world's light.
Laugh so much
that hearing you, my soul
will beat through space.

Tu risa me hace libre,
me pone alas.
Soledades me quita,
cárcel me arranca.
Boca que vuela,
corazón que en tus labios
relampaguea.

Es tu risa la espada
más victoriosa,
vencedor de las flores
y las alondras.
Rival del sol.
Porvenir de mis huesos
y de mi amor.

La carne aleteante,
súbito el párpado,
el vivir como nunca
coloreado.
¡Cuánto jilguero
se remonta, aletea,
desde tu cuerpo!

Desperté de ser niño:
nunca despiertes.
Triste llevo la boca:
ríete siempre.
Siempre en la cuna,
defendiendo la risa
pluma por pluma.

Ser de vuelo tan alto,
tan extendido,
que tu carne es el cielo
recién nacido.
¡Si yo pudiera

Your laughter frees me,
gives me wings.
It banishes loneliness,
tears down these walls.
Mouth that flies,
heart that flashes
on your lips.

Your laughter is
the supreme sword,
conqueror of flowers
and larks.
Rival of the sun.
Future of my bones
and of my love.

The flesh flutters
as sudden as an eyelid;
life, as never before,
takes on new color.
How many linnets,
wings beating, take off
from your body!

I woke from childhood:
don't you ever.
I wear my mouth sadly:
always laugh.
Stay always in your cradle
defending laughter
feather by feather.

You are a flight
so high, so wide,
that your flesh is heaven
just born.
If only I could climb

remontarme al origen
de tu carrera!

Al octavo mes ríes
con cinco azahares.
Con cinco diminutas
ferocidades.
Con cinco dientes
como cinco jazmines
adolescentes.

Frontera de los besos
serán mañana,
cuando en la dentadura
sientas un arma.
Sientas un fuego
correr dientes abajo
buscando el centro.

Vuela, niño, en la doble
luna del pecho:
él, triste de cebolla,
tú, satisfecho.
No te derrumbes.
No sepas lo que pasa
ni lo que ocurre.

to the origin
of your flight!

In the eighth month you laugh
with five orange blossoms.
With five little
ferocities,
with five teeth
like five young
jasmine buds.

They will be the frontier
of kisses tomorrow
when you feel a gun
in your mouth.
When you feel a burning
past the teeth
searching for the center.

Fly, child, on the double moon
of her breast:
it is saddened by onions,
you are satisfied.
Never let go.
Don't ever know what's coming,
what goes on.

TRANSLATED BY PHILIP LEVINE

LA RAÍZ

No lo puedes decir, pero lo vives,
como vive la tierra el cuerpo de los muertos
y los va transformando en trigo o en madera que devuelvan
     el calor que tuvieron;
y tu silencio te ilumina y te embellece mortalmente,
igual que la sequía dora las hojas de los árboles en
     primavera aún,
y nadie sabe de qué raíz brota tu vida en tanto que caminas
     como un río que se viste a diario el mismo cielo,
o se desnuda de las aguas durmientes y oficiales donde vas
     tramitando tu vida,
mientras callas una palabra sola,
una sola palabra que persiste en tu cuerpo
arremolinándolo todo interiormente como el viento en un
     pajar cerrado;
mientras callas una palabra sola,
que no puedes decir,
que no puedes abrir como una puerta porque te quedarías
     deshabitada,
desamparadamente dicha y varonil,
porque te quedarías escrita para siempre igual que un
     nombre en una lápida.

THE ROOT

You can't talk about it, but you live it,
as the earth lives the bodies of the dead,
and it gradually transforms them into wheat or wood that
    returns the heat that they once had;
and your silence makes you throw off light and makes you
    mortally beautiful,
just as the drought reddens the leaves of the trees still in spring,
and nobody knows from what root your life sprouted, as you
    move along like a river that daily dresses itself in the
    same sky,
or undresses itself of the sleeping and official waters where you
    go along transacting your life,
while you keep a single word under your breath,
a single unfading word in your body
stirring everything around inside like the wind in a locked barn,
while you keep a single word under your breath,
that you can't talk about,
that you can't open like a door because you would be left vacant,
helplessly uttered and overpowering,
because you would be left written forever like a name on a
    block of stone.

TRANSLATED BY RALPH NELSON
AND RITA GARCÍA NELSON

AGUA DESATÁNDOSE

El tiempo es un espejo en que te miras;
tú ya has entrado en el espejo y andas
a ciegas dentro de él; tú ya has entrado
en el espejo, nada
te puede desnacer: ya eres viviente;
tu carne sucesiva y simultánea
es igual que un trapecio donde un pájaro
a pie, se maniata
dando vueltas y vueltas procurando
sostenerse en el cuerpo, y se le lacra
la carne en la madera mientras gira,
—abajo, arriba, abajo—hasta que el alba
vuelva a girar el cielo y ya no pueda
seguirse sosteniendo y se le caigan
las manos, se le agrieten
las manos, temblorosas,
y al perder su sostén el cuerpo caiga
y caiga, desatándose, y sintiendo
un borbotón de música en las alas.

LOOSENING WATER

Time is a mirror in which you see yourself;
you have already stepped into the mirror, and there
you walk blindly; you have stepped
into the mirror; nothing
can annihilate your birth: you are among the living;
your continuous and simultaneous flesh
is like a trapeze where a bird
stands, locks himself
swinging around and around, trying
to hold himself within his body, and his flesh
is ripped on the wood as he rotates,
up and down and around, until the next time
the dawn rotates the sky and he can no longer
go on supporting himself,
and his hands fall,
his hands crack,
his hands open, trembling,
and losing his grip the body falls
and falls, loosening, feeling
a bubble of music in the wings.

TRANSLATED BY RALPH NELSON
AND RITA GARCÍA NELSON

EVOCACIÓN PARA GRABARLA
EN UNA CAJA DE MÚSICA

Brindis a Antonio Cabañete

Dime, Antonio, recuerdas que en el año 14
el sol se distraía descansando los sábados;
recuerdas que las damas bailaban de rodillas,
bailaban de rodillas llorando entre los brazos
del vals que las llevaba, como el agua de un río,
de la ribera lenta de un año hacia otro año;
recuerdas las muchachas cuyas bocas tenían
un beso únicamente sacramental y blanco,
las palabras corteses como calles con árboles,
la lenta hipocresía con su andar de galápago;
recuerdas que los hombres se mesaban la barba
con un gesto incoherente de honor inmaculado,
y un suspiro cifraba toda la biografía
de un general y a veces de un sabio catedrático;
recuerdas que las niñas soñaban por la noche
que el tren, hacia las doce, llegaba hasta su cuarto
y se sentían inermes y pequeñitas viendo
pasar el tren tan cerca que hacía temblar sus labios;
recuerdas la familia de silla en el paseo
con una sola lágrima que lloraban por turno,
primero el padre, luego la madre y los hermanos;
recuerdas las palabras decisivas, las nobles
palabras: ley, derecho, constitución, y un halo
de libertad que hacía que bajo las banderas
las manos comenzaran a aprender a ser manos...
Del arranque del siglo con sus años amigos
queda un copo de nieve como un escapulario,
queda sólo un recuerdo con yedra en las paredes:
tu corazón, Antonio, soñándolo y sonámbulo.

EVOCATION TO RECORD
A MUSIC BOX

For Antonio Cabañete

Tell me, Antonio, do you remember the year '14
when the sun amused itself resting on Saturdays;
do you remember that the ladies used to dance on their knees,
danced on their knees, shedding tears in the arms
of the waltz that swept them along, like the water of a river,
from the slow shore of one year toward another year;
do you remember the girls whose mouths had
only one sacramental and white kiss,
polite words like streets with trees,
the turtle's pace of slow hypocrisy;
do you remember that the men pulled at their beards
with an incoherent gesture of immaculate honor,
and their sighs summed up the biography
of a general or, sometimes, of a wise professor;
do you remember that the little girls used to dream at night
that the train, around twelve, came into their room
and they felt so defenseless and tiny watching
the train pass so close that their lips trembled;
do you remember the family in their chairs on the paseo
with only one tear to share between all of them,
one tear which they had to take turns to cry,
first the father, then the mother and the children;
do you remember the final words, the noble
words: law, justice, constitution, and a halo
of liberty beneath the banners, that inspired
the hands to start learning to be hands . . .
And what's left of the beginnings of the century with its friendly
          years?
Only a snowflake like a scapular,
a memory with ivy on its walls,
your heart, Antonio, a sleepwalker dreaming.

TRANSLATED BY RALPH NELSON
AND RITA GARCIA NELSON

CRECIENDO HACIA LA TIERRA

A José Coronel Urtecho

Cuando llegue la noche y sea la sombra un báculo,
cuando la noche llegue, quizás el mar se habrá dormido,
quizás toda su fuerza no le podrá servir para mover sólo un grano
      de arena,
para cambiar de rostro una sonrisa,
y quizás entre sus olas podrá nacer un niño
cuando llegue la noche;
cuando la noche llegue y la verdad sea una palabra igual a otra,
cuando todos los muertos cogidos de la mano formen una cadena
      alrededor del mundo,
quizás los hombres ciegos comenzarán a caminar como caminan las
      raíces en la tierra sonámbula;
caminarán llevando alegre el corazón igual que un árbol de coral,
y cuando al fin se encuentren se tocarán los rostros y los cuerpos en
      lugar de llamarse por sus nombres,
y sentirán una fe manual repartiendo entre todos su savia,
y quizás irán creciendo los vivos y los muertos, uno dentro de otros,
      hasta formar un bosque silencioso,
un bosque de raíces que formarán un árbol único
cuando llegue la noche.

GROWING TOWARD THE EARTH

For José Coronel Urtecho

When the night comes in and the darkness becomes a staff,
when the night comes in perhaps the sea will have been asleep,
perhaps all its strength won't help it to move a single grain of sand,
to change the face of a smile,
and perhaps among the waves a child could be born,
when the night comes in,
when the night comes in and truth becomes just another word,
when all the dead join hands and form a chain around the earth,
perhaps the blind men will begin to walk as the roots walk in the
        sleepwalking earth,
they will walk with joyful hearts like a tree of coral,
and when they finally meet instead of calling each other by name
        their faces and bodies will touch,
and they will feel a faith actually divide its sap among them,
and maybe the living and the dead will go on growing within each
        other, until they form a silent forest,
a forest of roots that will form the only tree
when the night comes in.

TRANSLATED BY RALPH NELSON
AND RITA GARCÍA NELSON

ABRAZADA A UNA LÁGRIMA

Como la hormiga testaruda lleva su carga sosteniéndose en ella,
así te encuentro siempre abrazada a una lágrima;
a una lágrima tuya que no has llorado todavía,
que no quieres llorar,
que no puedes llorar porque es más grande que tu cuerpo,
porque es más grande que tu cuerpo
y no la puedes contener como el mundo no contiene su noche;
y te apoyas en ella, sin llorarla, para que siga estando junta,
y duermes a su lado vigilándola un poco,
y la sostienes en tus brazos, sin abarcarla, como el rail sostiene el
      tren,
y la proteges con tu cuerpo de la profanación
para que el mundo, pequeñito, no la pueda enjugar en su pañuelo.

LOCKED WITH A TEAR

As the stubborn ant carries its load counting on it to stay alive,
that's how I find you always locked around a tear,
one of your tears that you haven't cried yet,
that you don't want to cry,
that you can't cry because it's larger than your body,
because it's larger than your body
and you can't hold it back, just as the world can't hold back its night,
against it you rest, without crying over it, to stay together,
sleeping beside it sometimes open-eyed,
and you hold it in your arms, without possessing it, the way the
     rails hold a train,
and you protect it with your body from desecration,
so that the world, so tiny now, can't soak it up in its handkerchief.

TRANSLATED BY RALPH NELSON
AND RITA GARCÍA NELSON

Y SÉ MUY CLARA Y TRISTEMENTE BIEN

Y sé muy clara y tristemente bien,
que hay personas que viven como teniendo invitado a su corazón,
y lo sientan
escogiendo su puesto en la cabecera de la mesa,
para poder colmarlo de atenciones,
porque lo viven como quieren vivirlo,
y lo disfrutan,
y lo tienen tranquilo y festejado,
y le sirven el vino cuando quieren;
pero yo sé muy bien,
muy tristemente bien,
que no tengo invitados,
que me estoy convocando y reuniendo a mí mismo
en partes dolorosas que no conviven juntas,
que nunca completaron su unidad,
que nunca podrán ser,
que nunca podré ser
sino tan sólo un hombre sucesivo que se escribe con sombras.

I KNOW TOO WELL AND SADLY ENOUGH

I know too well, and sadly enough,
that there are people in the world who live with their hearts as a
        guest,
they offer it a chair,
making room for it at the head of the table,
where they can shower it with attention,
because they give it the life they would like for themselves,
sharing in its pleasure,
and they make it feel at home and important,
and they pour it wine when the spirit moves them,
but I know only too well,
and sadly enough,
that I have no guests,
that I'm calling myself together, reuniting
the painful parts that don't like being together,
that never become whole,
that can never be,
that I can never be
anything except a man who endlessly follows himself, who writes
        himself down with shadows.

TRANSLATED BY RALPH NELSON
AND RITA GARCÍA NELSON

HE LLEGADO AL FINAL DE LA CASA
DONDE ESTÁN LA COCINA Y EL BAÑO

He llegado al final de la casa donde están la cocina y
    el baño,
y ahora me siento en el pasillo
igual que si estuviera circulando en mi propio sistema
    arterial,
y me rodea la sombra como si fuera sangre,
y me pesa en los hombros la estrechez de la tierra
comprimiendo mis brazos contra el cuerpo,
y me recorre un estremecimiento genital,
porque cerca de mí,
cerca de mí, crepitante y morena,
¿no estoy oyendo algo como una voz que arde?
como un desprendimiento de tierra que se agrieta, que
    se empieza a agrietar
en una voz en la que vibra esa tristeza que tú tienes,
esa tristeza humana
en que se está viviendo aún a Cristo mismo,
esa tristeza que es más antigua que la carne,
esa tristeza que está latiendo ahora
en esta habitación donde los libros
caminan y caminan y caminan.

I'VE COME TO THE BACK
OF THE HOUSE

I've come to the back of the house where the kitchen and the bath-
        room are,
and I feel like I'm in a narrow passage,
like I'm circulating through my own bloodstream,
and the shadows surround me as if they were blood,
and the snugness of the earth weighs on my shoulders,
pinning my arms against my sides,
and a shudder starting in my genitals runs through me,
because near me,
near me, crackling and dusky,
don't I hear something like a voice on fire?
like a landfall starting to crack open, that begins to crack
in a voice that resounds with this sadness that you embody,
this human sadness
where Christ himself is still being lived,
this sadness more ancient than the flesh,
this sadness that is throbbing now
in this room where the books
walk and walk and walk.

TRANSLATED BY RALPH NELSON
AND RITA GARCÍA NELSON

Gabriel Celaya

TEORÍA DE SILENCIOS

Hay un silencio antiguo convertido en estatua
que yace en el fondo de un transparente río.
Bajo música queda como el cuerpo desnudo
de esa virgen blanca que acaricia la noche.

Hay un silencio del año mil novecientos
refugiado dentro de una mustia berlina
llena de mariposas de un blanco nocturno
y olores a hule, y a flores de cera.

Hay otro silencio que es un laberinto
con puertas de vidrio y espejos que giran.
Los ángeles usan ese mecanismo
para aparecerse y efectuar prodigios.

Hay otro silencio con sus monumentos
y un mar en el fondo que sueña la nada:
Plaza de Chirico por cuyas arcadas
la muerte camina sonámbula y tiesa.

Hay otros silencios menos luminosos,
de mano enguantada, de gas violeta,
y hay maniquís que giran fijos en la enorme
luna que es un grito todo vuelto hacia dentro.

Son silencios, simas; son siempre peligros
de claridad que mata, de obsesión que aloca.
Son terribles silencios que ahora me rodean
como un corro de quietos perros sin cabeza.

THEORY OF SILENCES

There is an ancient silence changed into a statue
that lies on the bed of a clear river.
Under that music it lies like the nude body
of the bloodless virgin the night embraces.

There is a silence of the year 1900
huddled inside a musty carriage,
full of butterflies of a nocturnal whiteness
and odors of oilcloth and wax flowers.

There is another silence which is a maze
of revolving mirrors and glass doors.
Angels make use of this contraption
to take on flesh, their wonders to perform.

And still another silence with its monuments
and the ocean behind it, which the void is dreaming:
Plaza de Chirico through whose arcades
death sleepwalks on rigid legs.

There are other silences not so luminous,
silences of gloved hands, of violet gas,
and slowly turning manikins fixed in the huge
moon which is a cry turned entirely inward.

Silences, abysses; constant danger
of the brightness that kills, ideas that drive one mad—
horrible silences that surround me now
like a fixed circle of headless dogs.

TRANSLATED BY ROBERT MEZEY

SOBRE UN POEMA NATIVO DE
LAS ISLAS SALOMÓN QUE COMIENZA:
"TU VERGÜENZA GENITAL ES
EL GRAMÓFONO DEL HOMBRE BLANCO"

Tu vergüenza genital es el gramófono del hombre blanco,
y un embudo de sombra, y un paraguas cerrado,
y una culebra gorda que arrastra barro dulce:
Tu voz de espesas, largas plumas de un iris sedante.

La máquina de escribir te ha arrancado los dientes.
(¡Míralos, son estrellas de agua dura que brilla!)
Cuelgan hilos de baba y una canción gangosa
tan sensual que no puede dividirse por siete.

Las hormigas establecen caminitos en lo informe
de ese océano convulso que llamo amante, mi amante.
Bailemos, muerte viva, con ese escalofrío
que es, a falta de esqueleto, como un esquema en la carne.

Tu vergüenza genital es el frío de la hormiga,
móvil abstracto que pone, con patitas insensibles,
en evidencia los cuerpos de deseo que aún se ocultan.
Hombre blanco, tu mirada sólo es un grito inaudible.

AFTER A NATIVE POEM FROM THE SOLOMON ISLANDS THAT BEGINS: "YOUR SHAMEFUL PARTS ARE THE WHITE MAN'S GRAMOPHONE"

Your shameful parts are the white man's gramophone,
and a funnel of shadow, and a closed umbrella,
and a fat snake that drags sweet mud along:
your voice the long thick feathers of hypnotic iris.

The typewriter has pulled out all your teeth.
(Look, they are stars of hard, glittering water.)
Threads of spittle hang down, and a nasal song
so sensual it can't be divided by seven.

The ants lay down tiny roads on the shapelessness
of that oceanic seizure I call my lover.
And we shall dance, living death, with the shudder
that has no spine to run down, a tracery in the flesh.

Your shameful parts are the cold that pierces the ant,
abstract engine that with its numb little feet
lays bare the amorous bodies that still remain hidden.
White man, the look in your eyes is a cry nobody hears.

TRANSLATED BY ROBERT MEZEY

EL SENTIDO DE LA SOPA

"Han perdido el sentido de la sopa."
A. Gide

La vida va despacio, pisa tibio y mojado,
huele a río de fango, y a vaca y tierra lenta.
La mujer bajo un hombre sabe cómo huele.

Un olor sustancioso como una buena sopa,
un llanto nutritivo, unos días pacientes...
(Ahí comemos, bebemos, respiramos, amamos).

¿Debo aún explicarlo? ¿Hay alguien que lo ignore?
La vida dulce y negra es un humus cargado.
Tiene un calor de sexos y un empeño de llanto.

Es el río estancado de una mujer amada,
es el fruto ya dulce de unas horas cansadas,
y un trabajo, una casa, un instinto, rutinas.

Porque todos vivimos y vivir sólo es eso.
No es el amor, la dicha, una idea, el destino.
Es tan sólo una sopa caliente, espesa y sucia.

THE MEANING OF SOUP

"The meaning of soup has been lost."
A. Gide

Life moves slowly, with a warm, oozing tread,
it smells like river mud, like cows and slow earth.
The woman under a man knows that smell.

An odor as nourishing as good soup,
a nutritious weeping, a few patient days . . .
(Here's where we eat, drink, breathe, and make love.)

Must I explain? Is there anyone who doesn't know this?
Life is a heavy humus, sweet and black.
It has the heat of the loins and insists on shedding tears.

It's the dammed-up river of the woman we love,
the ripe fruit of exhausted hours,
and a job, a house, an impulse, a routine.

Because all of us live and life is just like that.
It's not love, or happiness, or ideas, or the future.
It's just a hot, thick, dirty soup.

TRANSLATED BY ROBERT MEZEY
AND HARDIE ST. MARTIN

LA VIDA QUE UNO LLEVA

Olía la cabaña
a madera fregada y a jabón de cocina.
Fuera, el sol zumbaba
como un compacto enjambre de mosquitos locos.
La puerta recortaba en luz hiriente un cuadro,
la arrastraba a una mesa euclidiana de pino,
y allí ardía en naranjas o vidriaba una loza,
y arrojaba a los fondos violetas y verdes
el resto de la choza.

Sobre una colchoneta suciamente caliente,
Uno—se llama Pedro—ronca cansadamente.
El mundo rumia triste su baba hedionda y tonta
con encías sin dientes, con soplos sin frescura,
con blasfemia en pingajos y lenta lengua larga.

A las seis de la tarde,
cuando pasa el expreso despertando nostalgias
(metales claros, brillos,
caminos excitantes que acarician la nada),
el hombre Pedro se alza,
recoge sus tirantes y se moja la cara,
y, en su mano callosa de cortos dedos torpes,
contempla diez monedas, diez vasos de mal vino.

Acaso en el derribo cuando vuelva borracho,
Adela esté esperando otros hombres más ricos,
(no mucho, se entiende).
Y Adela es buena chica.
Adela irá a la choza de Pedro si es que él quiere,
que sí querrá si bebe.

La hermosa luna lenta,
la noche como un río mirado desde el fondo,

THE LIFE ONE LEADS

The cabin gives off the odor
of scrubbed wood and strong kitchen soap.
Outside, the sun buzzes
like a dense swarm of mad mosquitoes.
The door carves out a blinding square of light
and lays it down as proof on a Euclidean pine table
where it burns orange and glazes an edge of porcelain,
leaving the rest of the shack
in a blackness of greens and violets.

On a narrow mattress, warm in its stench,
someone named Pedro is snoring monotonously.
His sour idiot spittle broods sadly over the world
with toothless gums and stale wheezes,
with tattered blasphemies and a long slow tongue.

At six in the evening
when the Express goes by, waking nostalgia
(bright steel, flashes,
burning road that mounts the emptiness),
the man Pedro gets to his feet,
hitches his suspenders, splashes some water on his face
and stares into his rough hand with its short clumsy fingers
at ten small coins, ten glasses of cheap wine.

Down at the ruined house, when he comes back drunk,
Adela may be waiting for others who have more money
(you understand, a little more).
And Adela's a good chick.
Adela will come to Pedro's shack if he wants her to,
and he's sure to, if he's been drinking.

Beautiful slow moon,
night like a river seen from its bed,

la brisa suave y densa,
las caderas y muslos de Adela cuando tiembla,
y el mal frío de dentro que nadie abrigó nunca,
y el mal vino que tiene,
y Adela que, callada, prepara el desayuno.

Al fin, un día dice: "Casémonos, Adela."
(Adela está asustada pero consiente siempre.)
Y el hombre Pedro escucha cómo pasa el expreso
(metales claros, brillos,
caminos excitantes que acarician la nada);
y siente una ternura,
y un gran frío por dentro,
y una nostalgia, y asco.
Y cree que eso es Adela, blanca, dulce, en camisa.

the soft heavy breeze,
Adela's hips and thighs when she starts to tremble,
and the ice inside him that no one has ever thawed,
and the cheap wine,
and Adela who wordlessly fixes breakfast.

One day he finally says, "Adela, let's get married."
(Adela is frightened but she always says okay.)
And the man Pedro listens to the Express roar by
(bright steel, flashes,
burning road that mounts the emptiness),
and he feels a tenderness,
and the immense chill deep inside,
and vague longings, and disgust.
And he thinks that's Adela, white, sweet, in her slip.

TRANSLATED BY ROBERT MEZEY
AND HARDIE ST. MARTIN

LA POESÍA ES UN ARMA
CARGADA DE FUTURO

Cuando ya nada se espera personalmente exaltante,
mas se palpita y se sigue más acá de la conciencia,
fieramente existiendo, ciegamente afirmando,
como un pulso que golpea las tinieblas,

cuando se miran de frente
los vertiginosos ojos claros de la muerte,
se dicen las verdades:
las bárbaras, terribles, amorosas crueldades:

Se dicen los poemas
que ensanchan los pulmones de cuantos, asfixiados,
piden ser, piden ritmo,
piden ley para aquello que sienten excesivo.

Con la velocidad del instinto,
con el rayo del prodigio,
como mágica evidencia, lo real se nos convierte
en lo idéntico a sí mismo.

Poesía para el pobre, poesía necesaria
como el pan de cada día,
como el aire que exigimos trece veces por minuto
para ser y en tanto somos dar un sí que glorifica.

Porque vivimos a golpes, porque apenas si nos dejan
decir que somos quien somos,
nuestros cantares no pueden ser sin pecado un adorno.
Estamos tocando el fondo.

Maldigo la poesía concebida como un lujo
cultural por los neutrales
que, lavándose las manos, se desentienden y evaden.
Maldigo la poesía de quien no toma partido hasta mancharse.

POETRY IS A WEAPON
LOADED WITH THE FUTURE

When finally one gives up all hope of personal exaltation,
but goes on anyway, quivering, just this side of awareness,
existing savagely, blindly contending,
like a pulse that strikes the darkness,

when the vertiginous
clear eyes of death are seen, face to face,
true things are said:
barbarous, terrible things, tender cruelties—

poems that breathe the spirit
into the starved lungs of so many men, men
who seek life, and music,
who seek some order for the things they feel too deeply.

With the speed of instinct,
with the luminous force of prodigy,
with magical evidence, the real
changes into something identical to itself.

Poetry for the poor, poetry as necessary
as our daily bread,
as the air that we require some thirteen times a minute,
for life, and while we're alive, for saying so with honor.

Because we live by blows, because they leave us
scarcely enough breath to say that we are who we are,
our singing can't just be an ornament and not be a crime.
We are touching bottom.

I curse that poetry conceived as a cultural
luxury for neutrals
who, washing their hands, pretend not to understand and slip away.
I curse the poetry of all who won't take sides till the knife's at their
        throat.

Hago mías las faltas. Siento en mí a cuantos sufren
y canto respirando.
Canto, y canto, y cantando más allá de mis penas
personales, me ensancho.

Quisiera daros vida, provocar nuevos actos,
y calculo por eso, con técnica, qué puedo.
Me siento un ingeniero del verso y un obrero
que trabaja con otros a España en sus aceros.

Tal es mi poesía: Poesía-herramienta
a la vez que latido de lo unánime y ciego.
Tal es, arma cargada de futuro expansivo
con que te apunto al pecho.

No es una poesía gota a gota pensada.
No es un bello producto. No es un fruto perfecto.
Es algo como el aire que todos respiramos,
y es el canto que espacia cuanto dentro llevamos.

Son palabras que todos repetimos sintiendo
como nuestras, y vuelan. Son más que lo mentado.
Son lo más necesario: Lo que no tiene nombre.
Son gritos en el cielo, y en la tierra son actos.

I make these failings my own. I feel so many people
suffering in me, and I sing by drawing breath.
I sing and sing, and singing out beyond my personal
suffering, I am multiplied.

I want to give you life, to incite new acts,
and I count on this with whatever art I have.
I think of myself as an engineer of verse, a worker
like others, who works on Spain, in her steel.

Such is my poetry: ironwork-poetry,
at the same time the heartbeat of something unanimous and blind.
That's what it is, a weapon loaded with expanding future,
and I am leveling it at your heart.

It is not a poetry thought out bit by bit.
It is not a beautiful product, not a perfect fruit.
It is something like the air we all breathe
and the music of space we carry deep inside.

Words which we all repeat, thinking
they're our own, and they vanish. They are more than talk.
They are what is needed most: what has no name.
They are cries out to heaven and, on earth, they are acts.

TRANSLATED BY ROBERT MEZEY

MOMENTOS FELICES

Cuando llueve, y reviso mis papeles, y acabo
tirando todo al fuego: poemas incompletos,
pagarés no pagados, cartas de amigos muertos,
fotografías, besos guardados en un libro,
renuncio al peso muerto de mi terco pasado,
soy fúlgido, engrandezco justo en cuanto me niego,
y así atizo las llamas, y salto la fogata,
y apenas si comprendo lo que al hacerlo siento,
¿no es la felicidad lo que me exalta?

Cuando salgo a la calle silbando alegremente
—el pitillo en los labios, el alma disponible—
y les hablo a los niños o me voy con las nubes,
mayo apunta y la brisa lo va todo ensanchando,
las muchachas estrenan sus escotes, sus brazos
desnudos y morenos, sus ojos asombrados,
y ríen ni ellas saben por qué sobreabundando,
salpican la alegría que así tiembla reciente,
¿no es la felicidad lo que se siente?

Cuando llega un amigo, la casa está vacía,
pero mi amada saca jamón, anchoas, queso,
aceitunas, percebes, dos botellas de blanco,
y yo asisto al milagro—sé que todo es fiado—,
y no quiero pensar si podremos pagarlo;
y cuando, sin medida, bebemos y charlamos,
y el amigo es dichoso, cree que somos dichosos,
y lo somos quizás burlando así la muerte,
¿no es la felicidad lo que trasciende?

Cuando me he despertado, permanezco tendido
con el balcón abierto. Y amanece: Las aves
trinan su algarabía pagana lindamente;
y debo levantarme pero no me levanto;
y veo, boca arriba, reflejada en el techo,

GREAT MOMENTS

When it rains, and I go over my papers and end up
throwing everything into the fire: unfinished poems,
bills still unpaid, letters from dead friends,
photographs, kisses preserved in a book,
I am throwing off the dead weight of my hard-headed past,
I am shining and growing just as fast as I disown myself,
so if I poke at the fire, leap over the flames,
and scarcely understand what I feel while I'm doing it,
is it not happiness that is lifting me up?

When I hit the streets, whistling in sheer delight
—a cigarette in my lips, my soul in good order—
and I talk to the kids or let myself drift with the clouds,
early May and the breeze goes lifting up everything,
the young girls begin wearing their low-cut blouses, their arms
naked and tanned, their eyes wide,
and they laugh without knowing why, bubbling over
and scattering their ecstasy which then trembles afresh,
isn't it happiness, what we feel then?

When a friend shows up and there's nothing in the house,
but my girl brings forth anchovies, ham, and cheese,
olives and crab and two bottles of white wine,
and I assist at the miracle—knowing it's all on credit—
and I don't want to worry about having to pay for it,
and we drink and babble like there's no tomorrow,
and my friend is well off and he figures we are too,
and maybe we are, laughing at death that way,
isn't that happiness which suddenly breaks through?

When I wake up, I stay stretched out
by the open balcony. And dawn comes: the birds
trill sweetly in their heathen arabics;
and I ought to get up, but I don't;
and looking up I watch the rippling light of the sea

la ondulación del mar y el iris de su nácar,
y sigo allí tendido, y nada importa nada,
¿no aniquilo así el tiempo? ¿No me salvo del miedo?
¿No es la felicidad lo que amanece?

Cuando voy al mercado, miro los abridores
y, apretando los dientes, las redondas cerezas,
los higos rezumantes, las ciruelas caídas
del árbol de la vida, con pecado sin duda,
pues que tanto me tientan. Y pregunto su precio,
regateo, consigo por fin una rebaja,
mas terminado el juego, pago el doble y es poco,
y abre la vendedora sus ojos asombrados,
¿no es la felicidad lo que allí brota?

Cuando puedo decir: El día ha terminado.
Y con el día digo su trajín, su comercio,
la busca del dinero, la lucha de los muertos.
Y cuando así cansado, manchado, llego a casa,
me siento en la penumbra y enchufo el tocadiscos,
y acuden Kachaturian, o Mozart, o Vivaldi,
y la música reina, vuelvo a sentirme limpio,
sencillamente limpio y, pese a todo, indemne,
¿no es la felicidad lo que me envuelve?

Cuando tras dar mil vueltas a mis preocupaciones,
me acuerdo de un amigo, voy a verle, me dice:
"Estaba justamente pensando en ir a verte."
Y hablamos largamente, no de mis sinsabores,
pues él, aunque quisiera, no podría ayudarme,
sino de cómo van las cosas en Jordania,
de un libro de Neruda, de su sastre, del viento,
y al marcharme me siento consolado y tranquilo,
¿no es la felicidad lo que me vence?

Abrir nuestras ventanas; sentir el aire nuevo;
pasar por un camino que huele a madreselvas;

dancing on the ceiling, prism of its mother-of-pearl,
and I go on lying there and nothing matters a damn—
don't I annihilate time? And save myself from terror?
Isn't it happiness that comes with the dawn?

When I go to the market, I look at the nectarines
and work my jaws at the sight of the plump cherries,
the oozing figs, the plums fallen
from the tree of life, a sin no doubt,
being so tempting and all. And I ask the price
and haggle over it and finally knock it down,
but the game is over, I pay double and it's still not much,
and the salesgirl turns her astonished eyes on me,
is it not happiness that is germinating there?

When I can say: The day is over.
And by day I mean its taxis, its business,
the scrambling for money, the struggles of the dead.
And when I get home, sweat-stained and tired,
I sit down in the dusk and plug the phonograph in
and Kachaturian comes on, or Mozart, or Vivaldi,
and the music holds sway, I feel clean again,
simply clean and, in spite of everything, unhurt,
is it not happiness that is closing around me?

When after turning things over and over again in my mind,
I remember a friend and go over to see him, he says
"I was just now thinking of going over to see you."
And we talk a long time, not about my troubles,
and he couldn't help me, even if he wanted to,
but we talk about how things are going in Jordan,
or a book of Neruda's, or his tailor, or the wind,
and as I leave I feel comforted and full of peace,
isn't that happiness, what comes over me then?

Opening a window; feeling the cool air;
walking down a road that smells of honeysuckle;

beber con un amigo; charlar o bien callarse;
sentir que el sentimiento de los otros es nuestro;
mirarse en unos ojos que nos miran sin mancha,
¿no es esto ser feliz pese a la muerte?
Vencido y traicionado, ver casi con cinismo
que no pueden quitarme nada más y que aún vivo,
¿no es la felicidad que no se vende?

drinking with a friend; chattering or, better yet, keeping still;
feeling that we feel what other men feel;
seeing ourselves through eyes that see us as innocent,
isn't this happiness, and the hell with death?
Beaten, betrayed, seeing almost cynically
that they can do no more to me, that I'm still alive,
isn't this happiness, that is not for sale?

TRANSLATED BY ROBERT MEZEY

LO ETERNO

Un mundo como un árbol desgajado.
Una generación desarraigada.
Unos hombres sin más destino que
apuntalar las ruinas.

       Rompe el mar
en el mar, como un himen inmenso,
mecen los árboles el silencio verde,
las estrellas crepitan, yo las oigo.

Sólo el hombre está solo. Es que se sabe
vivo y mortal. Es que se siente huir
—ese río del tiempo hacia la muerte—.

Es que quiere quedar. Seguir siguiendo,
subir, a contramuerte, hasta lo eterno.
Le da miedo mirar. Cierra los ojos
para dormir el sueño de los vivos.

Pero la muerte, desde dentro, ve.
Pero la muerte, desde dentro, vela.
Pero la muerte, desde dentro, mata.

...El mar—la mar—, como un himen inmenso,
los árboles moviendo el verde aire,
la nieve en llamas de la luz en vilo...

THE ETERNAL

A world like a mutilated tree.
An uprooted generation.
Men whose single destiny is to prop
ruins.

The sea breaks
on the sea like an enormous hymen,
trees rock the green silence,
the stars crackle, I hear them.

Only man is alone. Because he knows
he is alive and mortal. Because he feels
himself running—river of time towards death—.

Because he wants to stay. To keep going,
to ascend, against death's current, to the eternal.
He is afraid to look. He closes his eyes
to sleep the sleep of those who are alive.

But death sees, from within.
But death waits there, within.
But death strikes, from within.

. . . The sea—the sea—like an enormous hymen,
the trees stirring the green air,
the light suspended like snow on fire.

TRANSLATED BY HARDIE ST. MARTIN

A PUNTO DE CAER

Nada es tan necesario al hombre como un trozo de mar
y un margen de esperanza más allá de la muerte,
es todo lo que necesito, y acaso un par de alas
abiertas en el capítulo primero de la carne.

No sé cómo decirlo, con qué cara
cambiarme por un ángel de los de antes de la tierra,
se me han roto los brazos de tanto darles cuerda,
decidme qué haré ahora, decidme qué hora es y si aún hay
      tiempo,
es preciso que suba a cambiarme, que me arrepienta sin
      perder una lágrima,
una sólo, una lágrima huérfana,
por favor, decidme qué hora es la de las lágrimas,
sobre todo la de las lágrimas sin más ni más que llanto
y llanto todavía y para siempre.

Nada es tan necesario al hombre como un par de lágrimas
a punto de caer en la desesperación.

ABOUT TO FALL

A man needs nothing so much as a strip of sea
and a shore of hope on the other side of death,
that's all I need, and maybe a pair of wings
flung wide at the opening chapter of the body.

I don't know how to say it, if I have enough gall
to exchange myself for one of those angels that existed
        before the earth,
my arms have broken down from being wound up so often,
tell me what to do now, tell me what time it is, if there's
        still time,
it's time to go up and change, and repent without dropping
        a tear,
not one solitary orphaned tear,
please, tell me what is the right time for tears,
especially for tears that are nothing more nor less than
        weeping,
weeping now and forever.

A man needs nothing so much as a pair of tears
about to fall into despair.

TRANSLATED BY HARDIE ST. MARTIN

CAP. 10 LIB. II

Era deforme como un ángel caído en un patio entre algodones.
Como esas horribles esculturas donde la maternidad da a luz a la
belleza.
Porque he conocido cosas peores que la desesperación a mis treinta
y dos años,
y una mujer me acariciaba entre los muslos de las montañas llenas
de sangre
con una lentitud y una insistencia que hacía gemir a las mariposas
refugiadas en el bolsillo.

Me acuerdo que una vez estuve a punto de asesinar a mi sombra
solamente por una pequeña deformidad que se advertía debajo de
la tetilla izquierda de mi alma.
Pero ya pasó todo, así que afortunadamente el tiempo se desliza
entre los álamos
y la primavera restalla su gran látigo verde.

Cuando me asalta el recuerdo de lo espantoso que he sido conmigo
mismo
y de las noches trenzadas alrededor de mi garganta sin una pizca de
luna para aliviar la sed,
y vienen de golpe años y años pasados en la soledad de las aceras
públicas,
en el desamparo de las salas de recibir de los médicos,
al borde de los confesonarios,
junto a las faldas frías y las muchachas pálidas de la última remesa,
sin tener siquiera un libro a mano donde apoyar descuidadamente la
cabeza,
ni una pequeña flor ni nada que mereciese la pena de morir en aquel
instante,
cuando me asaltan estos recuerdos comprendo de repente la deformidad de todo, y me resigno a ser ceniza, solitaria ceniza
húmeda de lágrimas.

CHAP. 10 BOOK II

I was deformed like an angel fallen among cottons in a courtyard.
Like those terrible pieces of sculpture in which maternity gives birth
    to beauty.
Because at thirty-two I have known things worse than despair,
and a woman caressed me between the thighs of mountains filled with
    blood
so slowly and insistently that the butterflies sheltered in my pocket
    groaned.

I recall the time I was about to murder my shadow
simply because of a tiny deformity which could be observed under
    the left nipple of my soul.
But everything is over and done with, so that fortunately time glides
    in through the poplars
and spring cracks its long green whip.

When I am jolted by the memory of how horribly I have treated
    myself
and of the nights tangled around my throat without a drop of
    moonlight to take care of my thirst,
and all at once years and years spent in the solitude of public side-
    walks come rushing in,
years spent in the helplessness of doctors' waiting rooms,
on the edge of confessionals,
next to the cold skirts and the newest load of sallow girls shipped in,
without even a book handy to serve as makeshift pillow for my head
or a little flower or anything for which it would be worth dying at
    that moment;
when these memories jolt me, I suddenly realize how hideous every-
    thing is and I resign myself to being ashes, lonely ashes damp
    with tears.

TRANSLATED BY HARDIE ST. MARTIN

EL CLAUSTRO DE LAS SOMBRAS

. . . to the antique order of the dead
—Francis Thompson

En este momento, tengo treinta y tres años encima de la mesa
    del despacho
y un pequeño residuo de meses sobre el cenicero de plata.
He preguntado a mis hermanas si saben quién es este hombre
que viene, entre mi hombro y mi hombro, adonde yo vengo,
y vuelve
el rostro si yo lo torno...

Siento frío, y no sé qué ponerme por dentro
de la muerte, qué trozo de tierra es el mío,
qué noche es la noche de echarme a morir,
qué látigo verde me heñirá bajo el mar.

A veces me acomete un largo vértigo
y quisiera ser nada más un humoso lego en la orden antigua de
        los muertos,
servirles el silencio con mis propias manos
y meditar en un rincón del claustro de las sombras...

Del claustro de las sombras, allí
donde los sueños exaltan sus luces cándidas o pálidas.

THE CLOISTER OF THE SHADES

. . . to the antique order of the dead
—Francis Thompson

At the moment, I have thirty-three years on top of the table in
   my workroom
and a few months left over in the silver ashtray.
I've asked my sisters if they know this man
who comes, between my shoulders, wherever I come
and turns
his face if I turn mine. . . .

I feel cold, and I don't know what to put on
under my death, what plot of land is mine,
what night's the night I must make ready for death,
what green whip will knead me under the sea.

Sometimes I become light-headed for a while
and I want to be nothing but a smoky layman in the antique
   order of the dead,
to serve them silence, to serve it around with my own hands
and meditate in a corner of the cloister of the shades. . . .

Of the cloister of the shades, there
where dreams uplift their candid, pale lights.

TRANSLATED BY HARDIE ST. MARTIN

HIJOS DE LA TIERRA

Parece como si el mundo caminase de espaldas
hacia la noche enorme de los acantilados.
Que un hombre, a hombros del miedo, trepase por las faldas
hirsutas de la muerte, con los ojos cerrados.

Europa, amontonada sobre España, en escombros;
sin norte, Norteamérica, cayéndose hacia arriba;
recién nacida, Rusia, sangrándole los hombros;
Oriente, dando tumbos; y el resto, a la deriva.

Parece como si el mundo me mirase a los ojos,
que quisiera decirme no sé qué, de rodillas;
alza al cielo las manos, me da a oler sus manojos
de muertos, entre gritos y un trepidar de astillas.

El mar, puesto de pie,
le pega en la garganta con un látigo verde;
le descantilla; de
repente, echando espuma por la boca, le muerde.

Parece como si el mundo acabase, se hundiera.
Parece como si Dios, con los ojos abiertos,
a los hijos del hombre los ojos les comiera.
(No le bastan—parece—los ojos de los muertos.)

Europa, a hombros de España, hambrienta y sola;
los Estados de América, saliéndose de madre;
la bandera de Rusia, oh sedal de ola en ola;
Asia, la inmensa flecha que el futuro taladre.

¡Alzad al cielo el vientre, oh hijos de la tierra;
salid por esas calles dando gritos de espanto!
Los veintitrés millones de muertos en la guerra
se agolpan ante un cielo cerrado a cal y canto.

CHILDREN OF THE PLANET

It's as if the world were taking great steps backward
toward the giant night of the cliffs.
And a man, on the shoulders of fear, were climbing
the bristling foothills of death, with his eyes closed.

Europe, piled on top of Spain, in ruins;
North America, off its course, falling upward;
infant Russia, bleeding from its shoulders;
the East, staggering; and the rest, drifting.

It's as if the world were looking into my eyes,
wanting to tell me something, on its knees;
it lifts its hands to heaven, it gives me sheaves
of corpses to smell, among screams and quivering splinters.

The sea, now standing up,
strikes the throat of the world with a green whip;
splits it open; then
suddenly, froth leaping from its mouth, sinks its teeth in.

It's as if the world were ending, going under.
It's as if God, with his eyes open,
were feeding on the eyes of the children of men.
(Evidently the eyes of the dead are not enough.)

Europe, on Spain's shoulders, hungry, alone;
the United States of America, spilling over;
the Russian flag, oh line cast into wave after wave;
Asia, the immense arrow drilling into the future.

Lift your belly to the sky, oh children of the planet!
Run into the streets screaming with terror!
The twenty-three million corpses of this war
crowd before a heaven walled up with plaster and lime.

TRANSLATED BY HARDIE ST. MARTIN

JUICIO FINAL

Yo, pecador, artista del pecado,
comido por el ansia hasta los tuétanos,
yo, tropel de esperanza y de fracasos,
estatua del dolor, firma del viento.

Yo, pecador, en fin, desesperado
de sombras y de sueños: me confieso
que soy un hombre en situación de hablaros
de la vida. Pequé. No me arrepiento.

Nací para narrar con estos labios
que barrerá la muerte un día de éstos,
espléndidas caídas en picado
del bello avión aquel de carne y hueso.

Alas arriba disparó los brazos,
alardeando de tan alto invento;
plumas de níquel: escribid despacio.
Helas aquí, hincadas en el suelo.

Este es mi sitio. Mi terreno. Campo
de aterrizaje de mis ansias. Cielo
al revés. Es mi sitio y no lo cambio
por ninguno. Caí. No me arrepiento.

Ímpetus nuevos nacerán, más altos.
Llegaré por mis pies—¿para qué os quiero?—
a la patria del hombre: al cielo raso
de sombras ésas y de sueños ésos.

LAST JUDGMENT

I, sinner, poet of sin,
whom anxiety has eaten away to the bone,
I, a tangle of hope and disasters,
statue of suffering, signature of the wind.

I, sinner, in fact, driven to the wall
by shadows and dreams, confess I'm a man
in a position to talk to you
about life. I've sinned. And I'm not sorry.

I was born to describe with these lips
death will sweep away one of these days
how this fine aircraft of flesh and blood
went into marvelous nosedives.

He let his arms fly out like wings,
making too much of this high invention;
the feathers were nickel: write slowly.
Here they are, driven into the ground.

This is my place. My territory. Landing
strip of my anxieties. Heaven
upside down. It's my place, and I won't change it
for any other. I fell, and I'm not sorry.

New flights will be born, even higher.
I'll arrive on my feet—why else do I need you?—
in the country of man: in the open sky
full of those shadows and those dreams.

TRANSLATED BY HARDIE ST. MARTIN

MUY LEJOS

Unas mujeres, tristes y pintadas,
sonreían a todas las carteras,
y ellos, analfabetos y magnánimos,
las miraban por dentro, hacia las medias.

Oh cuánta sed, cuánto mendigo en faldas
de eternidad. Ciudad llena de iglesias
y casas públicas, donde el hombre es harto
y el hambre se reparte a manos llenas.

Bendecida ciudad llena de manchas,
plagada de adulterios e indulgencias;
ciudad donde las almas son de barro
y el barro embarra todas las estrellas.

Laboriosa ciudad, salmo de fábricas
donde el hombre maldice, mientras rezan
los presidentes de Consejo: oh altos
hornos, infiernos hondos en la niebla.

Las tres y cinco de la madrugada.
Puertas, puertas y puertas. Y más puertas.
Junto al Nervión un hombre está meando.
Pasan dos guardias en sus bicicletas.

Y voy mirando escaparates. *Paca
y Luz. Hijos de tal.* Medias de seda.
Devocionarios. Más devocionarios.
Libros de misa. Tules. Velos. Velas.

Y novenitas de la Inmaculada.
Arriba, es el jolgorio de las piernas
trenzadas. Oh ese barrio del escándalo...
Pero duermen tranquilas las doncellas.

FAR AWAY

A few women, sad and rouged,
used to smile at all the wallets
and in turn they, illiterate but generous,
looked inside *them*, up along their stockings.

Oh how much thirst, how many beggars in skirts
of eternity. City filled with churches
and public houses, where man stuffs himself
and hunger is passed out by the handful.

Blessed city covered with stains,
infested with adulteries and indulgences,
city where souls are made of clay
and clay muddies all the stars.

Industrious city, psalm of factories
where man says his *damns*, while the Chairmen
of the Board say their prayers: blast
furnaces, oh deep hells in the mist.

3:05 A.M.
Doors, doors, and doors. And more doors.
A man takes a piss down by the Nervion.
Two cops go by on bicycles.

And I walk along looking in shop windows.
"Paca & Luz." "Sons of such & such." Silk
stockings. Prayer books. And more prayer books.
Missals. Tulles. Veils. Candles.

And novenas to the Immaculate Conception.
Upstairs, a bang-up time of interlocked
legs. Oh that neighborhood of scandalous doings . . .
But nice girls sleep on peacefully.

Y voy silbando por la calle. Nada
me importas tú, ciudad donde naciera.
Ciudad donde, muy lejos, muy lejano,
se escucha el mar, la mar de Dios, inmensa.

CENSORIA

Se durmió en la cocina como un trapo.
No le alcanzaba el jornal ni para morirse.
Se dejó caer en la banqueta como un trapo
y se escurrió por el sueño, sin olvidar...

Usualmente, paren los humildes esas niñas
        escrofulosas
que portan únicamente una sayita deshilachada
        sobre los huesos.
¡Salid corriendo a verlas, hipócritas!
¡Escribid al cielo lo que aquí pasa!
¡Sobornad a vuestros monitores para admirar esto!
Españolitos helándose
al sol—no exactamente el de justicia.

Voy a protestar, estoy protestando desde hace mucho tiempo;
me duele tanto el dolor, que a veces
pego saltos en mitad de la calle,
y no he de callar por más que con el dedo
me persignen la frente, y los labios, y el verso.

And I go whistling down the street. You mean
nothing to me, city where I was born.
City where far away, a very long way off,
the sea can be heard, the immense sea of God.

TRANSLATED BY HARDIE ST. MARTIN

CENSORED

She fell asleep in the kitchen like a dishrag.
Her job didn't earn enough to die on.
She let herself slip onto the kitchen bench like a rag,
and slipped into sleep, without forgetting. . . .

The poor as a matter of course give birth to those scrofulous
        girls
who wear nothing but one old worn-out dress over their
        bones.

Run out and look at them, you hypocrites!
Write to heaven about the situation here!
Corrupt your student teachers into having a good look at this!
Spanish children freezing
in the sun . . . not exactly the sun of justice.

I'm going to protest, I've been protesting a long time;
their pain makes me suffer so much that sometimes
I jump up and down in the middle of the street,
and I won't shut up, no matter how much they make the sign
of the cross on my forehead, my lips, or my poems.

TRANSLATED BY HARDIE ST. MARTIN

ESCRITO CON LLUVIA

Ahora es cuando puedes empezar a morirte,
distráete un poco después de haber terminado tu séptimo libro,
ahora puedes abandonar los brazos a lo largo del tiempo
y aspirar profundamente entornando los párpados,
piensa en nada
y olvida el daño que te hiciste,
la espalda de Matilde
y su sexo convexo,
ahora mira la lluvia esparcida por el mes de noviembre,
las luces de la ciudad
y el dinero que cae en migajas los sábados a las seis,
espera
el despertar temible de iberoamérica
y comienza a peinarte, a salir a la calle, a seguir
laborando por todos
los que callan, y avanzan, y protestan y empuñan
la luz como cuchillo o la paz como un fusil.

WRITTEN IN RAIN

This is the time when you can begin to die,
take things easy after completing your seventh book,
now you can let your arms fall to your sides in the corridor
      of time,
and breathe deeply, pulling your eyelids shut,
think of nothing
and forget the wrong you've done yourself,
Mathilda's back
and the curve of her sex,
look now at the rain scattered among the days of November,
the city lights
and the money that falls in little crumbs on Saturdays at six,
wait
for the terrible awakening of Latin America
and start combing your hair, to go out, to keep on
working for all those
who say nothing, and keep on walking, and protest, and
      hold
the light in their fist like a knife or peace like a gun.

TRANSLATED BY HARDIE ST. MARTIN

UNA ESPECIE DE

la paz se ha destrozado, y el cielo es
una lamentable tienda de campaña

Y si yo en vez de ir esta noche al teatro me fuese a Viet-Nam.
¿Quién escribe, quién me coge la mano? No es mía.
Nada me pertenece: ni la máscara, ni el personaje.
Y si yo esta noche

                me fuese a Viet-Nam.
Un pobre diablo bebe un vaso de agua. No ocupa su localidad. Se
        sienta.
Somos dos. El Norte y los Títeres. Maese Pedro se llama el tercero,
        la celestina. Y si yo en vez de llamarme Murueta Sagarminaga
me fuese y me llamasen unión unión
contra el vaso de agua, la sed, el verso libre y el deber.
El día veinticinco de junio no teníamos armas.
El día veintiséis de julio no teníamos armas.
Sólo un soldado. Y millones de proyectos, hombres, pero carecíamos
        de armas.
Proyectiles en una palabra.
Aquí estoy sentado en medio de los escombros de Hue.
En mitad de la República Democrática y en mitad de la otra misma
        república democrática (*sic*).
Parado ante una piedra. En pie. Terriblemente desocupado
de invasores, sintiendo los aviones bajar subir sesgar
la noche— así el tirón rasgándose la tela.
¿Qué hacéis por ahí arriba? Pobres diablos, venid
a ver la función: sentaos tras la ametralladora.
Oíd. Vais a morir. No disparar, porque vais a morir de un momento
        a otro. Todos.
Tirad tirad tirad tirad tirad porque de todos modos vais a morir.

SOMETHING LIKE A

peace has been destroyed and
the sky is a pitiful tent

And what if instead of going to the theater this evening I went off
    to Vietnam.
Who is writing, who is holding my hand? It is not mine.
Nothing is mine. Neither the mask, nor the role.
And what if this evening
                        I went off to Vietnam.
Some poor devil drinks a glass of water. He's not in his theater seat.
    He sits down.
That makes two of us. The North and the Puppets. Maese Pedro is
    the third one's name, the pimp. And what if instead of being
    called Murueta Sagarminaga
I went off and they called out to me union union
against the glass of water, thirst, free verse and duty.
On June twenty-fifth we had no weapons.
On July twenty-sixth we had no weapons.
Just one soldier. And millions of projects, and men, but we lacked
    arms.
Missiles in one word.
Here I am sitting in the middle of the rubble of Hue.
Halfway into the Democratic Republic and halfway into the other
    same democratic republic (*sic*).
Standing in front of a stone. At attention. Terribly unworried
about invaders, hearing the airplanes descending climbing ripping
    through
the night—like fabric tearing at one jerk.
What are you doing up there? Poor devils, come
and see the performance: sit behind the machine gun.
Listen. You're all going to die. Don't shoot, because you're going to
    die any minute now. All of you.
Shoot shoot shoot shoot shoot because you'll die anyhow.

Un mínimo resplandor y el día, un día concreto, lunes dieciocho de
febrero rodea parte del cielo. Pronto os voy a ver la cara
machacada al pie de la letra, en el lugar donde brilló el avión. Venid,
tirad tirad tirad tirad, os queda sólo un hombre.

Una especie de verso que un perro husmea entre la basura.

A tiny glimmer and the day, a specific day, Monday February
      eighteenth circles part of the sky. I'll soon be seeing your face
literally pounded to bits, at the spot where the airplane flashed. Come
      on,
shoot shoot shoot shoot, you only have one more man to go.

Something like a line of poetry a dog sniffs at in the trash.

TRANSLATED BY HARDIE ST. MARTIN

ORACIÓN

Que estás en la tierra, Padre nuestro,
que te siento en la púa del pino,
en el torso azul del obrero,
en la niña que borda curvada
la espalda, mezclando el hilo en el dedo.
Padre nuestro que estás en la tierra,
en el surco,
en el huerto,
en la mina,
en el puerto,
en el cine,
en el vino,
en la casa del médico.
Padre nuestro que estás en la tierra,
donde tienes tu gloria y tu infierno
y tu limbo que está en los cafés
donde los pudientes beben su refresco.
Padre nuestro que estás en la escuela de gratis,
y en el verdulero,
y en el que pasa hambre
y en el poeta, ¡nunca en el usurero!
Padre nuestro que estás en la tierra,
en un banco del Prado leyendo,
eres ese Viejo que da migas de pan a los pájaros del paseo.
Padre nuestro que estás en la tierra,
en el cigarro, en el beso,
en la espiga, en el pecho
de todos los que son buenos.
Padre que habitas en cualquier sitio.
Dios que penetras en cualquier hueco,

PRAYER

You are here on earth, our Father,
for I see you in the pine needle,
in the blue torso of the worker,
in the small girl who embroiders
with bent shoulder, mixing the thread on her finger.
Our Father here on earth,
in the furrow,
in the orchard,
in the mine,
in the seaport,
in the movie house,
in the wine,
in the house of the doctor.
Our Father here on earth,
where you have your glory and your hell,
and your limbo in the cafés
where the rich have their cool drink.
Our Father who sits in school without paying,
you are in the groceryman,
and in the man who is hungry,
and in the poet—never in the usurer!
Our Father here on earth,
reading on a bench of the Prado,
you are the old man feeding breadcrumbs to the birds
        on the walk.
Our Father here on earth,
in the cigarette, in the kiss,
in the grain of wheat, in the hearts
of all those who are good.
Father who can live anywhere,
God who moves into any loneliness,

tú que quitas la angustia, que estás en la tierra,
Padre nuestro que sí que te vemos
los que luego te hemos de ver,
donde sea, o ahí en el cielo.

LOS PÁJAROS ANIDAN

Los pájaros anidan en mis brazos,
en mis hombros, detrás de mis rodillas,
entre los senos tengo codornices,
los pájaros se creen que soy un árbol.
Una fuente se creen que soy los cisnes,
bajan y beben todos cuando hablo.
Las ovejas me pisan cuando pasan
y comen en mis dedos los gorriones,
se creen que yo soy tierra las hormigas,
y los hombres se creen que no soy nada.

you who quiet our anguish, here on earth,
Our Father, yes we see you,
those of us who will see you soon,
wherever you are, or there in heaven.

TRANSLATED BY JOHN HAINES

BIRDS NEST

Birds nest in my arms,
on my shoulders, behind my knees,
between my breasts there are quails,
they must think I'm a tree.
The swans think I'm a fountain,
they all come down and drink when I talk.
When sheep pass, they pass over me,
and perched on my fingers, the sparrows eat,
the ants think I'm earth,
and men think I'm nothing.

TRANSLATED BY PHILIP LEVINE

LAS FLACAS MUJERES

Las flacas mujeres de los metalúrgicos
siguen pariendo en casa o en el tranvía.
Los niños van algunos a las Escuelas Municipales
ye se aprenden los ríos porque es cosa que gusta.
Las niñas van a las monjas que enseñan sus labores y
      a rezar.
De la ciudad se va borrando poco a poco la huella de
      los morteros.
¡Han pasado tantos meses!

          . . .

He visto en sueños que hay varios señores
hablando en una mesa de divisas,
de barcos, de aviones, de cornisas
que se van a caer cuando las bombas.

Y yo pido perdón al Gran Quien Sea
por desearles una buena caja
con cuatro cirios de los más curiosos.

THE SCRAWNY WOMEN

The scrawny women of the foundry workers
are still giving birth on trolley cars or at home.
The boys, some of them, go to the city schools
and learn about rivers, why not, it's harmless enough.
The girls go to the Sisters, who teach them
girl work
and how to say their prayers.
The traces of mortar fire slowly fade from the city.
So many months have gone by!

.   .   .

But in my dreams I am looking at certain gentlemen
who sit around a conference table discussing exchange
            rates,
discussing tankers and aircraft, and cornices
just about to fall as the bombs hit.

And I beg forgiveness of the Almighty Whoever He Is
for wishing them all a shining coffin
and four of the finest candles.

TRANSLATED BY ROBERT MEZEY

ESCALANDO

La Muerte estaba allí sentada al borde
—la Muerte que yo vi no era delgada,
ni huesuda, ni fría,
ni en sudario envolvía su espesa cabellera.

La Muerte estaba sola como siempre,
haciéndose un chaleco de ganchillo,
sentada en una piedra de la roca;
estaba distraída, no debió verme,
en seguida gritó: "¡No te tocaba!"
y se puso a tejer como una loca.

—Podrás llevarte entonces estos versos,
estas ganas de amar y este cigarro,
podrás llevarte el cuerpo que me duele,
pero cuidado con tocar mi alma.

A la Muerte la tengo pensativa
porque no ha conseguido entristecerme.

CLIMBING

Death was there, sitting by the roadside
—the death I saw wasn't skinny,
or all bones, or freezing,
and she didn't shroud her thick hair in a rag.

As usual death was alone
sitting on a rock of the crag
knitting herself a sweater.
She was so busy she didn't see me;
right off she shouted, "It's not your turn!"
and started knitting like mad.

"OK, you can take these poems away,
this wanting love and this cigarette,
you can take this body that's killing me,
but be careful not to finger my soul."

I've got death really thinking
because she couldn't make me sad.

TRANSLATED BY PHILIP LEVINE

LO DESCONOCIDO ATRAE TAMBIÉN
A LOS COBARDES

Delante de mi casa hay una viña
y pasa el sol delante de mi huerto,
al lado del jardín reposa el río
y aquí en el corazón reposa el sueño.
Hay un jardín que da peras al olmo
y hay una paz con música de incienso.
Existe en la comarca la justicia,
existen hombres puros en el techo.
Nadie tiene dolor, el aire es limpio,
puedes sentarte al lado de un labriego.

Pero esto que yo digo debe estar
detrás del cementerio.

EL AMOR TE CONVIERTE...

El amor te convierte en rosal
y en el pecho te nace
esa espina robusta como un clavo
donde el demonio cuelga su uniforme.

Al tocar lo que amas te quemas en los dedos,
y sigues sigues sigues hasta abrasarte todo;
después,
        ya en pie de nuevo,
tu cuerpo es otra cosa,
...es la estatua de un héroe muerto en algo,
al que no se le ven las cicatrices.

THE UNKNOWN ALSO
ATTRACTS COWARDS

In front of my house there's a vineyard
and the sun travels across my orchard,
the river lies down beside the garden
and sleep dozes here in my heart.
The garden grants pears to the elm
and peace is drenched in the music of incense.
In this country there's justice
and honest men are at the top.
No one's sick, the air is pure,
you can sit down beside a farmhand.

But what I'm talking about must be
behind the cemetery.

TRANSLATED BY PHILIP LEVINE

LOVE TURNS YOU INTO A ROSEBUSH

Love turns you into a rosebush
and in your heart grows
a thorn as big as a spike
from which the devil hangs his costume.

Playing with the parts you love you scorch your fingers,
and you go on and on and on until you're all ashes;
later,
        on your feet again,
your body's something else,
. . . the statue of a dead hero who got it somehow,
and none of the wounds show.

TRANSLATED BY PHILIP LEVINE

VENTANAS PINTADAS

Vivía en una casa
con dos ventanas de verdad y las otras dos pintadas
      en la fachada.
Aquellas ventanas pintadas fueron mi primer dolor.
Palpaba las paredes del pasillo,
intentando encontrar las ventanas por dentro.
Toda mi infancia la pasé con el deseo
de asomarme para ver lo que se veía
desde aquellas ventanas que no existieron.

LAS COSAS

Las cosas, nuestras cosas,
las gusta que las quieran;
a mi mesa la gusta que yo apoye los codos,
a la silla la gusta que me siente en la silla,
a la puerta la gusta que la abra y la cierre
como al vino le gusta que le compre y le beba,
mi lápiz se deshace si le cojo y escribo,
mi armario se estremece si le abro y me asomo,
las sábanas, son sábanas cuando me echo sobre ellas
y la cama se queja cuando yo me levanto.

¿Qué será de las cosas cuando el hombre se acabe?
Como perros las cosas no existen sin el amo.

PAINTED WINDOWS

I lived in a house
with two real windows and the other two painted on.
Those painted windows caused my first sorrow.
I'd touch the sides of the hall
trying to reach the windows from inside.
I spent my whole childhood wanting
to lean out and see what could be seen
from the windows that weren't there.

TRANSLATED BY PHILIP LEVINE

THINGS

These things, our things,
how they want to be wanted!
The table purrs under the weight of my elbows,
the chair when I collapse in it,
the door asks to be opened and closed,
the wine to be purchased and drunk,
my pencil undoes itself when I take it and write,
the closet shudders when I open and peek,
the sheets are sheets when I stretch out,
the bed moans when I get up.

What will come of things when we're gone?
They're like dogs that can't make it without their masters.

TRANSLATED BY PHILIP LEVINE

VIRGEN DE PLÁSTICO

Con su manto de nylon
y la corona eléctrica,
con pilas en el pecho
y una sonrisa triste,
se la ve en las vitrinas de todos los comercios
y en los sucios hogares de los pobres católicos.
En Nueva York los negros
tienen su virgen blanca
presidiendo el lavabo
junto a la cabecera...
Es un cruce de Virgen entre Fátima y Lourdes,
un leve vaciado con troquel "made in USA,"
tiene melena larga y las manos abiertas
es lavable y si cae no se descascarilla.
Las hay de tres colores,
blancas, azules, rosas
—las hay de tres tamaños—
—aún la grande es pequeña—.
Así, sin angelitos,
Virgen de resultado,
me diste tanta pena,
Virgen pura de plástico,
se me quitó la gana
de pedirte un milagro.

PLASTIC VIRGIN

With her nylon veil
and electric crown,
with dry-cell batteries
in her breast, and a dismal smile,
she's on display in all the shops
and on the dusty shelves of poor Catholics.
In New York City, above the bedstead
this white virgin watches over
the washstands of Negroes. . . .
Crossbreed of Fatima and Lourdes,
lightweight model stamped "made in USA,"
with streaming hair and open hands,
she's washable and shatterproof.
Comes in three colors
—white, pink, and blue—
available in three sizes
though even the big one is small.
There without angels,
virgin Virgin,
I've felt so bad for you
—pure Virgin of plastic—
I can't bring myself
to ask for one miracle.

TRANSLATED BY PHILIP LEVINE

HAY QUE BAJAR

A Ricardo Juan

Hay que bajar sin miedo.
Hay que bajar
hasta el reino de las raíces
o de las garras,
a ese reino de las manos solitarias
cuya sangre no late,
donde las hormigas nos esparcerán bajo la tierra
con sus tenazas ardientes,
donde nuestra carne se abrirá como un grito
al cosquilleo escalofriante
de las patas de los insectos
y la viscosa masa de los gusanos
será como una lengua de perro babeante.
Al borde de la luz abandonarlo todo
y sepultarnos en la tierra
aunque nos crujan los huesos
y los nervios se nieguen a abandonarnos
estrangulando nuestra carne con un supremo abrazo.

Nos espera para besarnos la sangre de los volcanes
y el corazón de la tierra se abrirá silencioso para recibirnos.
Una voz nos dirá:
Al fin llegasteis, venid y purificaros.
(Nuestra sombra errante por la tierra, buscándonos
con un temblor inquietante sobre los ojos.)
Y nosotros, diseminados por las plantas, los árboles,
quizá en la niebla de aquel astro,

YOU HAVE TO GO DOWN

For Ricardo Juan

You have to go down without fear.
You have to go down
till you get to the kingdom of roots
or of claws,
to that realm of the hands
all alone
whose blood doesn't pulse any more,
where the ants are waiting to scatter us
under the ground with their hot pincers,
where our bodies will be zipped open like a scream
to the bone-freezing skitter
of the feet of insects
and the slithery mass of the worms
will be like the tongue of a slavering dog.
At the fringe of the light to give up everything
and bury ourselves in the ground
even though the bones may crack
and the nerves refuse to give us up,
throttling our bodies with a final embrace.

Waiting to give us a kiss is the blood of volcanoes
and the heart of the earth is going to open silently to take us.
A voice is going to say:
Finally you are getting here, come and be purified.
(Our shades will go wandering over the earth, searching for us,
with a disquieting shiftiness in their eyes.)
And we, scattered by plants, trees,
maybe in the mist of that star,

en la boca de esa serpiente muerta al borde de la noche
o en aquel cuerpo que está cayendo hace tantos años
sobre la luz azul de las nebulosas,
en cualquier masa inerte que se agita sin que la veamos.

Los minerales amarillos, el óxido,
las nubes, el agua
y hasta el fuego que se consume a sí mismo,
todo, todo, abrirá sus venas para recibirnos.

¿Tenéis miedo?
Yo os invito; bajemos juntos
y circulemos con la vida palpitante,
con esa vida oscura de los minerales
que nadie ha visto, pero que se presiente,
como el galope de los caballos con el oído en la tierra.

¿No oís la llamada?
Es la tierra,
la tierra que nos busca para purificarnos
y arrojarnos de nuevo a la luz con su sudor doloroso.

in the mouth of that serpent dead at the brink of night
or in that body which has been falling for so many years
into the blue light of the nebulae,
or in some dead mass or other that moves without our seeing.

The yellow dirt, the rust,
the clouds, the water
and even the fire which burns itself up,
all, all, will spread their veins to receive us.

You others, are you afraid?
I invite you, let's go down together
and move around with the pulsing life,
with that hidden life of minerals
which no one has seen, but which lurks
like the galloping of horses to the ear on the ground.

Don't you hear the call?
It is the earth,
the earth which is after us to purify us
and to fling us again into the light with its sadness and sweat.

TRANSLATED BY WILLIAM STAFFORD
AND HERBERT BAIRD

PEZ

Por entre manos húmedas que agitas blandamente
vas tú, pez desnudo, espada velocísima
que pasas y te olvidas de tu huella.

Como una estrella, mudo,
derivas a la tumba donde el sonido existe.
(Oscura sentencia,
frío corazón con branquias,
ya muy cerca de la tierra,
de la tierra donde se sostiene el agua.)
Arriba, no lo sabes, ¡las águilas!

FISH

You go between wet hands
that gently wave. Naked fish, flashing sword
that passes by, you forget where you cut the water.

A quiet star
drifting down to the grave where sound lives.
(Dark future,
frozen heart with gills,
already next to the earth,
the earth where the water makes its bed.)
Above, unknown to you, eagles!

TRANSLATED BY RALPH NELSON

ESPERA SIEMPRE

La muerte espera siempre, entre los años,
como un árbol secreto que ensombrece,
de pronto, la blancura de un sendero,
y vamos caminando y nos sorprende.

Entonces, en la orilla de su sombra,
un temblor misterioso nos detiene:
miramos a lo alto, y nuestros ojos
brillan, como la luna, extrañamente.

Y, como luna, entramos en la noche,
sin saber dónde vamos, y la muerte
va creciendo en nosotros, sin remedio,
con un dulce terror de fría nieve.

La carne se deshace en la tristeza
de la tierra sin luz que la sostiene.
Sólo quedan los ojos que preguntan
en la noche total, y nunca mueren.

IT'S ALWAYS WAITING

Death is always waiting, among the years,
hidden away like a tree that suddenly throws
its shadow over the whiteness of a road—
we come along and it stops us in our tracks.

Then an odd trembling comes over us
at the edge of its shadow.
We lift our eyes and, strangely enough,
they give off light, like the moon.

And we slip into the night like a moon,
not sure of the road, and death starts to grow
inside us, who have no other choice,
with the gentle terror of cold snow.

The body breaks down in the sadness
of the earth that holds it close, in the dark.
Only our questioning eyes are left
with night all around them, and they never die.

TRANSLATED BY HARDIE ST. MARTIN

FLORES BAJO LOS MUERTOS

Bajo los puros muertos, a veces, brotan flores,
blancas y dolorosas, que levemente gimen,
porque crecer es duro, porque crecer es triste,
cuando un cuerpo sin vida en las espaldas pesa.

Entonces—escuchad—un pájaro detiene
el vuelo de sus alas y se apaga, se apaga,
mientras el hombre muerto, sin saberlo, transcurre
arriba, más arriba, sobre la tierra, solo.

Si en un mundo vacío crecieran estas flores,
qué vivamente irían al aire, a la alegría,
pero esta muerte mata su breve primavera,
como un gusano dulce, pisado y amarillo.

¿Y qué? Todo es lo mismo: crecer o derrumbarse,
tener sobre la carne una nube o la muerte,
doblarse ciegamente, doblarse como un río,
con estas blancas flores, leves y detenidas.

FLOWERS UNDER THE DEAD

Heartbreaking white flowers come up sometimes
from under the purifying dead, crying weakly
because it's hard to grow, and sad too,
when a corpse presses its weight down on your back.

Then—listen—a bird holds back its wings
in midflight and flickers, flickers out,
but the dead man, who doesn't know this, goes on
alone, higher and higher over the earth.

If these flowers came up in an empty world
they would climb to the air, to happiness, filled with life,
but death kills their short-lived spring
like a harmless worm crushed and turned yellow by some foot.

So? It's all the same, growing or breaking down,
having a cloud or death on top of your body,
blinded, buckling, buckling like a river
under these white flowers, lightbodied, pressed down.

TRANSLATED BY HARDIE ST. MARTIN

SOL DE LA MUERTE

Sueño un sol misterioso, hoja de un viejo otoño,
que pasa levemente por los cuerpos sin dicha,
atardecer de un mundo que nadie ha visto nunca,
donde sólo los muertos con ojos quietos miran.

Fuente de un oro triste, como una antigua luna,
manando de un sol vago, sin luz de mediodía;
sombrío sol, que roza sobre los muertos lívidos
y de las almas muertas su lento fulgor liba.

Cuando en la noche helada mi carne se deshaga,
también yo he de llamarte con voz atardecida;
también daré mi alma para que tú fulgures,
por ver si con tu llama mi cuerpo se ilumina.

Pero no has de quererme. Mi alma estará sola.
Las almas de los tristes a Dios sólo iluminan,
y en su noche infinita, inacabablemente,
como un espectro ardiendo, con luz opaca brillan.

HAS BAJADO

Has bajado a la tierra, cuando nadie te oía,
y has mirado a los vivos y contado tus muertos.
Señor, duerme sereno; ya cumpliste tu día.
Puedes cerrar los ojos que tenías abiertos.

SUN OF DEATH

In my dreams a strange sun, a leaf in an autumn
that's growing old, goes softly into unhappy bodies:
a twilight in a world no one has seen yet,
where only the dead, whose eyes look straight ahead, can see.

Headwaters of bleak gold, like an aging moon,
poured from a dull sun without its brightness at noon,
a cheerless sun that brushes up against the pale dead
and soaks up its heavy light from their lifeless souls.

When my flesh flakes away on a frosty night,
I too will call you with my twilight voice,
I too will throw my soul in to help you beam,
to see if my body draws light from your flame.

And yet, you won't want me. My soul will be alone.
Sad people's spirits spend all their light on God
and burn forever in the endless night
with a faint glow, like a ghost on fire.

TRANSLATED BY HARDIE ST. MARTIN

YOU CAME DOWN

You came down to the earth when no one was listening
and you looked at the living and counted your dead.
Rest in peace, Lord; your day is over.
Your eyes were open, you can close them now.

TRANSLATED BY HARDIE ST. MARTIN

ORILLA DE LA NOCHE

Toda la noche de la tierra
se me derrama entre las manos,
igual que un agua fugitiva
entre los juncos y los pájaros.

Quiero apresarla con mis dedos
y detener su oscuro paso.
Se me ha secado la garganta.
Quiero beberla con mis labios.

Un agua negra la tristeza
ha de beber, para su canto.
Tengo la noche recogida
en este cuenco de las manos.

SHORE OF NIGHT

All of the night on this earth
is running out between my hands
like water trying to run away
between bulrushes and birds.

I want to trap it in my fingers
and stop its dark flow.
My throat has dried up.
I want to drink it with my lips.

In order to sing, sadness
will have to drink black water.
I have the night cupped
in the hollow of these hands.

TRANSLATED BY HARDIE ST. MARTIN

José Hierro ❦

UNA TARDE CUALQUIERA

Yo, José Hierro, un hombre
como hay muchos, tendido
esta tarde en mi cama,
volví a soñar.
                    (Los niños,
en la calle, corrían.)
Mi madre me dió el hilo
y la aguja, diciéndome:
"Enhébramela, hijo;
veo poco."
                    Tenía
fiebre. Pensé: "Si un grito
me ensordeciera, un rayo
me cegara..." (Los niños
cantaban.) Lentamente
me fué invadiendo un frío
sentimiento, una súbita
desgana de estar vivo.

Yo, José Hierro, un hombre
que se da por vencido
sin luchar. (A la espalda
llevaba un cesto, henchido
de los más prodigiosos
secretos. Y cumplido,
el futuro, aguardándome
como a la hoz el trigo.)
Mudo, esta tarde, oyendo
caer la lluvia, he visto
desvanecerse todo,

ANY AFTERNOON

I, José Hierro, a man
like so many others, stretched out
this afternoon in my bed,
dreamed again.
                        (Children
down in the street, running.)
My mother gave me a needle
and thread, saying
"Thread it for me, son;
my eyes are bad."
                        I had a
fever. I thought: "If a cry
deafened me, a ray of light
would blind me. . . ." (The children
were singing.) Slowly
a cold thought was invading
me, a sudden
revulsion at being alive.

I, José Hierro, a man
who gives himself up to defeat
without a struggle. (Behind me
I was dragging a basket, crammed
with the most fantastic
secrets. And the future,
accomplished, waiting for me
like a sickle for the wheat.)
This afternoon, listening dumbly
to the rain falling, I saw
everything blow away,

quedar todo vacío.
Una desgana súbita
de vivir. ("Toma, hijo,
enhébrame la aguja,"
dice mi madre.)

        Amigos:
yo estaba muerto. Estaba
en mi cama, tendido.
Se está muerto, aunque lata
el corazón, amigo.

Y se abre la ventana
y yo, sin cuerpo (vivo
y sin cuerpo, o difunto
y con vida), hundido
en el azul. (O acaso
sea el azul, hundido
en mi carne, en mi muerte
llena de vida, amigos:
materia universal,
carne y azul sonando
con un mismo sonido.)
Y en todo hay oro, y nada
duele ni pesa, amigos.
A hombros me llevan. Quién:
la primavera, el filo
del agua, el tiemblo verde
de un álamo, el suspiro
de alguien a quien yo nunca
había visto.

Y yo voy arrojando
ceniza, sombra, olvido.
Palabras polvorientas
que entristecen lo limpio:

leaving only emptiness.
A sudden revulsion
at being alive. ("Here, son,
thread the needle for me,"
my mother said.)

            Friends,
I was dead. I was
sprawled on my bed.
One can be dead, my friends, even if
the heart is beating.

And the window opens
and I, bodiless (alive
and bodiless, or dead
yet somehow alive), immersed
in the blue. (Or maybe
I am the blue, trapped
in my flesh, in my death
full of life, my friends:
primal matter,
flesh and blue resounding
with the same sound.)
And there is gold in everything, and nothing
is heavy or painful, friends.
They carry me on their shoulders. They are:
the spring, the blade
of water, the green shivering
of a poplar, the breath
of someone I have
never seen.

And I go scattering
ashes, shadow, forgetfulness.
Dust-covered words
that bring down what is shining:

Funcionario,
tintero,
30 días vista,
diferencial,
racionamiento,
factura,
contribución,
garantías...

Subo más alto. Aquí
todo es perfecto y rítmico.
Las escalas de plata
llevan de los sentidos
al silencio. El silencio
nos torna a los sentidos.
Ahora son las palabras
de diamante purísimo:
    Roca,
    águila,
    playa,
    palmera,
    manzana,
    caminante,
    verano,
    hoguera,
    cántico...

...cántico. Yo, tendido
en mi cama. Yo, un hombre
como hay muchos, vencido
esta tarde (¿esta tarde
solamente?), he vivido
mis sueños (esta tarde
solamente), tendido
en mi cama, despierto,
con los ojos hundidos

       bureaucrat,
       inkwell,
       30-day permit,
       differential,
       rationing,
       bill of lading,
       contribution,
       guarantee . . .

I climb higher. Here
everything is perfect and rhythmic.
Ladders of silver
reach from our senses
to the silence and the silence
restores us to our senses.
Now the words
are of purest diamond:
       rock,
       eagle,
       beach,
       palm tree,
       apple,
       traveler,
       summer,
       bonfire,
       canticle . . .

. . . canticle. I, stretched out
on my bed. I, a man
like many another, beaten
this afternoon (only
this afternoon?), have lived out
my dreams (only
this afternoon), stretched out
awake on my bed,
my eyes sunk

aún en las ascuas últimas,
en las espumas últimas
del sueño concluido.

REQUIEM

Manuel de Río, natural
de España, ha fallecido el sábado
11 de mayo, a consecuencia
de un accidente. Su cadáver
está tendido en D'Agostino
Funeral Home. Haskell. New Jersey.
Se dirá una misa cantada
a las 9,30, en St. Francis.

Es una historia que comienza
con sol y piedra, y que termina
sobre una mesa, en D'Agostino,
con flores y cirios eléctricos.
Es una historia que comienza
en una orilla del Atlántico.
Continúa en un camarote
de tercera, sobre las olas
—sobre las nubes— de las tierras
sumergidas ante Platón.
Halla en América su término
con una grúa y una clínica,
con una esquela y una misa
cantada, en la iglesia St. Francis.

to the last
embers, the last
froth
of the dream
now finished.

TRANSLATED BY ROBERT MEZEY

REQUIEM

Manuel del Río, born
in Spain, died Saturday
the 11th of May, the result
of an accident. The body
is laid out at the D'Agostino
Funeral Home. Haskell. New Jersey.
There will be a sung Mass
at 9:30, in St. Francis.

It is a story that opens
in sunlight and stone, and ends
on a table, in D'Agostino's,
among flowers and electric candles.
It is a story that opens
on one shore of the Atlantic,
continues in a third-
class cabin over the waves
—or is it over the clouds?—
of those lost continents
sunk long before Plato,
and comes to an end in America
with a tow truck and a clinic,
a death notice and a sung mass
in the church of St. Francis.

Al fin y al cabo, cualquier sitio
da lo mismo para morir:
el que se aroma de romero,
el tallado en piedra o en nieve,
el empapado de petróleo.
Da lo mismo que un cuerpo se haga
piedra, petróleo, nieve, aroma.
Lo doloroso no es morir
acá o allá...

Requiem aeternam,
Manuel del Río. Sobre el mármol
en D'Agostino, pastan toros
de España, Manuel, y las flores
(funeral de segunda, caja
que huele a abetos del invierno),
cuarenta dólares. Y han puesto
unas flores artificiales
entre las otras que arrancaron
al jardín... *Libera me Domine
de morte aeterna...* Cuando mueran
James o Jacob verán las flores
que pagaron Giulio o Manuel...

Ahora descienden a tus cumbres
garras de águila. *Dies irae.*
Lo doloroso no es morir
Dies illa acá o allá;
sino sin gloria...
                Tus abuelos
fecundaron la tierra toda,
la empapaban de la aventura.
Cuando caía un español
se mutilabe el universo.
Los velaban no en D'Agostino
Funeral Home, sino entre hogueras,

In the long run it makes no difference
where we die. Whether it smells
of rosemary, or is carved out of stone
or snow, or soaked in gasoline
—and whether a body turns into stone,
gasoline, snow, or just a smell—
what difference does it make?
The misery's not in dying
here, there, or somewhere else. . . .

> *Requiem aeternam,*
Manuel del Río. Over the slab
in D'Agostino's the bulls of Spain
are grazing, Manuel, and there are flowers
(second-class funeral, coffin
smelling of winter fir),
which cost forty bucks. And they have stuck
some artificial ones
in with the ones picked
from the garden. . . . *Libera me Domine
de morte aeterna* . . . When a James dies,
or a Jacob, he will stare
at these same flowers, compliments
of Giulio or Manuel. . . .

Now down to the crest of your life
eagle talons. *Dies irae.*
The misery's not in dying
Dies illa here or there,
but so ingloriously . . .
>   Your fathers
swelled the entire earth
with the seed of their daring.
When a Spaniard fell down dead
a wound opened in the cosmos.
Not in D'Agostino's Funeral Home
did they keep their dead watches

entre caballos y armas. Héroes
para siempre. Estatuas de rostro
borrado. Vestidos aún
sus colores de papagayo,
de poder y de fantasía.

El no ha caído así. No ha muerto
por ninguna locura hermosa.
(Hace mucho que el español
muere de anónimo y cordura,
o en locuras desgarradoras
entre hermanos: cuando acuchilla
pellejos de vino derrama
sangre fraterna.) Vino un día
porque su tierra es pobre. El mundo
Libera me Domine es patria.
Y ha muerto. No fundó ciudades.
No dió su nombre a un mar. No hizo
más que morir por diecisiete
dólares (él los pensaría
en pesetas) *Requiem aeternam.*
Y en D'Agostino lo visitan
los polacos, los irlandeses,
los españoles, los que mueren
en el week-end.

Requiem aeternam.
Definitivamente todo
ha terminado. Su cadáver
está tendido en D'Agostino
Funeral Home. Haskell. New Jersey.
Se dirá una misa cantada
por su alma.

but by campfires, in the midst
of their horses and weapons. Heroes,
always. Statues, with the faces
obliterated. Yet decked out
in the old parrot colors, the colors
of might and imagination.

He did not die that way. He did not die
for any beautiful madness.
(For a long time now Spaniards have died
anonymous and prudent
or else in some stupid madness
between brothers: whenever you
slash a wineskin, your brother's blood
jumps out.)
He came one day to this place
because his country is poor. The world
Libera me Domine is the homeland.
And he died. Having founded no city,
having given his name to no ocean.
All he did was die for seventeen
bucks (which he'd translate
into pesetas) *Requiem aeternam.*
And now in D'Agostino's they visit him,
Poles, Irish,
Spaniards, those who died
over the weekend.

Requiem aeternam.

It is really over.
Finished. The body
lies in D'Agostino's
Funeral Home. Haskell. New Jersey.
There will be a sung mass
for his soul.

Me he limitado
a reflejar aquí una esquela
de un periódico de New York.
Objetivamente. Sin vuelo
en el verso. Objetivamente.
Un español como millones
de españoles. No he dicho a nadie
que estuve a punto de llorar.

EL NIÑO DE LA JAULA VACÍA

Con tus manos hiciste libres
—con tus propias manos—las aves.
Hijo: qué sueñas, sombra, símbolo
del hombre que rompe sus cárceles,

del que libera pensamientos,
palabras que se lleva el aire;
del que dio canto y dio consuelo
y no halló quien lo consolase.

Solitario, mudo, ceñidas
las sienes de hojas otoñales.
En la boca reseca, el gusto
de la sal de todos los mares.

La sal que dejaron las olas
de los días al derrumbarse.

I have confined myself here
to thinking about an obituary clipped
from a New York newspaper.
Objectively. Without flying off
into verse. Objectively.
A Spaniard like millions
of Spaniards. And I have said
nothing to anyone
about being on the verge of tears.

TRANSLATED BY ROBERT MEZEY

THE BOY WITH THE EMPTY CAGE

With your hands you freed
—with your own hands—the birds.
Son: what a dreamer you are, a shadow,
a symbol of the man who breaks his chains,

of the man who frees thoughts,
words that the air carries off;
of the man who sang, who gave comfort
and found no one who would comfort him.

Solitary, mute, your temples
garlanded with autumn leaves.
In your dry mouth, the taste
of salt from all the seas.

The salt left by the waves of days
as they crashed down and sank away.

TRANSLATED BY RACHEL BENSON

EL ENCUENTRO

A Rafael Alberti

Diré un día: bienvenido
a la casa. Esta es tu lumbre.
Bebe en tu copa tu vino,
mira el cielo, parte el pan.
Cuánto has tardado. Anduviste
bajo las constelaciones
del Sur, navegaste ríos
de son diferente. Cuánto
duró tu viaje. Te noto
cansado. No me preguntes.
Da de comer a tus perros,
oye la canción del álamo.
No me preguntes por nada,
no me preguntes.

       Si hablase,
llorarías. Si enfrentases
tus espectros al espejo,
seguro que no verías
imágenes reflejadas.
Lo vivo lejano ha muerto;
lo mató el tiempo. Tú solo
puedes enterrarlo. Dale
tierra mañana, después
de descansar. Bienvenido
a tu casa. No preguntes
nada. Mañana hablaremos.

THE MEETING

To Rafael Alberti

Someday I'll say: welcome
to this house. Here is your fire.
Drink your wine in your cup,
look at the sky, break the bread.
How long it's been. You traveled
beneath the constellations
of the South, you sailed rivers
with other voices. How long
your voyage lasted. I notice
that you're tired. Don't ask me anything.
Give your dogs something to eat,
listen to the song of the poplar.
Don't ask me about anything.
Don't ask.

　　　　If I were to speak,
you'd weep. If you were to face
your phantoms in the mirror,
I'm sure that you wouldn't see
images reflected.
What once was a life has died;
time killed it. Only you
can bury it. Lay it to rest
tomorrow, after you
have slept. Welcome
to your house. Ask
nothing. Tomorrow we'll talk.

TRANSLATED BY RACHEL BENSON

ACELERANDO

Aquí, en este momento, termina todo,
se detiene la vida. Han florecido luces amarillas
a nuestros pies, no sé si estrellas. Silenciosa
cae la lluvia sobre el amor, sobre el remordimiento.
Nos besamos en carne viva. Bendita lluvia
en la noche, jadeando en la hierba,
trayendo en hilos aroma de las nubes,
poniendo en nuestra carne su dentadura fresca.
Y el mar sonaba. Tal vez fuera su espectro.
Porque eran miles de kilómetros
los que nos separaban de las olas.
Y lo peor: miles de días pasados y futuros nos separaban.
Descendían en la sombra las escaleras.
Dios sabe a dónde conducían. Qué más daba. "Ya es hora
—dije yo—, ya es hora de volver a tu casa."
Ya es hora. En el portal, "Espera," me dijo. Regresó
vestida de otro modo, con flores en el pelo.
Nos esperaban en la iglesia. "Mujer te doy." Bajamos
las gradas del altar. El armonio sonaba.
Y un violín que rizaba su melodía empalagosa.
Y el mar estaba allí. Olvidado y apetecido
tanto tiempo. Allí estaba. Azul y prodigioso.
Y ella y yo solos, con harapos de sol y de humedad.
"¿Dónde, dónde la noche aquella, la de ayer...?", preguntábamos
al subir a la casa, abrir la puerta, oir al niño que salía
con su poco de sombra con estrellas,
su agua de luces navegantes,
sus cerezas de fuego. Y yo puse mis labios
una vez más en la mejilla de ella. Besé hondamente.
Los gusanos labraron tercamente su piel. Al retirarme
lo vi. Qué importa, corazón. La música encendida,
y nosotros girando. No: inmóviles. El cáliz de una flor
gris que giraba en torno vertiginosa.
Dónde la noche, dónde el mar azul, las hojas de la lluvia.

ACCELERANDO

Here, at this moment, everything ends,
life stops. Yellow lights have bloomed
at our feet, perhaps they are stars. Silently
the rain falls upon love, upon remorse.
Our kisses open wounds. Blessed rain
in the night, throbbing on the grass,
drawing down in slim threads the scent of the clouds,
setting its cold teeth in our flesh.
And we could hear the sea. The ghost of the sea perhaps.
Because there were thousands of miles
separating us from the waves.
And worse: thousands of days, past and future, separating us.
The stairs went down into shadow.
God knows where they led. What did it matter. "Now it's time,"
I said, "now it's time you went back to your house."
Now it's time. At the door, "Wait," she told me. She came back
in a different dress, with flowers in her hair.
They were waiting for us in the church. "I give you this woman."
We went down the altar steps. The organ was playing.
And a violin that rippled out its cloying melody.
And the sea was there. Forgotten and hungered for
all the time. There it was. Blue and prodigious.
And she and I alone with tatters of sun and dampness.
"Where, where is that night? It was just yesterday . . ." we asked
as we went up to the house, opened the door, listened to the child
who was coming out with his little bit of starred shadow,
his small sea with sailing lights,
his cherries of fire. And I put my lips
to her cheek one more time. Deeply I kissed.
Worms were laboring stubbornly at her skin. I saw it
as I drew back. It doesn't matter, my love. The music on fire,
and we spinning. No: motionless. The calyx of a gray flower
spinning giddily around us.
Where is the night, the blue sea, the leaves of rain.

Los niños —quiénes son, que hace un instante
no estaban—, los niños aplaudieron, muertos de risa:
"Qué ridículos, papá, mamá." "A la cama," les dije
con ira y pena.   Silencio.   Yo besé
la frente de ella, los ojos con arrugas
cada vez más profundas. Dónde la noche aquella,
en qué lugar del universo se halla. "Has sido duro
con los niños." Abrí la habitación de los pequeños,
volaron pétalos de lluvia. Ellos estaban afeitándose.
Ellas salían con sus trajes de novia. Se marcharon
los niños —¿por qué digo niños?— con su amor,
con sus noches de estrellas, con sus mares azules,
con sus remordimientos, con sus cuchillos de buscar pureza
bajo la carne. Dónde, dónde la noche aquella,
dónde el mar... Qué ridículo todo: este momento detenido,
este disco que gira y gira en el silencio,
consumida su música...

The children—who are they; they weren't here
a moment ago—the children applauded, dying of laughter:
"Oh papa, mama, how ridiculous." "To bed," I told them
in anger and sorrow.   Silence.   I kissed
her brow, her eyes with the wrinkles deepening
more and more. Where is that night,
in what part of the universe can it be found. "You were harsh
with the children." I opened the door of the little ones' room,
petals of rain flew. There were the boys, shaving.
There were the girls dressed as brides, leaving. The children
walked away—why do I say children?—with their loves,
with their starry nights, with their blue seas,
with their remorse, with their knives for seeking purity
under the flesh. Where, where is that night,
where the sea. . . . How ridiculous it all is: this stopped moment,
this record that spins in silence,
its music consumed . . .

TRANSLATED BY RACHEL BENSON

Carlos Bousoño

TRES POEMAS SOBRE LA MUERTE

I

Hay veces que los hombres tristemente
a la muerte cantamos.
Allá en el esqueleto está escondida,
dura, fija, aguardando.

Pero los hombres nunca saben.
La muerte flota entre sus labios,
y mirando los cielos transitorios
hablan de amor y eternos cánticos.

Mas el hueso en el fondo de sus vidas
espera tierra y muerte sin descanso.
Está tranquilo, porque luz no habita
su funeral reposo milenario.

Yo sé lo mismo que los huesos saben
y miro, sin embargo,
el viento puro, y sin tristeza
suspiro en él, y algunas veces amo.

2

Sólo los huesos son eternos.
La muerte son que espera su reinado.
La muerte que se sabe victoriosa
allá en su fondo solitario.

Los huesos son antiguos. De su origen
nada sabemos los humanos,

THREE POEMS ON DEATH

1

There are times when we men write
sad poems dedicated to death.
It lurks there in our skeleton,
hard, firm, waiting.

And yet men never know it.
Death floats between their lips,
and as they watch the changing skies
they talk of love and everlasting songs.

But the bone at the bottom of their lives
restlessly waits for earth and death.
It's peaceful because light doesn't inhabit
its timeless place of rest.

I know the same things bones know,
and yet I stare
at the clean wind and sigh in it
without sadness, and sometimes I love.

2

Only the bones are eternal.
They are death waiting for its kingdom,
death that realizes it is sovereign
there in its lonely pit.

Bones are ancient. We human beings
know nothing of their origin,

mas hundido en el cuerpo nos habita
lo que seremos bajo el campo.

No la semilla de los vientos
ni la alegría de lo iluminado,
sino un duro esqueleto indescifrable
de irredenta mudez bajo los astros.

3

Quizá los huesos fueron roca,
montaña, río, fuego o valle
antes que el hombre hubiese aparecido
como un dolor bajo los aires.

Por eso el hueso es el deseo
de otra vez ser pura extensión sin nadie,
y allá dentro parece un duro otoño,
un triste otoño inexplicable.

Pero los huesos mandan su ola lenta
hasta los ojos, que no saben,
y creyendo de dicha su alba espuma
morimos bajo el cielo interminable.

but sunk in our body there lives in us
what we'll be under the ground.

Not the seed of the winds
nor the joy of things covered with light,
but a hard inscrutable skeleton
unredeemed and silent under the stars.

3

Maybe our bones were rock,
a mountain, a river, a fire or a valley
before man had appeared
like a pain under the winds.

For that reason the bone is a desire
to be a clean bodiless space once more,
and deep inside a hard autumn seems to go on,
a sad inexplicable autumn.

But the bones send their heavy wave
up to the eyes which are unaware,
and believing in the happiness of its white foam
we meet death under the endless sky.

TRANSLATED BY CHARLES GUENTHER

LA PUERTA

(Plaza Mayor de Madrid)

Sobre la calle estamos
aún. Después acaso
subimos una escalera de piedra, gastada
por otros pasos tercos, confiados,
allá en el fondo oscuro de un pasado remoto. Y tocamos,
tocamos con ansiedad, con disimulada agonía,
esta gruesa puerta de madera pesada,
que dura, que ha durado, que ha contemplado con impasibilidad y
      silencio
desde su abrupta altivez o insensibilidad de materia,
unas manos tras otras golpear en el pesadísimo picaporte de hierro.
Se ha dejado gastar muy levemente
por el roce presuroso de unos dedos. Ha visto
envejecer el rostro humano muy poco a poco,
tan poco a poco que nadie fijaba su atención distraída
en el menudo pormenor de una arruga incipiente.
Esta puerta está aquí como entonces.
Se ha acallado el tráfago.
Los caballeros han desaparecido de la plaza frontera.
Los caballos
no están.
Las divisas de los jinetes en la tarde de toros,
la altiva majestad de algún rey contemplando
la plaza, el señorío opaco de un atuendo,
la indiferencia de una mirada distraída,
las lentas horas que un reloj anuncia,
las nubes lentas, pausadas, que a ratos cubren el azul... No sé,
no sabría decir cuáles son esos otros,
ese público denso que algo mira,
algo que les absorbe en la tarde de estío
un momento.
        ¡Qué silencio se ha hecho de pronto!

THE DOOR

(Plaza Mayor, Madrid)

We're on the street
even now. Maybe later
we'll climb a flight of stone steps, worn
by other unerring, stubborn footsteps,
there in the dark hole of the remote past. And we knock,
we knock anxiously, hiding our pain,
on this thick door made of heavy timber
which lasts, has lasted, has watched silent and undisturbed
out of its rough pride or material insensibility
hand after hand strike the massive iron knocker.
The fingers' friction
has worn it gently. It has seen
human faces age gradually,
so gradually that no one noticed
the small detail of an incipient line.
This door exists here now as it was then.
The traffic has been silenced.
The horsemen have disappeared from the square opposite.
The horses
are gone.
The colors of the horsemen of the afternoon's bullfight,
the proud majesty of some king contemplating
the square, the dark nobility of court dress,
the indifference of a distracted glance,
the slow hours a clock announces,
the slow, deliberate clouds fitfully covering the blue . . . I don't know,
I wouldn't know who the rest are,
that crowded audience watching something,
something absorbing them for a moment
on a summer afternoon.
                How soon silence comes!

¡Qué quietud tan extraña en la fiesta!
Desierta ha quedado la plaza.
Ya todo, como un vapor, se ha extinguido.
Un reloj da las horas
despacio. Mi corazón de pronto da las horas.
Y yo delante de esta puerta,
de esta pesada puerta,
pregunto.
Sin intención de ofenderte, Señor, sin pretender injuriarte
pregunto. Yo quisiera inquirir, yo desearía indagar el hecho mismo
        que ahora contemplo,
el hecho mínimo de esta puerta que existe,
con su cerradura de hierro.
Esta implacable puerta que la carcoma ha respetado.
Y aquí está segura, cerradísima,
implacable en su sin soñar
su materia sobrevivida, su materia resuelta a vivir.
Y he aquí la humana tristeza de unos ojos que miran,
que no saben, que inquieren, que examinan con lentitud cada porción
        de materia,
preguntándose cómo ha sido posible,
cómo ha llegado hasta nosotros cierta,
cómo ha llegado sin detrimento, con integridad, sin falacia,
esta puerta que miro y señalo,
esta puerta cerrada que yo quisiera ver entre la noche abrirse,
girar despacio,
abrirse en medio del silencio,
abrirse sigilosa y finísima,
en medio del silencio, abrirse pura.

What a strange quiet in the festival!
The square is left deserted.
Now everything has faded like mist.
A clock tolls the time
slowly. Suddenly my heart tolls the time.
And in front of this door,
this cumbersome door,
I ask questions.
Not meaning to offend you, Lord, not trying to hurt you,
I ask questions. I'd like to explore, I want to examine the very act
        I am looking at now,
the least act of this door that remains
with its iron lock.
This implacable door the termite has respected.
And now it's secure, locked,
implacable in its dreamlessness,
its persistent matter, its matter resolved to live.
And here I have the human sorrow of gazing eyes
that don't know, that ask, that slowly examine each particle of
        matter,
asking how it has been possible,
how it has come down to us so safe,
how it has come down intact, whole, flawless,
this door I see and point at,
this closed door that I'd like to see open in the night,
slowly swing
open in the surrounding silence,
open secretly and gently
in the silence, open free.

TRANSLATED BY CHARLES GUENTHER

EN LA CENIZA HAY UN MILAGRO

A Guillermo Carnero

En la ceniza hay un milagro.
Allí respira el mundo.

En la ceniza hay un despertar y un oír y un relampaguear
        y un absorto tener y un erguirse.
En la ceniza hay día y brilla el sol
futuro.
En la ceniza hay miedo.
Todo vuelve a empezar.

En la ceniza hay hombres.
Hay amor, hay desdicha.
En la ceniza hay noche y un crujido en la noche,
y hay soplo entre las sombras y hay suspiros.
En la ceniza hay lágrimas.

¿Por qué entre la ceniza no se oye
respirar ese mundo que respira
el aire irrespirable,
la fuerza irrespirable que ha de surgir? Callad.

En la ceniza hay viento y no se oye.
Y una paloma vuela bajo el sol.

THERE'S A MIRACLE GOING ON IN THE ASHES

For Guillermo Carnero

There's a miracle going on in the ashes.
The world is breathing in there.

In the ashes there's a desire to wake up and hear and give off light
        and possess completely and a desire to rise up.
In the ashes there is daylight and the sun shining
tomorrow.
The ashes are full of fear.
Everything goes back to begin again.

There are people in the ashes.
There's love, there's misery.
In the ashes there is night and a rustling noise in the night,
and a wind blows through the shadows and something is sighing.
There are tears in the ashes.

Why can't you hear the other world breathing
in there, the world that breathes the air
no one can breathe, the force no one can breathe,
the force that has to rise out of the ashes? Don't ask.

A wind is blowing in the ashes and you can't hear it.
And a dove is flying under the sun.

TRANSLATED BY LEWIS HYDE

PERO CÓMO DECÍRTELO

Pero cómo decírtelo si eres
tan leve y silenciosa
como una flor. Cómo te lo diré
cuando eres agua,
cuando eres fuente, manantial, sonrisa,
espiga, viento,
cuando eres aire, amor.

Cómo te lo diré,
a ti, joven relámpago,
temprana luz, aurora,
que has de morirte un día
como quien no es así.

Tu forma eterna,
como la luz y el mar, exige acaso
la majestad durable
de la materia. Hermosa
como la permanencia del océano
frente al atardecer, es más efímera
tu carne que una flor. Pero si eres
comparable a la luz, eres la luz,
la luz que hablase,
que dijese "te quiero,"
que durmiese en mis brazos,
y que tuviese sed, ojos, cansancio
y una infinita gana
de llorar, cuando miras
en el jardín las rosas
nacer, una vez más.

HOW AM I TO TELL YOU

But how am I to tell you,
you who are light and silent
like a flower. How am I to tell you
when you are water,
a fountain, a spring, a smiling mouth,
an ear of wheat, a wind,
when you, my love, are air.

How am I to tell you,
you, child lightning,
morning light, dawn,
that some day you'll have to die
like others who aren't all these things.

Like the light and the sea
your timeless body may be asking
for the sustained dignity
of matter. Lovely
like the sea's settlement
at dusk, your body is more
perishable than a flower. But not only are you
like the light, you are the light
itself, the light speaking,
saying, "I love you,"
falling asleep in my arms,
with its thirst, its eyes, its tired feeling
and an everlasting desire
to cry, when you look
at the roses in the garden
starting to bud again.

TRANSLATED BY HARDIE ST. MARTIN

PRECIO DE LA VERDAD

A Ángel González

En el desván antiguo de raída memoria,
detrás de la cuchara de palo con carcoma,
tras el vestuario viejo ha de encontrarse, o junto al muro
desconchado, en el polvo
de siglos. Ha de encontrarse acaso más allá del pálido gesto de una
      mano
vieja de algún mendigo, o en la ruina del alma
cuando ha cesado todo.
Yo me pregunto si es preciso el camino
polvoriento de la duda tenaz, el desaliento súbito
en la llanura estéril, bajo el sol de justicia,
la ruina de toda esperanza, el raído harapo del miedo, la desazón
      invencible a mitad del sendero que conduce al torreón
      derruido.
Yo me pregunto si es preciso dejar el camino real
y tomar a la izquierda por el atajo y la trocha,
como si nada hubiera quedado atrás en la casa desierta.
Me pregunto si es preciso ir sin vacilación al horror de la noche,
penetrar el abismo, la boca de lobo,
caminar hacia atrás, de espaldas hacia la negación,
o invertir la verdad, en el desolado camino.
O si más bien es preciso el sollozo de polvo en la confusión de un
      verano
terrible, o en el trastornado amanecer del alcohol con trompetas de
      sueño
saberse de pronto absolutamente desiertos, o mejor,
es quizá necesario haberse perdido en el sucio trato del amor,
haber contratado en la sombra un ensueño
comprado por precio, una reminiscencia de luz, un encanto
de amanecer tras la colina, hacia el río.
Admito la posibilidad de que sea absolutamente preciso
haber descendido, al menos alguna vez, hasta el fondo del edificio
      oscuro,

THE COST OF TRUTH

For Ángel González

It must be there. In the ancient storeroom
above our faded memory, in back of the worm-eaten wooden spoon,
behind the old dresser, or by the wall
with its fallen plaster, or in the dust
of centuries. It must be there. Maybe just beyond the bloodless
     motion
of an old beggar's hand or in the ruins of the soul
when everything is over.
I wonder if we have to have all this: the clinging
doubt with its dusty road, the sudden weariness
out on the dry prairie, under the sun of justice
and every hope in ruins, the frayed rags of fear, the uneasiness you
     can't hold back when you're halfway down the road to the
     ruined fortress.
I wonder, do we have to leave the high road
and go by foot through the old trail to the left
as if nothing had been left for us in the deserted house?
I wonder if we have to go straight into the horrible night,
and climb down into the sinkhole, the wolf's mouth,
and walk backwards, back into nothingness,
and turn the truth upside down, out on the empty highway.
I mean, do we have to put the dust in our mouths and whimper
     during the terrible summer's
confusion, or do we have to wake up all alone
when the dream-trumpets announce the bewildering alcoholic dawn?
     Or better:
maybe we're supposed to get lost in the dirty traffic of love,
or go into the shadows and hire
a fantasy, paying its price, a souvenir of light, a lovely dawn
on the other side of the hill, toward the river.
I admit it's possible, maybe there's no other way,
maybe we should have gone down, at least once, deep into the
     shadowy building,

haber bajado a tientas el peligro de la desvencijada escalera, que
    amenaza ceder a cada paso nuestro,
y haber penetrado al fin con valentía en la indignidad, en el sótano
    oscuro.
Haber visitado el lugar de la sombra,
el territorio de la ceniza, donde toda vileza reposa
junto a la telaraña paciente. Haberse avecindado en el polvo,
haberlo masticado con tenacidad en largas horas de sed
o de sueño. Haber respondido con valor o temeridad
al silencio
o la pregunta postrera y haberse allí percatado y rehecho.
Es necesario haberse entendido con la malhechora verdad
que nos asalta en plena noche y nos desvela de pronto y nos roba
hasta el último céntimo. Haber mendigado después largos días
por los barrios más bajos de uno mismo, sin esperanza de recuperar
    lo perdido,
y al fin, desposeídos, haber continuado el camino sincero y entrado
    en la noche absoluta con valor todavía.

maybe we should have felt our way down the shaky staircase that
       threatens to collapse at every step
and pushed bravely into the filthy thing, into the dark basement.
We should have gone to the shadow place,
the land of ashes, where all the ugly things rest
beside the patient spiderweb. We should have set up house in the
       dust
and kept on chewing it during the endless hours of thirst
or drowsiness. We should have answered—bravely or foolishly—
to the silence
or to the last question, and then looked after ourselves and regained
       our strength.
We should have taken lessons from the truth that hurts us,
that attacks us in the middle of the night and keeps us awake and
       steals
every penny we own. Then we should have spent long days begging,
walking through the lowest parts of ourselves, knowing it's impossible
       to get back what we lost,
and finally, when we had no home at all, we should have stayed on
       the true road and kept our nerve going into the night that
       never ends.

TRANSLATED BY LEWIS HYDE

MUERTE EN LA TARDE

De los cientos de muertes que me habitan,
ésta de hoy es la que menos sangra.
Es la muerte que viene con las tardes,
cuando las sombras pálidas se alargan,
y los contornos se derrumban,
y se perfilan las montañas.

Entonces alguien pasa pregonando
su mercancía bajo la ventana,
a la que yo me asomo para ver
las últimas farolas apagadas.

Por la ceniza de las calles cruzan
sombras sin dejar huella, hombres que pasan,
que no vienen a mí ni en mí se quedan,
a cuestas con su alma solitaria.

La luz del día huye hacia el oeste.
El aire de la noche se adelanta,
y nos llega un temor agrio y confuso,
casi dolor, apenas esperanza.

Todo lo que me unía con la vida
deja de ser unión, se hace distancia,
se aleja más, al fin desaparece,
y muerto soy,
                    ...y nadie me levanta.

DEATH IN THE AFTERNOON

Of the hundreds of deaths that inhabit me,
this one today bleeds the least.
It's the death that comes with the afternoons,
when the pale shadows grow longer,
and contours collapse
and the mountains show themselves.

Then someone passes hawking
his merchandise under my window,
where I lean out to see
those streetlamps that are still unlit.

Shadows cross the ashes of the streets
without leaving tracks, men that pass
who do not come to me and do not stay
with their lonely soul on their backs.

The daylight escapes toward the west.
The night air comes in before time,
and a bitter, confused fear, almost
pain, hardly hope, reaches me.

Everything that tied me to life
becomes untied, becomes distance,
goes farther off, disappears at last,
and I'm a dead man,

                    . . . and no one raises me.

TRANSLATED BY DAVID IGNATOW

MUNDO ASOMBROSO

Mundo asombroso
surge bruscamente.

Me da miedo la luna
embalsamada
en las aguas del río,
el bosque silencioso
que araña con sus ramas
el vientre de la lluvia,
los pájaros
que aúllan en el túnel de la noche
y todo
lo que súbitamente
hace un gesto y sonríe
para marchar de pronto.

En medio
de la cruel retirada de las cosas
precipitándose en desorden hacia
la nada y la ceniza,
mi corazón naufraga en la zozobra
del destino del mundo que lo cerca.
¿A dónde va ese viento y esa luz,
el grito
de la roja amapola inesperada,
el canto de las grises
gaviotas de los puertos?

¿Y qué ejército es ese que me lleva
envuelto en su derrota y en su huída
—fatigado rehén, yo, prisionero
sin número y sin nombre, maniatado
entre escuadras de gritos fugitivos—
hacia la sombra donde van las luces,
hacia el silencio donde la voz muere?

WITHOUT WARNING

Without warning
a strange world looms up.

I am afraid of the moon
shrouded
in the river water,
the soundless forest
its branches
clawing the belly of the rain,
the birds
wailing in the tunnel of night,
of everything
that suddenly shrugs
and smiles
only to leave abruptly.

In the midst
of the bitter retreat of things
rushing in headlong flight
towards emptiness and ashes,
my heart is dragged under, the wreckage
of everyone's fate swirling around it.
Where is the wind off to, and the light
and the scream
of the shocking red poppy,
the singsong of the gray
seagulls above the harbors?

And what army is it that carries me off
caught up in its rout,
—bone-tired hostage, captured
without papers or dogtags, bound
among squads of runaway screams—
to the darkness where the lights are going,
to the silence where the voice dies?

TRANSLATED BY ROBERT MEZEY AND
HARDIE ST. MARTIN

EL CAMPO DE BATALLA

Hoy voy a describir el campo
de batalla
tal como yo lo vi, una vez decidida
la suerte de los hombres que lucharon
muchos hasta morir,
otros
hasta seguir viviendo todavía.

No hubo elección:
murió quien pudo,
quien no pudo morir continuó andando,
los árboles nevaban lentos frutos,
era verano, invierno, todo un año
o más quizá: era la vida
entera
aquel enorme día de combate.

Por el oeste el viento traía sangre,
por el este la tierra era ceniza,
el norte entero estaba
bloqueado
por alambradas secas y por gritos,
y únicamente el sur,
tan sólo
el sur,
se ofrecía ancho y libre a nuestros ojos.

Pero el sur no existía:
ni agua, ni luz, ni sombra, ni ceniza
llenaban su oquedad, su hondo vacío:
el sur era un enorme precipicio,
un abismo sin fin de donde,
lentos,
los poderosos buitres ascendían.

THE BATTLEFIELD

Today I am going to tell about the field
of battle
just as I saw it, one time that decided
the fate of the men who struggled
many to death
others
to go on living today.

There wasn't any choice:
whoever could, died;
whoever couldn't die went on walking;
the trees rained a heavy fruit;
it was summer, winter, a whole year
or more maybe: it was a whole
life
that tremendous day of fighting.

From the west the wind brought blood,
from the east the earth was ashes,
the whole north was
blocked
by harsh barbed-wire barricades and by cries,
and the south only,
that alone
the south,
offered itself wide and free to our eyes.

But the south did not exist:
not water, not light, not shadow, not ashes
filled its nothingness, its deep vacancy:
the south was an enormous cliff,
an endless abyss from which
slowly,
the ponderous vultures were ascending.

Nadie escuchó la voz del capitán
porque tampoco el capitán hablaba.
Nadie enterró a los muertos.
Nadie dijo:
"dale a mi novia esto si la encuentras
un día."

Tan sólo alguien remató a un caballo
que, con el vientre abierto,
agonizante,
llenaba con su espanto el aire en sombra:
el aire que la noche amenazaba.

Quietos, pegados a la dura
tierra,
cogidos entre el pánico y la nada,
los hombres esperaban el momento
último,
sin oponerse ya,
sin rebeldía.

Algunos se murieron,
como dije,
y los demás, tendidos, derribados,
pegados a la tierra en paz al fin,
esperan
ya no sé qué
—quizá que alguien les diga:
"amigos, podéis iros, el combate..."

Entre tanto,
es verano otra vez,
y crece el trigo
en el que fue ancho campo de batalla.

No one listened to the voice of the captain
because the captain was not talking.
No one buried the dead.
No one said:
"Give my sweetheart this if you meet her
some day."

The only thing, someone finished off a horse
which, with its belly opened,
struggling to death,
filled with its fright the shadowy air:
the air that the night was threatening.

Quietly, pinned to the hard
earth,
caught between panic and nothingness,
the men were waiting for the moment,
the end,
already without resistance,
without rebellion.

Some died,
as I mentioned,
and the others, wracked out, struck down,
pinned to the earth in peace at last,
are holding on—
but what for, I don't know—
maybe for someone to tell them:
"Friends, you can leave; the battle . . ."

This far along
it's summer again,
and the wheat is thriving
on what was a wide field of battle.

TRANSLATED BY WILLIAM STAFFORD
AND HERBERT BAIRD

ESTÍO EN BIDONVILLE

Languidez de las cosas subalternas,
inútiles objetos, olvidados,
grises
plataformas del polvo
cotidiano,
sucios cristales ante turbios cielos,
contra los que los gatos
mayan, duermen, se aburren,
paseando
su felino desdén, su desenfado
torvo, su angulosa
y erizada estructura, en el tejado
musgoso y apacible como
un prado.

Allí, en esa silla baja, es donde
el niño
      cojo
         se ha sentado
para ver las palomas...
—¿Qué palomas? No es cierto.
Yo estaba equivocado:
para ver
los papeles oscuros casi blancos
izados por el viento,
levantados
—lloverá— en un remedo
de vuelo sucio, inútil, fracasado.

Para ver a la cabra comeárboles
atada a un árbol carcomido y lacio,
para gustar el polvo en la saliva,
para oir a los grillos enjaulados
en su cárcel de alambre y de madera,

SUMMER IN SLUMVILLE

Torpor of trivial things,
no-good stuff, abandoned,
gray
heaps of dust
—the customary—
dirty glass under a muddy sky,
against which the cats
mew, drowse, get bored,
prowling
their cat disdain, their mean
unconcern, their angular
and bristly bodies, on the roof
which is as mossy and tranquil as
a lawn.

Over there, in that low chair, is where
the child
      —lame—
             has sat down
to see the doves . . .
—What doves? It's not true.
I made a mistake:
in order to see
the dirty off-white papers
swept up by the wind,
whipped up
—it's going to rain—in a mockery
of dirty flight, no good, failed.

In order to see the tree-chewing goat
staked to a withered, worm-eaten trunk,
in order to taste the dust in his mouth,
in order to hear the jailed crickets
in their cell of wire and wood,

para cerrar los ojos deslumbrados
ante el destello súbito y violento
del sol en vidrios rotos reflejado,
para sentir las uñas de la tarde
clavándose en sus leves, blancos párpados,
y abrir después los ojos, y...

       Silencio.
La ciudad rompe contra el campo
dejando en sus orillas amarillas,
en el polvo de hoy que será barro
luego,
los miserables restos de un naufragio
de colosales dimensiones: miles
de hombres sobreviven. Enseres y artefactos
—como ellos rotos, como ellos
oxidados—·
flotan aquí y allá, o bien reposan
igual que ellos, salvados
hoy por hoy —¿sólo hoy?—, sobre esta tierra.

Mañana es un mar hondo que hay que cruzar a nado.

in order to shut dazzled eyes
before the sudden, violent flash
of the sun bounced from broken windows,
in order to feel the nails of the afternoon
stabbing into his fluttering white eyelids,
and to open his eyes afterwards, and . . .

Silence.

The city breaks against the countryside
leaving on its yellow shore,
on today's dust which is going to be mud
later,
the dingy trash of a shipwreck
of colossal dimensions: thousands
of men survive. Furniture and junk
—like them broken, like them
rusted—
float here and there, or else rest
just like them saved
for today—only today?—, on this earth.

Tomorrow is a deep sea that will have to be crossed
    by swimming.

Translated by William Stafford
and Herbert Baird

CADÁVER ÍNFIMO

Se murió diez centímetros tan sólo:
una pequeña muerte que afectaba
a tres muelas careadas y a una uña
del pie llamado izquierdo y a cabellos
aislados, imprevistos.
Oraron lo corriente, susurrando:
"Perdónalas, Señor, a esas tres muelas
por su maldad, por su pecaminosa
masticación. Muelas impías,
pero al fin tuyas como criaturas."
El mismo estaba allí,
serio, delante
de sus restos mortales diminutos:
una prótesis sucia, unos cabellos.
Los amigos querían consolarle,
pero sólo aumentaban su tristeza.
"Esto no puede ser, esto no puede
seguir así. O mejor dicho:
esto debe seguir a mejor ritmo.
Muérete más. Muérete al fin del todo."
El estrechó sus manos, enlutado,
con ese gesto falso, compungido,
de los duelos más sórdidos.
                              "Os juro
—se echó a llorar, vencido por la angustia—
que yo quiero morir mi sentimiento,
que yo quiero hacer piedra mi conducta,
tierra mi amor, ceniza mi deseo,
pero no puede ser, a veces hablo,
me muevo un poco, me acatarro incluso,
y aquellos que me ven, lógicamente
deducen que estoy vivo,
mas no es cierto:
vosotros, mis amigos,

THE LEAST CORPSE

He had died only a few inches:
a tiny death that had its effect
on three rotten molars and one toenail
on his so-called left foot and, surprise!
a few hairs here and there.
They mumbled the usual prayers:
"O Lord, forgive those three molars
their iniquity, their sinful
chewing. Godless teeth,
but your own creatures, after all."
He was there himself,
solemn before
what there was of his mortal remains:
a filthy prosthesis and some hair.
Friends had come to comfort him
but they only deepened his sadness.
"This is impossible, it can't go on
this way. Or maybe we should say:
This ought to be speeded up.
Die some more. Die once and for all."
Dressed in mourning, he shook their hands
with that phony regret
you see at the worst funerals.
                        "I swear"
—overcome, he burst into tears—
"I want to extinguish my feelings,
I want to turn my life into stone,
my love into earth, my desire to ashes,
but I can't help it, I talk sometimes,
I move a bit, I even catch cold,
and naturally those who see me
deduce that I'm alive,
but it's not so:
you ought to know this, my friends,

deberíais saber que, aunque estornude,
soy un cadáver muerto por completo."

Dejó caer los brazos, abatido,
se desprendió un gusano de la manga,
pidió perdón y recogió el gusano
que era sólo un fragmento
de la totalidad de su esperanza.

even if I sneeze,
I'm a corpse, I couldn't be more dead."

Despondently he let fall his arms,
flicked a worm from his sleeve,
said, "Pardon me," and picked up the worm.
After all it was only a scrap
of all he was looking forward to.

TRANSLATED BY ROBERT MEZEY

José Ángel Valente

LA MAÑANA

A José Agustín Goytisolo

La mañana desnuda, el diamante
purísimo del día...
                    Vale más despertar.

Las caravanas de los mercaderes,
los pescados resbalando otra vez hacia el mar.
En larguísimos carros, cubiertos de deseos,
veo pasar
a los pobres de espíritu
y a los pobres de pan,
los pobres de palabra
y de solemnidad.

Pero la mañana es azul y las montañas
beben su claridad.

¿Quién me llama, quién
desde el vagido del hambre —el sol es alto arriba—
se ha atrevido a llorar?
Las despedidas y los regresos
con iguales pañuelos; el sabor de la sal
como el amor amarga.
Nadie debe llorar.

La mañana desnuda: árboles, altos pájaros,
el invierno, el otoño... Paz.

MORNING

For José Agustín Goytisolo

Naked morning, the day's transparent
diamond . . .
                    Better shake off sleep.

Caravans of merchants,
fish sliding back into the sea.
I watch the poor in spirit
going past
in such long carts, covered with desires,
the poor in bread,
the poor in words
and in formalities.

But the morning is blue, the mountains
soak up its clean light.

Who is calling me, who
in the cradle's wail of hunger—the sun is riding high—
has dared to cry?
Goodbyes and homecomings
with the same handkerchiefs, the taste of salt
bitter like love.
People shouldn't cry.

Naked morning: trees, birds far overhead,
winter, fall . . . Peace.

Los campesinos muerden las semillas
que han de multiplicar;
alrededor del mismo miedo
aprietan el hogar.

Oh, nadie, nadie debe
llorar.

La luz es alta y pura para cuanto respira.

Y más allá
de su belleza,
y más allá ¿qué hay?

Pongo nombre a mis hijos,
edifico amistad.
Mas mi casa es de tiempo.

Qué claro despertar.

Peasants bite into the seed
that will have to multiply.
They pull their homes tight
around the terror they share.

Oh, no one, no one
should cry.

The tall, open light takes in everything that breathes.

And out there past
its loveliness,
farther off, what's there?

I give my children names,
I build friendship.
But my house is made of time.

                Everything is so clear this morning.

            TRANSLATED BY HARDIE ST. MARTIN

LA VÍSPERA

El hombre despojóse de sí mismo,
también del cinturón, del brazo izquierdo,
de su propia estatura.

Resbaló la mujer sus largas medias,
largas como los ríos o el cansancio.

Nublóse el sueño de deseo.
                Vino
ciego el amor
batiendo un cuerpo anónimo.
                   De nadie
eran la hora ni el lugar
ni el tiempo ni los besos.

Sólo el deseo de entregarse daba
sentido al acto del amor,
pero nunca respuesta.

El humo gris.
            El abandono.
                El alba
como una inmensa retirada.
                Restos
de vida oscura en un rincón caídos.
Y lo demás vulgar, ocioso.
               El hombre
púsose en orden natural, alzóse
y tosió humanamente.
            Aquella hora
de soledad. Vestirse de la víspera.
Sentir duros los límites.
             Y al cabo
no saber, no poder reconocerse.

THE EVENING BEFORE

The man freed his body of itself,
of its belt, of its left arm,
of its own height.

The woman slid her long stockings off,
long like rivers or weariness.

Oncoming sleep clouded up with desire.
                              Love
came along, blinded,
fighting a body that didn't have a name.
                        No one
owned the hour, the place,
the weather, the kisses.

Only the desire to let themselves go
gave the act of love a meaning,
but it was never the answer.

Gray smoke.
          Abandon.
                    Daybreak
like a mass withdrawal.
                    Remnants
of obscure living dumped into a corner.
And everything else vulgar, pointless.
                              The man
came to a natural position, pulled himself
together and coughed like a man.
                        That hour
of loneliness. Putting the evening back on with their clothes.
Feeling the hard edges.
                  And in the end
not knowing anything, not knowing themselves.

TRANSLATED BY HARDIE ST. MARTIN

TIERRA DE NADIE

La ciudad se ponía
amarilla y cansada
como un buey triste.

     Entraba
la niebla lentamente
por los largos pasillos.

Pequeña ciudad sórdida, perdida,
municipal, oscura.

      No sabíamos
a qué carta poner
la vida
para no volver siempre
sin nada entre las manos
como buceadores del vacío.

Palabras incompletas o imposibles
signos.

    Adolescentes en el orden
reverencial de las familias.

Y los muertos solemnes.

        Lunes,
domingo, lunes.

     Ríos
de soledad.

     Pasaban largos trenes
sin destino.

     Y bajaba la niebla
lamiendo los desmontes
y oscureciendo el frío.

Por los largos pasillos me perdiera
del recinto infantil ahora desnudo,
cercenado, tapiado por la ausencia.

NO MAN'S LAND

The city used to grow
yellow and tired
like a heavy-eyed ox.
                    Fog
pushed in slowly down
the long passageways.

Tiny, sordid city, lost,
municipal, dark.
            We didn't know
what card to lay
our lives on
in order not to come back time after time
with nothing in our hands,
like deep-sea divers of emptiness.

Unfinished words or impossible
dumb show.
            Adolescents in the
respectable order of families.

And the dead-serious dead.
                    Monday,
Sunday, Monday.
            Rivers
of solitude.
            Long trains wandered
past.
      And the fog rolled down,
licking the cleared mountainsides,
throwing a cloud over the cold.

If I could only slip back into the long
passageways of childhood, empty,
cut off, boarded up by absence now.

TRANSLATED BY HARDIE ST. MARTIN

CON PALABRAS DISTINTAS

La poesía asesinó un cadáver,
decapitó al crujiente
señor de los principios principales,
hirió de muerte al necio,
al fugaz señorito de ala triste.
Escupió en su cabeza.
                            No hubo tiros.
Si acaso, sangre pálida,
desnutrida y dinástica,
o el purulento suero de los siempre esclavos.
Cayeron de sí mismas
varias pecheras blancas en silencio.
Se abrió el horizonte. Sonó el látigo
improvisado y puro.
Hubo un revuelo entre los mercaderes
del profanado templo.
                    Ya después del tumulto,
llegaron retrasadas cuatro vírgines
de manifiesta ancianidad estéril.
Mas todo estaba consumado.
                              Huyó la poesía
del ataúd y el cetro.
                      Huyó a las manos
del hombre duro, instrumental, naciente,
que a la pasión directa llama vida.
Se alzó en su pecho, paseó sus barrios
suburbanos y oscuros,
gustó el sabor del barro o de su origen,
la obstinación del mineral,
la luz del brazo armado.
                      Y vino a nuestro encuentro
con palabras distintas, que no reconocimos,
contra nuestras palabras.

WITH PLAIN WORDS

Poetry murdered a corpse,
it beheaded a creaking
high-principled gent,
it butchered him, the fool,
the flighty dude with his sad wing.
It spit on his head.
                    There was no shooting.
If anything, pale blood,
undernourished, dynastic,
or the puslike serum of lifelong slaves.
Several white dickeys fell silent,
all by themselves.
The horizon flew open. A whip cracked,
makeshift and pure.
Merchants milled hysterically
in the defiled temple.
                    When things calmed down,
four virgins rushed in, old, barren, obviously
on their last legs. Too late,
it was all over.
                    Poetry fled
from the coffin and the staff.
                    Ran into the hands
of the tough guy, the rising instrument,
the existentialist.
It rose up in his chest, it walked through dark
neighborhoods at the edge of town,
it tasted the mud, tasted his origins,
the stubbornness of the mineral,
the light of the fighting arm.
                    And came out to meet us,
drowning out our words with plain words
we didn't recognize.

TRANSLATED BY ROBERT MEZEY AND
HARDIE ST. MARTIN

LUGAR VACÍO EN LA CELEBRACIÓN

Yo nací provinciano en los domingos
de desigual memoria,
nací en una oscura ratonera vacía,
asido a dios como a un trapecio a punto
de infinitamente arrojarme hacia el mar.

Nací viscosamente pegado a los residuos de mi vida,
rodeado de amor,
de un amor al que aún amo más que a mis propios huesos
y al que tan sólo puedo odiar sin tregua
por habérseme dado para dejarse así morir
de triste, de irrisorio,
siendo mayor que tantas muertes juntas.

Yo nací vestido de mimético niño
para descubrir en tanta reverencia sólo un óxido triste
y en las voces que inflaban los señores pudientes
enormes anos giratorios
de brillante apariencia en el liso exterior.

Los pudientes señores llevaban bisoñé.

Después, un viento hosco barrió la faz de aquella tierra.

Hubo prudentes muertos, cadáveres precoces
y muertos poderosos cuya agonía aún dura,
cuya muerte de pulmones horrendos
aún sopla como un fuelle inagotable.

Y yo empecé a crecer entonces,
como toda la historia ritual de mi pueblo,
hacia adentro o debajo de la tierra,
en ciénagas secretas, en tibios vertederos,
en las afueras sumergidas
de la grandiosa, heroica, orquestación municipal.

AN EMPTY PLACE AT THE CELEBRATION

I was born a country boy on Sundays,
some remembered better than others,
born in a dark, empty mousehole,
handcuffed to god like a trapeze
about to hurl me endlessly into the sea.

I was born slimy, stuck to the leftovers
of my life, with love all around me,
a love that means more to me than my own bones,
and I have to keep on hating it
because it let itself die
of sadness, from being laughed at,
when it was greater than so many deaths together.

I was born in the clothes of a boy who puts on an act
only to find a sad rust in all the bowing and scraping,
and in the bloated voices of rich men
enormous revolving assholes
whose smooth cheeks had a brilliant shine.

And the rich men wore their toupees.

And then an ugly wind swept the face of the land.

There were timid dead bodies, corpses before their time
and iron-handed dead whose death agony is still going on,
whose death from corrupted lungs
still puffs up and collapses like a bellows that can't stop.

And I started growing then,
like all the history of my people, a mere ritual,
inward or under the ground,
in hidden-away swamps, in warm sewers,
on the submerged edges
of the grand, heroic orchestration of the city.

Nací en la infancia, en otro tiempo, lejos
o muy lejos y fui
inútilmente aderezado para una ceremonia
a la que nunca habría de acudir.

UNA ELEGÍA INCOMPLETA

Había la miseria,
miserable miseria del llanto en las familias,
las urnas, hornacinas, las capillas azules
con una lamparilla,
y un gran muerto inocente
depositado en medio
de las horas, los días, los semestres, los años,
sí, los años nudosos, nodulares, negados.

El aire tibio de perpetuamente
conllevar aquel rezo
y el maullido larguísimo del triste
gato perdido en el viscoso invierno.

Blasfemias en cuclillas,
masturbadas, no dichas, indecibles.
Y tantos dioses en sus claras vitrinas
con velos y azucenas de intocada blancura.

La mísera miseria, la invasora miseria,
el llanto en las familias,
la secreción oscura del subrepticio semen
perturbador y el odio
todavía sin nombre.

I was born into childhood, in other times, far
or far, far away and I was trained for nothing,
for a ceremony
I would never attend.

TRANSLATED BY HARDIE ST. MARTIN AND
RALPH NELSON

AN ELEGY THAT WAS NEVER FINISHED

There was misery,
the unbearable misery of weeping in whole families,
urns, vaulted niches, blue chapels
with vigil lamps,
and a huge innocent dead body
set down in the middle of the hours,
the days, the semesters, the years,
yes, the snarled-up, knotted, useless years.

And the air lukewarm, from putting up
with the same old prayer
and the endless whimper of the poor stray
cat out in the winter slush.

Squatting down with our blasphemies—
masturbated, bitten back, unsayable.
And all the gods in their lit-up glass show-
cases, with veils and lilies, whose whiteness no one ever touched.

Unbearable misery, creeping into everything;
the weeping in the families,
the upsetting trickle of secret semen
in the dark, and hate
that still didn't have its name.

Antes de huir, cuando las grandes lluvias,
cuando los grandes vientos derribaron el cielo,
arrasamos las tiendas, los altares, los ídolos,
la raíz, los residuos de la triste parodia.

Before we beat a retreat, in the heavy rains,
in the heavy winds that brought the sky crashing down,
we sacked stores, altars, idols,
the roots, the only thing left of the sad mock show.

TRANSLATED BY HARDIE ST. MARTIN

Jaime Gil de Biedma

ARTE POÉTICA

A Vicente Aleixandre

La nostalgia del sol en los terrados,
en el muro color paloma de cemento
—sin embargo tan vívido— y el frío
repentino que casi sobrecoge;

la dulzura, el calor de los labios a solas
en medio de la calle familiar,
igual que un gran salón donde acudieran
multitudes lejanas como seres queridos,

y sobre todo la eternidad del tiempo,
el gran boquete abriéndose hacia dentro del alma
mientras arriba sobrenadan promesas
que desmayan, lo mismo que si espumas...

Es sin duda el momento de pensar
que el hecho de estar vivo exige algo,
acaso heroicidades ¿o basta simplemente
alguna humilde cosa común

cuya corteza de materia terrestre
tratar entre los dedos— con un poco de fe?
Palabras, por ejemplo.
Palabras de familia gastadas tibiamente.

THE ART OF POETRY

For Vicente Aleixandre

A longing for the sun on flat roofs,
on the gray, pigeon-colored wall of stone
—yet it stands out so clear— and the sudden rush
of cold that comes almost with a shock.

The sweetness, the warmth of lips alone
in the middle of the street, familiar
as a big hall filling with strange people,
come together like our loved ones.

Above everything, time's endlessness,
the deep fissure that opens toward the soul,
while promises drift overhead
and break like surf against the shore.

Isn't it time we started thinking
that just being alive demands something
of us, big things maybe, or perhaps
some simple thing would be enough,

something with an earthy crust
that fingers can shape, with a little faith?
Words, for one thing.
Household words well worn with warmth.

TRANSLATED BY TIMOTHY BALAND

NOCHE TRISTE DE OCTUBRE, 1959

A Juan Marsé

Definitivamente
parece confirmarse que este invierno
que viene, será duro.

Adelantaron
las lluvias, y el Gobierno,
reunido en consejo de ministros,
no se sabe si estudia a estas horas
el subsidio de paro
o el derecho al despido,
o si sencillamente, aislado en un océano,
se limita a esperar que la tormenta pase
y llegue el día en que, por fin,
las cosas dejen de venir mal dadas.

En la noche de octubre,
mientras leo entre líneas el periódico,
me he parado a escuchar el latido
del silencio en mi cuarto, las conversaciones
de los vecinos acostándose,

                    todos esos rumores
que recobran de pronto una vida
y un significado propio, misterioso.

Y he pensado en los miles de seres humanos,
hombres y mujeres que en este mismo instante,
con el primer escalofrío,
han vuelto a preguntarse por sus preocupaciones,
por su fatiga anticipada,
por su ansiedad para este invierno,

SAD NIGHT OF OCTOBER 1959

For Juan Marsé

It does look
as if this winter coming in
will be a hard one.

The rains
started early, and no one knows
if the Government, huddled now in its ministries,
is mulling over
insurance for the unemployed
or the right to unemploy them,
or if it's lost at sea and doing nothing
but wait for the storm to wear itself out
and day to come, the day at long last
when things will stop going from bad to worse.

This night in October,
reading between the lines of the newspaper,
I've stopped to listen to the silence
pulsing in my room, to the conversations
of neighbors turning in,
                      all those muffled sounds
that suddenly take on a life
and a hidden meaning of their own.

And I've thought of the thousands of human beings,
men and women, who at this very moment,
shivering for the first time,
have started brooding on their troubles again,
the exhaustion that's waiting for them,
the fear of the winter,

mientras que afuera llueve.
Por todo el litoral de Cataluña llueve
con verdadera crueldad, con humo y nubes bajas,
ennegreciendo muros,
goteando fábricas, filtrándose
en los talleres mal iluminados.
Y el agua arrastra hacia la mar semillas
incipientes, mezcladas en el barro,
árboles, zapatos cojos, utensilios
abandonados y revuelto todo
con las primeras Letras protestadas.

while it rains outside.
It's raining along the whole coast of Catalonia
with real cruelty, with smoke and low clouds,
blackening walls,
leaking into factories, seeping
into poorly lighted workshops.
And the rainwater sweeps out to sea
opening seeds mixed in with the mud,
trees, one-legged shoes, broken tools,
all of it swirling together
with the first defaulted payments.

TRANSLATED BY HARDIE ST. MARTIN
AND ROBERT MEZEY

DE LOS AÑOS CUARENTA

Media España ocupaba España entera
con la vulgaridad, con el desprecio
total de que es capaz, frente al vencido,
un intratable pueblo de cabreros.

Barcelona y Madrid eran algo humillado.
Como una casa sucia, donde la gente es vieja,
la ciudad parecía más oscura
y los Metros olían a miseria.

Con luz de atardecer, sobresaltada y triste,
se salía a las calles de un invierno
poblado de infelices gabardinas
a la deriva, bajo el viento.

Y pasaban figuras mal vestidas
de mujeres, cruzando como sombras,
solitarias mujeres adiestradas
—viudas, hijas, o esposas—

en los modos peores de ganar la vida
y suplir a sus hombres. Por la noche,
las más hermosas sonreían
a los más sinvergüenzas de los vencedores.

IN THE FORTIES

Half of Spain occupied the whole of Spain
with all the coarseness, the utter
contempt for the defeated,
a stubborn nation of goatherds is capable of.

Madrid and Barcelona had been forced to their knees.
Like a dirty house where the people are old,
the city seemed darker
and the subways gave off an odor of misery.

In the confused, sad glow of dusk
we would go out into the streets
of a winter peopled by unhappy raincoats
blown about in the wind.

Women would pass by, shabbily dressed,
crossing like shadows,
solitary women—wives, daughters,
widows—schooled

in the worst ways of making a living
and taking care of their men. At night
the best-looking ones would smile
at the most brutal of the conquerors.

TRANSLATED BY TIMOTHY BALAND

The last line of this poem echoes the line: "And the loveliest/smiles at the fiercest of the conquerors," from Rubén Darío's "Marcha triunfal" ("Triumphal March").

ELEGÍA Y RECUERDO
DE LA CANCIÓN FRANCESA

C'est une chanson
qui nous resemble.
Kosma y Prevert:
"Les Feuilles Mortes"

Os acordáis: Europa estaba en ruinas.
Todo un mundo de imágenes me queda de aquel tiempo
descoloridas, hiriéndome los ojos
con los escombros de los bombardeos.
En España la gente se apretaba en los cines
y no existía la calefacción.

Era la paz—después de tánta sangre—
que llegaba andrajosa, tal cual la conocimos
los españoles durante cinco años.
Y todo un continente empobrecido,
carcomido de historia y de mercado negro,
de repente nos fue más familiar.

Estampas de la Europa de postguerra
que parecen mojadas en lluvia silenciosa,
ciudades grises adonde llega un tren
sucio de refugiados: cuántas cosas
de nuestra historia próxima trajisteis, despertando
la esperanza en España, y el temor!

Hasta el aire de entonces parecía
que estuviera suspenso, como si preguntara,
y en las viejas tabernas de barrio
los vencidos hablaban en voz baja...
Nosotros, los más jóvenes, como siempre esperábamos
algo definitivo y general.

Y fue en aquel momento, justamente
en aquellos momentos de miedo y esperanzas

IN MOURNFUL PRAISE AND MEMORY
OF THE FRENCH SONG

C'est une chanson
qui nous resemble.
—Kosma and Prevert:
"Les Feuilles Mortes"

Europe was a mess: it will come back to you.
I have a whole world of faded images
left from that time, the bomb-gutted
buildings so hard on the eyes.
All over Spain people jammed together at the movies
and central heating didn't exist.

It was peace—after all that blood—
that showed up in tatters, unchanged from the way
we Spaniards had known her those five years.
And a whole continent gone to seed,
rotting away with history and the black market,
was all of a sudden more familiar to us.

Sketches of postwar Europe
that seem to be soaked in silent rain,
drab cities where a train pulls in
filthy with refugees: how many things
of our recent history you brought for us, stirring up
hope and also fear throughout our country.

Even the air then became somehow
suspended, as though asking a question,
and in the rundown corner bars
the losers spoke in low voices. . . .
We, the youngest ones, hoped as always
for something definite for everyone.

And it was at that point,
in that time of hope mixed with fear

—tan irreales, ay—que apareciste,
oh rosa de lo sórdido, manchada
creación de los hombres, arisca, vil y bella
canción francesa de mi juventud!

Eras lo no esperado que se impone
a la imaginación, porque es así la vida,
tú que cantabas la heroicidad canalla,
el estallido de las rebeldías
igual que llamaradas, y el miedo a dormir solo,
la intensidad que aflige al corazón.

Cuánto enseguida te quisimos todos!
En tu mundo de noches, con el chico y la chica
entrelazados, de pie en un quicio oscuro,
en la sordina de tus melodías,
un eco de nosotros resonaba exaltándonos
con la nostalgia de la rebelión.

Y todavía, en la alta noche, solo,
con el vaso en la mano, cuando pienso en mi vida,
otra vez más *sans faire du bruit* tus músicas
suenan en la memoria, como una despedida:
parece que fue ayer y algo ha cambiado.
Hoy no esperamos la revolución.

Desvencijada Europa de postguerra
con la luna asomando por las ventanas rotas,
Europa anterior al milagro alemán,
imagen de mi vida, melancólica!
Nosotros, los de entonces, ya no somos los mismos,
aunque a veces nos guste una canción.

—so hard to believe—that you suddenly came to be,
O sordid rose, stained
and man-made, shy, grimy and beautiful
French song of my youth.

You were the undreamed-of thing that captures
the imagination, for life is like that;
you who sang of disreputable courage,
the uprisings that broke out like flames,
and the fear of sleeping alone,
the deep feelings that end in heartbreak.

How we all loved you from the start!
Yours was a world of nights, of lovers
standing locked in the shadow of a doorstep,
we heard an echo of ourselves in the
muted sound of your melody, and it filled us
with frustrated longing for rebellion.

And even now, alone, late at night,
a drink in my hand, when I think of my life
your melody comes back
like a goodbye: *sans faire du bruit.*
It's as if it were yesterday again—with a difference.
Today there's no hope of revolution.

Splintered postwar Europe
with the moon looming up through broken windows,
Europe before the German miracle,
bitter image of my lifetime!
We lived through that, and are no longer the same,
though now and then we can still be moved by a song.

TRANSLATED BY TIMOTHY BALAND

PRÍNCIPE DE AQUITANIA,
EN SU TORRE ABOLIDA

Una clara conciencia de lo que ha perdido,
es lo que le consuela. Se levanta
cada mañana a fallecer, discurre por estancias
en donde sordamente duele el tiempo
que se detuvo, la herida mal cerrada.
Dura en otro lugar este otro mundo,
y vuelve por la noche en las paradas
del sueño fatigoso... Reino suyo
dorado, cuántas veces
por él pregunta en la mitad del día,
con el temor de olvidar algo!
Las horas, largo viaje desabrido.
La historia es un instante preferido,
un tesoro en imágenes, que él guarda
para su necesaria consulta con la muerte.
Y el final de la historia es esta pausa.

THE PRINCE OF AQUITANIA
IN HIS TORN-DOWN TOWER

What comforts him is a clear understanding
of what he's lost. He gets up every morning
to die, he wanders in and out of rooms
where the unhealed wound, the time
that stopped, aches with its dull pain.
This other world goes on somewhere else
and comes back at night through the stations
of the weary dream. . . . So often
during the day he asks about his golden kingdom,
afraid he may have forgotten something!
The hours: long lifeless journey.
The story he tells is a favorite bit of time,
a treasure stored in images that he's keeping
for his conference with death when it comes.
And the end of the story is this pause.

TRANSLATED BY LEWIS HYDE

Claudio Rodríguez ₂❧

SIEMPRE SERÁ MI AMIGO...

Siempre será mi amigo no aquel que en primavera
sale al campo y se olvida entre el azul festejo
de los hombres que ama, y no ve el cuero viejo
tras el nuevo pelaje, sino tú, verdadera

amistad, peatón celeste, tú, que en el invierno
a las claras del alba dejas tu casa y te echas
a andar, y en nuestro frío hallas abrigo eterno
y en nuestra honda sequía la voz de las cosechas.

EUGENIO DE LUELMO

Que vivió y murió junto al Duero

I

Cuando amanece alguien con gracia, de tan sencillas
como a su lado son las cosas, casi
parecen nuevas, casi
sentimos el castigo, el miedo oscuro
de poseer. Para esa
propagación inmensa del que ama
floja es la sangre nuestra. La eficacia de este hombre,
sin ensayo, el negocio
del mar que eran sus gestos, ola a ola,
flor y fruto a la vez, y muerte, y nacimiento
al mismo tiempo, y ese gran peligro
de su ternura, de su modo de ir

WHO WILL BE MY FRIEND ALWAYS...

Not he who in spring goes out to the field
and loses himself in the blue festivities
of men whom he loves, and is blind to the old
leather beneath the fresh down, shall be my friend always

but you, true friendship, celestial pedestrian who in winter
leave your house in the breaking dawn and set out
on foot, and in our cold find eternal shelter
and in our deep drought the voice of the harvests.

TRANSLATED BY W. S. MERWIN

EUGENIO DE LUELMO

Who lived and died near the Duero

I

When someone wakens with grace, so simple
are the things beside him, they almost
seem new, we almost
feel the judgment, the dark fear
of possession. Our blood
is too thin to pass on the immensity
of someone who loves. The worthiness of this man,
untested, his actions equal
the business of the sea, wave after wave,
both flower and fruit, and death, and birth
at once, and the great hazard
of his tenderness, of his style of walking

por las calles, nos daban
la única justicia: la alegría.
Como quien fuma al pie
de un polvorín sin darse cuenta, íbamos con él
y, como era tan fácil
de invitar, no veíamos
que besaba al beber y que al hacerle trampas
en el tute, más en el mus, jugaba
de verdad, con sus cartas
sin marca. El, cuyo oficio sin horario
era la compañía, ¿cómo iba
a saber que su Duero
es mal vecino?

2

Caminos por ventilar
que oreó con su asma,
son de tambores del que él hizo arrullo
siendo de guerra, leyes que dividían
a tajo hombre por hombre
de las que él hizo injertos para poblar su agrio
vacío no con saña,
menos con propaganda,
sino con lo más fértil: su llaneza,
todo ardía en el horno de sus setenta y dos años.
Allí todo era llama
siempre atizada, incendio sin cenizas
desde el sueldo hasta el hijo,
desde las canas hasta la ronquera,
desde la pana al alma. Como alondra
se agachaba al andar, y se le abría un poco
el compás de las piernas, con el aire
del que ha cargado mucho (tan distinto
del que monta a caballo o del marino).
Apagada la oreja,
oliendo a cal, a arena, a vino, a sebo,

the streets, gave us
the one justice: joy.
Like someone in the dark smoking
beside a powder keg, we trailed after him
and, because he couldn't say no,
we didn't see
that he kissed as he drank and though he was cheated
at Blackjack and even worse at Hearts, he played
truly, with unmarked
cards. He, whose business without hours
was companionship, how could
he know his Duero
is a bad neighbor?

2

Roads he took,
to ease his asthma,
the drumrolls he turned to lullabys
although they were the drums of war, laws that cut
man from man,
of which he made graftings to stock his bitter
emptiness not with fury,
less with propaganda,
but with what is most fertile: his simplicity,
all of these fuel for the oven of his seventy-two years.
There everything was fire
flaring up always, burning without ashes
from his wages to his child,
from his white hairs to his hoarse throat,
from his denims to his soul. He stooped
like a lark when he walked, and the measure
of his stride opened a bit, with the air
of one who has carried many loads (so different
from the horseman or the sailor).
His hearing burned out,
smelling of whitewash, sand, wine, tallow,

iba sin despedida:
todo él era retorno.
Esa velocidad conquistadora
de su vida, su sangre
de lagartija, de águila, y de perro,
se nos metían en el cuerpo como
música caminera. Ciegos para el misterio
y, por lo tanto, tuertos
para lo real, ricos solo de imágenes
y solo de recuerdos, ¿cómo vamos ahora
a celebrar lo que es suceso puro,
noticia sin historia, trabajo que es hazaña?

3

No bajo la cabeza,
Eugenio, aunque yo bien sé que ahora
no me conocerían ni aún en casa.
La muerte no es un río, como el Duero,
ni tampoco es un mar. Como el amor, el mar
siempre acaba entre cuatro
paredes. Y tú, Eugenio, por mil cauces
sin crecida o sequía,
sin puentes, sin mujeres
lavando ropa, ¿en qué aguas
te has metido?
Pero tú no reflejas, como el agua;
como tierra, posees.
Y el hilván de estas calles
de tu barriada al par del río,
y las sobadas briscas,
y el dar la mano sin dar ya verano
ni realidad, ni vida
a mansalva, y la lengua
ya tonta de decir "adiós," "adiós,"
y el sol ladrón y huído,
y esas torres de húmeda

he went without goodbyes:
all of him a constant coming back.
The winning speed
of his life, his blood
of lizard, of eagle, of dog,
seeped into our bodies like
the music of the road. Blind to the mysterious
and therefore with one eye only
on the actual, rich only in images
and remembered things, how can we now
celebrate what is pure happening,
heroic work, tidings without history?

3

I'm not lowering my head,
Eugenio, and I'm sure
that no one would know me, even at home.
Death is not a river, like the Duero,
neither is it a sea. Like love, the sea
always ends between four
walls. And you, Eugenio, down a thousand riverbeds
without flood or drought,
without bridges, without women
washing clothes, what waters
have you gotten into?
But you're not given to reflection like water;
you possess, like earth.
And the raw stitches of these streets
of your neighborhood alongside the river,
and the thumb-worn hands of cards,
and this giving a handshake without giving summer
or reality, or life
without danger, and the tongue
gone dumb from saying "goodbye," "goodbye,"
and the sun a thief slipping off,
and these towers of damp

pólvora, de calibre
perdido, y yo, con este aire de primero de junio
que hace ruido en mi pecho,
y los amigos... Mucho,
en poco tiempo mucho ha terminado.
Ya cuesta arriba o cuesta abajo,
hacia la plaza o hacia tu taller,
todo nos mira ahora
de soslayo, nos coge
fuera de sitio.
Nos da como vergüenza
vivir, nos da vergüenza
respirar, ver lo hermosa
que cae la tarde. Pero
por el ojo de todas las cerraduras del mundo
pasa tu llave, y abre
familiar, luminosa,
y así entramos en casa
como aquel que regresa de una cita cumplida.

explosives, the force
lost, and I, with this wind of the beginning of June
crashing in my chest,
and our friends . . . Much,
so much has ended in a little time.
Uphill or down,
toward the plaza or toward your shop,
everything sneaks a look at us
now, catching us
out of place.
To be alive shames us
a little, it shames us
to breathe, to see how beautifully
the evening ends. But
through the eye of all the world's locks
your key passes, and it opens
friendly, shining,
and we come home
like someone returning from an appointment fulfilled.

TRANSLATED BY PHILIP LEVINE

ESPUMA

Miro la espuma, su delicadeza
que es tan distinta a la de la ceniza.
Como quien mira una sonrisa, aquella
por la que da su vida y le es fatiga
y amparo, miro ahora la modesta
espuma. Es el momento bronco y bello
del uso, el roce, el acto de la entrega
creándola. El dolor encarcelado
del mar, se salva en fibra tan ligera;
bajo la quilla, frente al dique, donde
existe amor surcado, como en tierra
la flor, nace la espuma. Y es en ella
donde rompe la muerte, en su madeja
donde el mar cobra ser, como en la cima
de su pasión el hombre es hombre, fuera
de otros negocios: en su leche viva.
A este pretil, brocal de la materia
que es manantial, no desembocadura,
me asomo ahora, cuando la marea
sube, y allí naufrago, allí me ahogo
muy silenciosamente, con entera
aceptación, ileso, renovado
en las espumas imperecederas.

FOAM

I watch the foam, its delicacy nothing
like the delicacy of ashes.
I'm like a man who looks at a smile
he would give his life for, that wears him out
and warms him—I look now
at the unassuming foam.
              It is the wild
and beautiful moment of spending itself,
of contact, the act of abandonment,
self-form. The locked-in grief of the sea
breaks free on just so light a thread;
under the keel, facing the dock, wherever
love is plowed, like a flower on the earth
foam is born. And it's in foam
that death erupts, in foam's loose skein
that the sea has its fullness of being,
as at the height of his passion
man is man, whatever else he may be:
in the living cream.
And at this rail, parapet made of the stuff
which is the source and not the mouth,
I lean out now as the tide
comes in, and there I founder, there I drown
in utter silence, utter
acceptance, unharmed, made whole again
in the imperishable foam.

TRANSLATED BY ROBERT MEZEY

GORRIÓN

No olvida. No se aleja
este granuja astuto
de nuestra vida. Siempre
de prestado, sin rumbo,
como cualquiera, aquí anda,
se lava aquí, tozudo,
entre nuestros zapatos.
¿Qué busca en nuestro oscuro
vivir? ¿Qué amor encuentra
en nuestro pan tan duro?
Ya dió al aire a los muertos
este gorrión, que pudo
volar, pero aquí sigue,
aquí abajo, seguro,
metiendo en su pechuga
todo el polvo del mundo.

TIEMPO MEZQUINO

Hoy con el viento del Norte
me ha venido aquella historia.
Mal andaban por entonces
mis pies y peor mi boca
en aquella ciudad de hosco
censo, de miseria y de honra.
Entre la vieja costumbre
de rapiña y de lisonja,
de pobre encuesta y de saldo
barato, iba ya muy coja
mi juventud. ¿Por qué lo hice?

SPARROW

He doesn't forget. Shrewd waif,
he doesn't move off
one step from our life. Always
on borrowed time, aimless
like anyone else, there he goes,
stubbornly washing himself
between our shoes.
What's he looking for in the darkness
of our living? What love
can he hope to find in our hard bread?
Already gave the dead away to the air,
this sparrow,
who could have flown but stays on
here below, trusting,
filling his breast
with all the dust of the world.

TRANSLATED BY ROBERT MEZEY

PETTY TIME

Today with the north wind
that story came back to me.
Things went badly for me in those days
and my mouth worse,
in that city with its
thinning herd, its poverty
and its good name.
What with the old traditions
of fawning and stealing you blind,
the bored interview
and the cheap rummage sale, my youth
went on one leg. And for what?

Me avergüenzo de mi boca
no por aquellas palabras
sino por aquella boca
que besó. ¿Qué tiempo hace
de ello? ¿Quién me lo reprocha?
Un sabor a almendra amarga
queda, un sabor a carcoma;
sabor a traición, a cuerpo
vendido, a caricia pocha.

Ojalá el tiempo tan solo
fuera lo que se ama. Se odia
y es tiempo también. Y es canto.
Te odié entonces y hoy me importa
recordarte, verte enfrente
sin que nadie nos socorra
y amarte otra vez, y odiarte
de nuevo. Te beso ahora
y te traiciono ahora sobre
tu cuerpo. ¿Quién no negocia
con lo poco que posee?
Si ayer fue venta, hoy es compra;
mañana, arrepentimiento.
No es la sola hora la aurora.

I'm ashamed of my mouth
not for its words
but for a mouth that
it kissed. How long ago
was that? And who blames me?
All I have left is a taste
of bitter almond, a taste of gall,
of treachery, the body
sold out, the spoiled caress.

I wish to God that time
were merely what we love. We hate
and that's time too. And poems.
I hated you then and today I have to
remember you, I have to have you
in front of me, with no one to help us out,
and love you once more and hate you
once more. I kiss you now
and I betray you now, on top of
your body. Everyone does business
as best he can with the little he has.
If yesterday was selling, today is buying;
tomorrow, repentance.
Dawn isn't the only time of day.

TRANSLATED BY ROBERT MEZEY

CENIZA EN OXFORD

Os miro,
y veo despojados vuestros jóvenes cuerpos,
y apenas reconozco vuestras antiguas diferencias.
Sólo algún diente de metal, porque aquellas sonrisas
se han transformado en el horror de un bostezo profundo.
Tampoco reconozco la distinción de vuestra raza,
hecha de timidez y de rapiña,
mientras mi voz os suena funeral, en la distancia breve
que va de un esqueleto a otro esqueleto.
Porque os hablo de un muerto,
de alguien que está alojado en la humedad perpetua,
y no es verdad que esté más vivo que nosotros,
como pretendo aseguraros.
Cae ceniza detrás de las ventanas,
muertas hojas sin savia, y el espectro del cielo
sin color.

(Tan sólo un poderoso cadáver que soñara
nos pudiera crear de esta manera.)

ASHES IN OXFORD

Looking at you
I see young bodies stripped of everything,
and I can hardly tell the old faces apart.
Only a metal tooth, here and there. Those grins
have opened into the horror of a bottomless yawn.
I can't tell now what made you a different race of people,
timidity in the bird of prey.
And all this time my voice comes to you like a dead man's
           over the short distance
that keeps one skeleton away from another.
Because I am speaking to you about a dead man,
someone lodged in perpetual dampness,
and I am lying to you when I try to make you believe
that he is more alive than we are.

Ashes settle on the other side of the windows,
dead leaves drained of sap, and the sky a ghost
all color gone out of it.

(Only a dead man with a lot of power could have made us
like this, in one of his dreams.)

Translated by Hardie St. Martin

EL DOLOR

La niña,
con los ojos dichosos,
iba—rodeada
de luz, su sombra por las viñas—
a la mar.
Le cantaban los labios,
su corazón pequeño le batía.
Los aires de las olas
volaban su cabello.

Un hombre, tras las dunas,
sentado estaba,
al acecho del mar.
Reconocía la miseria humana
en el gemido de las olas,
la condición reclusa de los vivos
aullando de dolor,
de soledad, ante un destino ciego.
Absorto las veía
llegar del horizonte, eran
el profundo cansancio del tiempo.

Oyó, sobre la arena,
el rumor de unos pies
detenidos.
Ladeó la cabeza, pesadamente
volvió los ojos:
la sombría visión que imaginara
viró con él, todavía prendida,
con esfuerzo.
Y el joven vio que el rostro
de la niña
envejecía misteriosamente.

GRIEF

With eyes happy
the small girl
surrounded by light
was on her way to the sea,
her shadow falling among the vines.
Her lips were singing,
her small heart beating fast.
The breezes from the waves
blew her hair.

Behind the dunes
sat a man, spying on the sea.
In the moan of the waves
he recognized human misery,
the secluded condition of those alive
howling with grief,
loneliness, before a blind fortune.
Absorbed, he watched the waves
coming in from the horizon, they were
the deep-seated weariness of time.

He heard the rustle
of feet stopping
on the sand,
tilted his head, turned
his eyes, heavy-laden;
the gloomy vision he was imagining
turned with him,
still holding on to him.
And the young man saw how the child's face
grew old mysteriously.

Con ojos abrasados
miró hacia el mar: las aguas
eran fragor, ruina.
Y humillado vio un cielo
que, sin aves, estallaba de luz.
Dentro le dolía una sombra
muy vasta y fría.
Sintió en la frente un fuego:
con tristeza se supo
de un linaje de esclavos.

He looked toward the sea
with burning eyes: the waters
were crashing down, a ruin.
And humbled, he saw a birdless sky
erupting into light.
Inside him a vast cold shadow hurt.
On his forehead he felt a fire:
sadly realized
he came from a line of slaves.

TRANSLATED BY DAVID IGNATOW

MIRÁNDOSE

Así que el hombre ha hundido su barbilla en la mano,
y ha cerrado los ojos para ver
el humo de su vida,
tan sólo ha visto sucesión de gestos, cansados pasos, sombras
y sombras:
allá, en un punto de su vida, algún terror,
y, más terrible aún, las alegrías ahora vanas.
Y a unas sombras que pugnan por formar de nuevo el bulto
(son las que fueron para él más vivas
que aquella misma vida suya),
en la memoria las derriba el tiempo.

Abre los ojos, en torno de su cuarto,
y es noche oscura.
De nuevo deja la barbilla humosa
caer en el estrago de la mano.
De toda aquella vana polvareda
sólo un dolor pervive,
que rompe las cadenas, en su pecho, de una bestia de fuego.
La vida muerde aún,
mientras la sombra de la tarde viene
para apagarle su dolor,
su vida toda.

Y un aire llega que deshace el humo.

HAVING SUNK HIS CHIN IN HIS HAND

Having sunk his chin in his hand
and closed his eyes to see
the smoke of his life
he has seen only gestures, tired footsteps, shadows
and shadows:
there, at a point in his life, some terror,
and even more terrifying, the good times now of no use to him.
And some shadows struggling to reform in his mind
as time collapses them in memory—
these more vivid to him than the life itself.

He opens his eyes on the room around him
and the night is dark.
Again he lets his smoky chin
fall into the ruin of his hand.
Out of all that vain smokedrift
only a grief survives
that breaks the chains of a fiery beast in his chest.
Life yet can kill,
while the shadow of late afternoon comes
to put out his grief,
his whole life.

And a wind comes to dissolve the smoke.

TRANSLATED BY DAVID IGNATOW

EL MENDIGO

Extraño, en esta noche, he recordado
una borrada imagen. El mendigo
de mi niñez, de rostro hirsuto, torna
desde otro mundo su mirada dura.
Llegaba al mediodía, y un gruñido
de animal viejo le anunciaba. (Toda
la casa estaba abierta, y el verano
llegaba de la mar.) Andaba el niño
con temor a la puerta, y en su mano
depositaba una moneda. Era
hosca la voz, los ojos fríos de odio,
y sentía un gran miedo al acercarme,
la piedad disipada. Violenta
la muerte me rondaba con su sombra.
Sólo después, al ver a los mayores
hablar indiferentes, ya de vuelta,
se serenaba el pecho. Me quedaba
cerca de la ventana, y frente al mar
recordaba las sombrías historias.

Esta noche, pasado tanto tiempo,
su presencia terrible y misteriosa
me ha desvelado el sueño. Ningún daño
he sufrido de aquella voluntad,
y el hombre ya habrá muerto, miserable
como vivió. Aquellos años, otros,
muchos mendigos iban por las casas
del pueblo. Todos, sin venganza, yacen.
Los extinguió el olvido. Vagas, rotas,
surgen sus sombras: la memoria turba
un reino frío y solitario y vasto.
Poderosos, ahora me devuelven
la mísera limosna: la piedad
que el hombre, cada día, necesita

THE BEGGAR

Strange, tonight I've remembered
an image I'd blotted out. The beggar
from my childhood, with his hairy face, turns
his hard gaze on me from the other world.
He used to come at noon; you could hear him
grunting like an old animal. (The whole
house stood open, and summer
drifted up from the sea.) The child would go
to the door fearfully and deposit a coin
in his hand. His voice was sullen
and his eyes cold with hate,
and I felt very frightened when I got close to him;
my pity vanished. Violent
death enveloped me in its shadow.
Only afterward when I went inside and saw
the grownups had come back and were talking, unconcerned,
did my heart calm down. I stayed
near the window and, facing the sea,
remembered gruesome stories.

Tonight, so many years later,
his terrible and mysterious presence
has kept me from sleep. No harm
have I suffered from my benevolence,
and the man must have died by now, as wretchedly
as he lived. During those years,
many other beggars passed by the houses
in the village. All are dead and bear no grudges.
Neglect extinguished them. Restless, broken,
their ghosts rise up; memory disturbs
a kingdom that is cold and lonely and vast.
Powerful beings, they now repay
my puny alms: the pity
that man needs each day

para seguir viviendo. Y aquel miedo
que de niño sentí, remuerde ahora
mi vida, su fracaso: un anciano
me miraba con ojos inocentes.

HAY UNA LUZ QUE
CUBRE TODO EL CAMPO

Hay una luz que cubre todo el campo
de sombra, y va a la noche. Reposan
los naranjos, y casas de abandono,
y los montes se tienden en la nada.
La paz está conmigo, no sucede
sino el sueño más libre de la dicha:
amo el vivir, y el mundo incomprensible.

Ya en los pueblos del llano, y en la costa
del mar oscilan luces rosas: queman,
antes que las estrellas, las ventanas.
El mar ha ennegrecido en lo lejano,
y se enciende la fiebre de la carne:
pues me llama al placer lo que allá vive.

to go on living. And that fear
I felt as a child gnaws now
at my life, its ruin: an ancient man
was watching me with innocent eyes.

TRANSLATED BY RACHEL BENSON

THERE IS A LIGHT THAT
SHROUDS THE WHOLE FIELD

There is a light that shrouds the whole field
with shadow and leads into night. The orange trees
rest, and the abandoned houses,
and the mountains stretch out in the emptiness.
Peace is with me, only the most innocent
dreams of happiness invade me:
I love living, and this world I don't understand.

Now in the villages on the plain, and along
the seacoast, rose-colored lights waver: they flame,
those windows, sooner than the stars.
The sea has blackened in the distance,
and a fever is kindling in my flesh:
whatever lives there summons me to pleasure.

TRANSLATED BY RACHEL BENSON

Carlos Sahagún

EN EL PRINCIPIO, EL AGUA

En el principio, el agua
abrió todas las puertas, echó las campanas al vuelo,
subió a las torres de la paz —eran tiempos de paz—,
bajó a los hombros de mi profesor
—aquellos hombros suyos tan metafísicos,
tan doctrinales, tan
florecidos de libros de Aristóteles—,
bajó a sus hombros, no os engaño,
y saltó por su pecho como un pájaro vivo.

Ah, no te olvido,
a ojos cerrados te recuerdo tapiando las ventanas,
sobre el papel en blanco de la vida
dejando caer tinteros y palabras de piedra.
Y era lo mismo: yo seguía puro;
los últimos de clase, los expulsados por llevar ternura
       en los bolsillos,
seguíamos puros como el viento.
Antes de Thales de Mileto,
mucho antes aún de que los filósofos fueran canon-
      izados,
cuando el diluvio universal,
el llanto universal,
y un cielo todavía universal,

el agua contraía matrimonio con el agua,
y los hijos del agua eran pájaros, flores, peces, árboles,
eran caminos, piedras, montañas, humo, estrellas.
Los hombres se abrazaban, uno a uno,
como corderos, las mujeres

IN THE BEGINNING

In the beginning, the water
opened all doors, it shouted from the housetops,
went up to the towers of peace—this was in peacetime—,
it landed on my teacher's shoulders
—those metaphysical shoulders of his,
so doctrinal, so
heavy with blossoms from Aristotle's books—,
it landed on his shoulders, I swear this happened,
and hopped across his chest like a live bird.

Oh I can't forget you,
I close my eyes and I remember you walling up windows,
dropping inkwells and words of stone
on the blank paper of my life.
And I remained pure, all the same;
those of us at the foot of the class, expelled for carrying
        tenderness in our pockets,
we remained pure as the wind.
Before Thales of Miletus,
long before philosophers were made into saints,
at the time of the Flood,
the universal weeping,
and a still universal heaven,

water entered into marriage with water,
and the sons of water were birds, flowers, fishes, trees,
they were roads, stones, mountains, smoke, stars.
Men hugged one another
like lambs, women

dormían sin temor, los niños todos
se proclamaban hijos de la alegría, hermanos
de la yerba más verde,
los animales se dejaban
llevar, no estaban solos —nadie estaba solo,
y era feliz el aire aun sin ponerse en movimiento,
y en el espejo de unas manos llenas de agua
iba a mirarse la esperanza, y estaba limpia, y sonreía.

(Aquí quisiera hablar, abrir un libro —aquí,
en este instante sólo—
de aquel poeta puro que sin cesar cantaba:
"El mundo está bien hecho, el mundo está
bien hecho, el mundo
está bien hecho..." —aquí, en este instante sólo—.)

¡Y cómo no iba a estar bien hecho,
si en aquel tiempo las palomas altas
se derretían como copos,
si era inocente amarse desesperadamente,
si las mañanas claras, recién lavadas, daban
su generoso corazón al hombre!

Aquello era la vida,
era la vida y empujaba,
                              pero,
cuando entraron los lobos, después, despacio, devorando,
el agua se hizo amiga de la sangre,
y en cascadas de sangre cayó, como una herida,
cayó sobre los hombres
desde el pecho de Dios, azul, eterno.

slept like babies, all the children
called themselves sons of joy, brothers
of greenest grass,
animals let themselves
be led along, they were not alone—no one was—,
and the air was happy even before it was set in motion,
and hope used to go look at itself in the mirror
of a handful of water, it was clean, and it smiled.

(Here I would like to open a book—here,
just for a second—
by that pure poet who sang without stopping:
"The world is well made, the world is
well made, the world
is well made . . ." —here, just for a second—.)

How could it not be well made,
when, at that time, the soaring pigeons
melted like flakes,
and loving one another desperately was something innocent,
and the clean mornings, freshly rinsed,
offered man their generous heart!

That was life,
it was life and it pushed ahead,
       but
afterward wolves came, stealthy, devouring,
water made friends with the blood
and poured down in bloody cataracts, like a wound,
poured down on men
from the blue, eternal breast of God.

TRANSLATED BY HARDIE ST. MARTIN

RÍO

El río adolescente se perdía en el llano,
gozosamente triste, como el corazón.
—Hölderlin

Le llamaron posguerra a este trozo de río,
a este bancal de muertos, a la ciudad aquella
doblada como un árbol viejo, clavada siempre
en la tierra lo mismo que una cruz. Y gritaron:
"¡Alegría! ¡Alegría!"
               Yo era un río naciente,
era un hombre naciente, con la tristeza abierta
como una puerta blanca, para que entrase el viento,
para que entrase y diera movimiento a las hojas
del calendario inmóvil... Castillos en el aire
y aun estando en el aire, derrumbados, los sueños
hechos piedra, maderas que no quieren arder,
rayos de sol manchando los cristales más puros,
altísimas palomas ya sin poder volar...

¿Lo estáis viendo? Vosotros, los que venís de lejos,
los que tenéis el brazo libre como las águilas
y lleváis en los labios una roja alegría,
pasad, miraos en mí, tened fe. Yo era un río,
yo soy un río, y llevo marcado a fuego el tiempo
del dolor bombardeado. Mi edad, mi edad de hombre,
sabedlo bien, un día se perderá en la tierra.

RIVER

The adolescent river was lost on the plain,
joyfully sad, like the heart.
—Hölderlin

They named this stretch of river Postwar,
this plot of the dead, city bent
like an old tree, always stuck
in the ground like a cross. And they shouted:
"Joy! Joy!"
           I was a river being born,
I was a man being born, with my sadness open
like a white door, for the wind to come in,
for it to come in and set in motion the leaves
of the motionless calendar. . . . Castles in the air
and even being in air, knocked down, dreams
turned to stone, chunks of wood that refused to burn,
sunlight staining the clearest windows,
the highest pigeons unable to fly . . .

Are you watching? You, who come from far away,
who have an arm as free as eagles
and wear a red joy on your lips,
come in, look at yourselves in me, have faith. I was a river,
I am a river, I carry branded on me the time
of bombed-out sorrow. My years, my years as man,
know it well, will some day disappear into the ground.

              TRANSLATED BY DAVID IGNATOW

AQUÍ EMPIEZA LA HISTORIA

Aquí empieza la historia. Fue una tarde
en que se habían puesto las palomas
más blancas, más tranquilas. Como siempre
salí al jardín. Alrededor no había
nadie: la misma flor de ayer, la misma
paz, las mismas ventanas, el sol mismo.
Alrededor no había nadie: un árbol,
un estanque, ceniza en aquel monte
lejano. Alrededor no había nadie.

Pero ¿qué es este viento, quién me coge
el corazón y lo levanta en vilo,
y lo hunde y lo levanta en vilo? Una
muchacha azul en la orfandad del aire
ordenaba los pájaros. Sus manos
acariciaban con piedad el árbol,
y el estanque, y aquel lejano monte
ceniciento. El jardín ardía al sol.

La miré. Nada. La miré de nuevo,
y nada, y nada. Alrededor, la tarde.

THE STORY BEGINS HERE

The story begins here. It was an afternoon
when the pigeons had turned more white,
more quiet. I went out into the garden
as usual. There was no one
around: the same flower as yesterday, the same
peace, the same windows, and the sun the same.
There was no one around: a tree,
a reservoir, ashes on the hill
out there. There was no one around.

But what is this wind, who takes hold
of my heart and lifts it into the air,
lowers and then lifts it into the air?
A blue girl sets the birds in order
in the orphanage of the air. Her hands
stroked the tree with pity,
and the reservoir, and the ashy hill
out there. The garden was burning in the sun.

I looked at her. Nothing. I looked at her again,
and nothing, nothing. Around me the afternoon.

TRANSLATED BY DAVID IGNATOW

FOTOGRAFÍA DE NIÑO

Cuando un niño nos mira serio
y en pie desde el retrato,
no queremos saber que ha sido
dueño de nuestros años.

Le volvemos la espalda, porque
no queremos tenerlo
tan cerca de nosotros, hombres
que ya no comprendemos.

Como a un extraño le decimos:
"Aparta, no es tu tierra
ésta que piso yo de ángeles
perdidos en la niebla.

Si te pusieron en la frente
mala ceniza un día,
cierra los ojos, porque ya
no podrás con la vida.

Angel cargado de blancura,
mirabas a lo alto,
pero un golpe fatal de arena
todo lo ha derribado.

El soldado de plomo, el caballo,
el barco de papel...
La vida es como un río grande.
No debimos crecer.

Nos arrastran como a aquel árbol
que el leñador cortó.
La primavera se ha perdido
para tu corazón."

PHOTOGRAPH OF A BOY

When a boy, serious and standing,
looks at us from a photograph
we don't want to know
he is owner of our years.

We turn our back on him,
we don't want him
so close to us
who no longer understand.

As if he were a stranger,
we tell him, "Go away,
this fogbound angels' country
we walk in is not yours.

"If one day they placed evil ashes
on your forehead
close your eyes, because
life already will be too much for you.

"Angel laden with whiteness,
you looked into the sky,
but a deadly sandstrike
knocked down everything.

"The lead soldier, the horse,
the paper boat . . .
Life is like a great river.
We shouldn't have grown up.

"We're dragged along like that tree
the woodsman cuts down.
In your heart
Spring has been lost."

Y nos sigue mirando serio
el niño, ese retrato.
Y se quiere venir con nosotros
cuando nos alejamos.

DE LA VIDA EN PROVINCIAS

Si es difícil trepar por la cucaña
a cuerpo descubierto, aún más difícil
resulta de este modo: acompañado
de un perro y de paraguas para el perro,
y de remilgos y renunciamientos.
Pero el esfuerzo humano siempre vence
cuando desde la cuna han preparado
al hijo del converso para el triunfo:
abdicar, doblegarse, sonreír,
darse al mejor postor con voluntad
de servicio, aceptar humildemente
las migajas del gran festín, ¿qué son
sino el más puro ejemplo de hidalguía
española? Ofenderse, rechazar,
protestar, rebelarse ante lo injusto,
¿no son más bien ideas foráneas, algo
orquestado por mentes extranjeras,
ay, para nuestro daño?
                    Nuestro hombre
lo entiende así, y separa blandamente
la espiga y la cizaña, porque piensa
que está llamado a puestos responsables,
cuando exista vacante, cualquier día.
Por ello se prepara ardientemente,
viste ya trajes preministeriales,
y escucha, ausculta el variar del viento,

And the boy, that photograph,
continues looking at us seriously.
And wants to come with us
when we go away.

TRANSLATED BY DAVID IGNATOW

LIFE IN THE PROVINCES

If it's hard to climb the greased pole
stripped to the waist, it's twice as hard
going up with a dog,
an umbrella for the dog,
a tight ass and a small mouth.
But human effort always does the trick
when the convert's son has been raised
from the cradle to his consummation:
to bow and scrape and smile,
to sell himself to the highest bidder
body and soul, humbly accepting
the crumbs from the banquet table—what's this
but the purest example of Spanish
chivalry? To be indignant, to say no,
to cry out and struggle against injustice,
these are foreign notions, aren't they?
something cooked up by foreign minds
to poison ours.
                    Our man
sees it that way, and cautiously separates
the wheat from the chaff, for he thinks
important positions are waiting for him,
when there's an opening, any day now.
He trains religiously for this,
already he wears the gray suits of his superiors,
and he listens, and tests which way the wind blows,

no en las altas esferas de Fray Luis,
sino en las más prosaicas de un imperio
de gángsters mediocres. Mientras tanto,
se esfuerza, toma aliento y, poco a poco,
trepa por la cucaña provinciana,
eso sí, acompañado de su perro,
y su paraguas, y su pañuelito,
su flor en el ojal, su tontería.

not in the high realms of Fray Luis de León
but in the backwaters of a government
of mediocre racketeers. And meanwhile
he keeps trying, takes heart, and little by little
mounts the provincial pole,
yes he does, along with his dog
and his umbrella,
his pocket handkerchief,
his buttonhole flowers,
and all his bullshit.

TRANSLATED BY ROBERT MEZEY

IN MEMORIAM

A una profesora de Historia

Aprendí
la interminable lista
de reyes godos y el mundo
no fue mío
   ni tu historia
violeta como tus ojeras de doncella

si acaso
en las cálidas tardes con principiante trompeta
como fondo melódico
tu mano de profesora culta
dividió mi mundo proletario

       saber o no saber

la cuestión era aceptar
un blanco destino de burócrata
o emigrar al mundo
de los que nada habían perdido
nunca, ni tan siquiera cuando
cruzó el estrecho el último rey godo

fabulosas tus historias de hijos
buenos, redentores de su madre
lavandera, cajeros de Banco, aspirantes
a directores de Banco, asépticos
buenos, higiénicos, sin remordimientos

IN MEMORIAM

For a history teacher

I learned
the interminable list
of the kings of the Visigoths and the world
was not mine
              neither was your history
violet as the circles under your girlish eyes

if by chance
in the warm afternoons with the trumpet starting up
background music
your well-bred teacher's hand
severed my working class world

                      to know or not to know

the question was to accept
the colorless destiny of a clerk
or emigrate to the world
of those who had never lost
anything, not even when
the last king of the Visigoths crossed the Strait

fantastic your stories of good
sons, redeemers of their mother
the washerwoman—bank tellers, dreaming
of the Board of Directors, germless,
righteous, hygienic, without regrets

inútil historia la de mi clase,
por ti y por mí desconocida entonces
cuando eras una princesa omnipotente
y yo tu juglar de versos vergonzosos
                                    ni siquiera
conocedor de tu sexo, ni tu tiempo

pasaron rápidos años como tardes,
aprendí tu lista y tu frontera, tu nombre
tu nostalgia y cuando acaso
tenía respuesta a tus palabras
incluso a tu bella patraña de hijos —godos
reyes—buenos
                    ya era tarde

Y te enterraron ignorante de mi sabiduría
que tú empezaste y nadie concluirá,
de mi amor de juglar
                        princesa de un Historia
nada dialéctica, por la que tú pasaste
como pasa un rey bueno, con majestad.

useless the history of my class
unknown to either of us in those days
when you were an omnipotent princess
and I your minstrel of shy verses

$\qquad\qquad\qquad\qquad$ not even
familiar with your sex, or your times

the years passed quickly like afternoons,
I learned your lists and your frontiers, your name
your nostalgia and when I was almost
ready to answer your words
including your beautiful fairy tale of good
sons Visigoth kings

$\qquad\qquad\qquad$ it was too late

and you were buried before you knew about my learning
which you began and no one will ever finish,
of my minstrel's love

$\qquad\qquad\qquad\qquad$ princess of a history not even
vaguely dialectical, through which you moved
magnificent, like a great king.

$\qquad\qquad\qquad\qquad$ TRANSLATED BY ROBERT MEZEY

VERANO Y HUMO

Ya sabemos lo que cuesta
vencer la resistencia tenaz
de dos piernas unidas
     el sabor
de algún aliento amargó el aire
de madrugada en nuestras fauces
y el cuerpo resultó torpe al despertar
o se quejó triste por un frío olvidado

y sin embargo
más de una vez se nos otoñizan los árboles,
brilla la calle bajo la lluvia amarilla,
damos lumbre a un paseante solitario
por el puerto
    y silbamos una melodía
ramplona, ya tarde, cuando los veleros
mienten puertos ansiados y el aire
salino no pregunta
      ¿quién,
quién no teme perder lo que no ama?

SUMMER AND SMOKE

Now we know what it costs
to beat down the bitter resistance
of two locked legs
    the taste
of someone's breath embittered the air
of the small hours in our throat
and the body felt sluggish waking up
or sadly mourned for some forgotten coldness

and nevertheless
more than once the trees grow through autumn for us
the street glistens under the yellow rain
we give some lonesome walker
of the waterfront a light
    and whistle a rough
tune, already late, while the sailboats
lie about the longed-for ports and the salt
air doesn't ask
   who?
who's not afraid to lose what he doesn't love?

TRANSLATED BY ROBERT MEZEY

GAUGUIN

Periodista
su padre
escribió artículos notables
la libertad —decía—
es una dignidad popular
y sin embargo
murió rumbo a Lima
donde Pablo cumpliría once años
una mañana —a las once y cuarto—
de junio
       mil ochocientos cincuenta y nueve

marinero
después en un buque de carga
descubrió los olores
el salazón las brumas de Bretaña
siempre amaría
las bajamares infinitas
          entonces
cuando parece que la huida
del mar lleva consigo
nuestros males oscuros
         la ira abstracta

pero todavía
sirvió en las filas de aquel ejército
que no supo cortar
el avance prusiano
       —Bismarck comentaba
que el soldado francés era cobarde
y tan ligero como su ropa interior—
          nada experto
en socialismo utópico
recordaría tal vez a su padre
        cuando

GAUGUIN

His journalist
father
wrote some remarkable articles
liberty—he said—
is the dignity of the people
notwithstanding
he died on his way to Lima
where Paul would turn eleven
one morning—11:15—
June
   1859

later
deck hand on a merchantman
he discovered the smells
seasonings mists of Brittany
he would always love
the vast stretch of low tide
                        that moment
when the retreat of the sea
seems to carry off
our shadowy ills
              abstract rage

but still
he served in the ranks of that army
that had no way of stopping
the Prussian advance
              —Bismarck remarked
that the French soldier is a coward
and as lightweight as his underwear—
                     knowing nothing
of utopian socialism
perhaps he would think of his father
                when

el ejército de Thiers fusilaba
a los redactores del Journal Official

no muy al día
nunca supo que Marx
                 —judío alemán—
hubiera escrito "...esos mártires
han penetrado en el gran corazón
de la clase obrera"
                 inútil aclararlo:
eran los días de la Commune

               atraído
por los café concierto
la sensación caldosa del buen mundo
Gauguin quiso tener faltriquera
y el suelo firme
para una sombra por todos respetada

pintaba los domingos paisajes inseguros
                 —el impresionismo
ya no era una pirueta y las duquesas
de la tercera república tenían su Monet—
durante la semana
era un probo agente bursátil
muy alabado por M. Arosa
coleccionista de Pissaro y gran connaisseur

en la agencia de cambio Bertin
le describen como un joven severo
de impecable levita y bigote
algo provocativo pero correcto
hasta el bostezo
               incluso algo lento
en las respuestas como los pajes
o los gobernadores del Banco de Francia

Thiers' army was emptying its rifles
into the editors of the Official Journal

not very hip
he never knew that Marx
     —the German Jew—
had written ". . . those martyrs
are lodged in the great heart
of the working class"
     useless to try to explain:
those were the days of the Commune

    drawn
by cabaret music
the cozy sensation of high society
Gauguin wanted some cash in his pockets
and his feet on the ground
to cast a shadow everyone would respect

Sundays he painted hesitant landscapes
      —impressionism
no longer a pirouette and the duchesses
of the Third Republic had their Monet—
during the week
he was an upright stockbroker
much praised by M. Arosa
collector of Pissaro and noted connoisseur

in the Bertin office
he is described as a severe young man
impeccable frock coat mustache
a bit provocative but polite
even to his yawn
    even a little slow
in his responses like the pages
or the Directors of the Bank of France

casado en Copenhague,
tuvo hijos y siguió pintando los domingos

en la Bolsa, aseguraban,
cada vez estaba más distante
y los clientes se complacían en la tristeza
por un joven antaño tan prometedor

nadie sabe cómo consiguiera romper el abrazo
mañanero de un cuerpo blando
y propicio aunque fétido el aliento
amanecido recuerde la elemental biología
que respalda al amor

                    ni cómo consiguiera
prescindir de las raíces
                —sus hijos
le tenían por un padre severo
pero humano, en suma un padre
de manual pedagógico finisecular—

viajero en Panamá
París, Bruselas o Bretaña
sus pinceles fueron debilitando
el cosquilleo de cualquier remordimiento
su derecho a la locura
fue ratificado por Vincent Van Gogh
aunque en Arlés todo demuestra que durmieron
en habitaciones separadas
                  en el café Voltaire
intentó comprender los versos que leía Mallarmé
Stéphane insistía
                c'était le jour beni
de ton premier baiser
                pero Gauguin
permanecía silencioso
                hubiera querido

married in Copenhagen
he had children and went on painting on Sundays

at the Bourse we are told
he grew steadily more remote
and the clients enjoyed commiserating
over this young man once so very promising

no one knows how he managed to break loose
from the early morning embrace
of that easy bland body though her bad breath
recalls the simple biology
that backs love up

                     nor how he managed
to forget his beginnings
                  —his sons
knew him for a strict father
but human, in short a father
out of a fin-de-siècle Manual Advice to Fathers—

traveling in Panama
Paris Brussels or Brittany
his brushes fought off
the prickles of any remorse
his right to madness
was confirmed by Vincent Van Gogh
although in Arles everything indicates that they slept
in separate rooms
                in the Café Voltaire
he tried to understand the poems Mallarmé read aloud
Stéphane was dogged
                  c'était le jour beni
de ton premier baiser
                but Gauguin
remained silent
            he would have liked

pintar aquellos versos mas no tenían
color ni tan siquiera una emoción humana

no bastaba
la huida de la Bolsa del desayuno
normativo
las mismas palabras se repiten
siempre si los cuerpos no cambian

en Tahití
las autoridades miran con recelo
al extranjero blanco amante de canacas
no entendieron que intentaba objetivar
lo subjetivo
         y que la animalidad
tierna de las canacas era casi el fin
del viaje vital de Paul Gauguin

desterrado a las Marquesas
conoció la cárcel por sospechoso
de no infundir sospechas
         en París
se le tenía por un snob empedernido
sólo algunas nativas conocían su impotencia
pasajera
         y que l'or de ses corps
               era un pretexto
para olvidar las negras sillerías de las lonjas
el cucú de un comedor de Copenhague
un viaje a Lima con una madre triste
las pedantes charlas del café Voltaire
           y sobre todo
los incomprensibles versos de Stéphane Mallarmé.

to paint those verses but they had no
color not even any human feeling

it wasn't enough
the flight from the Bourse from the
decorous breakfast
the same words repeated endlessly
while the flesh doesn't change

in Tahiti
the authorities look with mistrust
on the white foreigner lover of native girls
they didn't understand that he was trying to objectify
the subjective
              and that the tender
animal warmth of those girls was almost the end
of the road for Paul Gauguin

banished to the Marquesas
he was jailed on suspicion
of not inspiring suspicion
                  in Paris
he was put down as a hardened snob
only a few natives knew about his spells
of impotence
              and that "the gold of their bodies"
                            was a pretext
for not being forced to think
about the rows of black seats in the Stock Exchange
the cuckoo clock in that dining room in Copenhagen
the voyage to Lima the weeping of his mother
the pedantic smalltalk of the Café Voltaire
                       and above all
the incomprehensible poems of Stéphane Mallarmé.

TRANSLATED BY ROBERT MEZEY

YRAMÍN Y EL MAR

Mar sin marinos, ni buques fantasmas
inútilmente esperó
algún regreso
        no vuelve el tiempo
                ni las naves
del rey Mark con Iseo la Blanca
              y Tristán
puede bañarse de once a una entre Creixell
y Torredembarra o en el chamizo de cañas
sorber un granizado de planetas helados

                    la muchacha
lleva bikini y suda despacio,
habla de Alfredo,
de cuando Alfredo estuvo en las cruzadas
y al regreso traficó con camiones de harina,
                 bielas
o cojinetes, no precisamente para patinetes
de niños desdentados, en situación de crecer
o morirse de arrepentimiento

              algunos hijos
de madres anchas arenizan castillos de arena
junto al mar, exprimen limones
sobre los ojos blancos de almejas silenciosas

                más tarde
por el camino que bordea la antigua marisma
descienden
       pantalones tejanos y blusas amarillas
los diecisiete bárbaros de padres calvos, madres
de pies con manicura y amante malcriado
a la sombra de blancas villas con pararrayos,
geráneos tras las rejas y azuladas muchachas
con incipientes niños en ataúd de hule

YRAMÍN AND THE SEA

Sea without sailors, or phantom ships
he waited pointlessly
for someone to come back
          the time doesn't come twice
                    nor the ships
of King Mark with Iseult the Pale One
              and Tristan
can swim from eleven to one between Creixell
and Torredembarra or else suck on a snowcone
of frozen planets in a thatched hut

             the girl
wears a bikini and sweats lightly,
she talks of Alfred,
of when Alfred fought in the Crusades
and came back to go into business with trucks full of flour,
                connecting rods
or bearings, not exactly for the skates
of toothless kids, who happen to be growing up
or dying of remorse

        the offspring
of ample mothers are tamping sandcastles
by the sea, and squeezing lemon
on the blank eyes of speechless clams

           later
they go down the road that runs beside the ancient
swamp
      blue jeans and yellow blouses
the seventeen wild kids of bald fathers, mothers
with manicured feet and surly lovers
in the shade of white villas guarded by lightning rods,
geraniums behind the grilles, and uniformed girls
wheeling embryos in coffins of oilskin

hablan

de la aventura nocturna ayer, cuando
en las cámaras del mar bajo la encesa
se perpetró el cotidiano genocidio de los peces

ella se abrió como un humilde mejillón al calor
sobre la arena (la dejaron lavándose en el mar)

todo lo vio desde la terraza más alta
cuando seguía el rumbo de los astros
tal vez los mismos que en el cielo de Yramín
que nunca volvería
                que nunca huiría del rey Mark
porque Yramín también tenía un bikini
con topos amarillos y amantes en la playa

o tal vez sólo tuviera otros vientos, otras naves
otras velas,
           y una carta concisa que no quiso enviar.

they talk
of last night's adventures, when
in the chambers of the sea under the lure lights
the fish suffered their daily genocide

she spread herself open on the sand like a simple
mussel in the heat (they left her to wash herself off in the sea)

he saw it all from the highest terrace
while he followed the drift of the stars
perhaps the same that appeared in the sky of Yramín
who would never come back
                              who would never flee from King Mark
because Yramín also had a bikini
with yellow polka dots and lovers on the beach

or maybe she only had other winds, other ships
other sails
            and a curt letter she didn't want to mail.

                    TRANSLATED BY ROBERT MEZEY

In general, only the poet's most important or comprehensive books of poetry, accompanied by the earliest date of publication, appear after each biographical note. More than one date after a book title means that each new edition carried previously unpublished work. In the limited space allowed me, I make brief reference to the content and style of a poet's work only when he is new to English readers or when the selection of his poems in this anthology is too small to give a fair idea of his work.

RAFAEL ALBERTI (1902-   ) was born in Puerto de Santa María (Cádiz) where he studied in a Jesuit school until 1917, when his family moved to Madrid. There he discovered the Prado and decided to become a painter. He started writing four years later but it wasn't until 1923–1924, while living in the Guadarrama mountains to recover his health, that he wrote his first book of poems, *Marinero en tierra*, which won him the National Award (Antonio Machado was on the award committee). From then on he dedicated himself to literature, writing poetry and plays, although he never gave up his drawing entirely (he has recently had one-man shows of lithographs and drawings in important European art galleries). He took part in the student uprisings against the dictator Primo de Rivera in 1929 and that same year he wrote his first "social" poem, "Elegía cívica." In 1933 he recited some of his poems at political rallies. With the defeat of the Republicans in the Spanish Civil War, he left his country to live in exile, first in Argentina and now in Rome.

Marinero en tierra, 1924; *La amante, canciones*, 1925; *El alba de alhelí*, 1927; *Cal y canto*, 1929; *Sobre los ángeles*, 1929; *De un momento a otro*, 1937; *Entre el clavel y la espada*, 1941; *Pleamar*, 1944; *A la pintura*, 1948; *Retornos de lo vivo lejano*, 1952; *Ora marítima*, 1953; *Baladas y canciones del Paraná*, 1954; *Poesías completas*, 1961; *Roma, peligro para caminantes*, 1968; *Los ocho nombres de Picasso*, 1970; *Poesía*, 1972; *Canciones del Alto Valle del Aniniene*, 1972; *Desprecio y maravilla*, 1972.

VICENTE ALEIXANDRE (1898–) was born in Seville but spent most of his childhood in Malaga, moving to Madrid when he was eleven. There he studied business administration as well as law. In 1920 he taught in a business school and a year later took a job in a railroad company, where he remained until 1925. He had been writing poems for several years but only published his first poems in 1926, in *Revista de Occidente*, the cultural review founded by Ortega y Gasset. Like Alberti before him, Aleixandre moved into the Guadarrama mountain area because of poor health in 1925. During his two years there, he wrote his first book of poems, *Ámbito*. His early work seems detached and cold, but he discovered Freud and the French surrealists around 1928, and his poems took on freer form and tremendous passion. With the years his poetry turned from the dark corners of the subconscious to the light of the world outside. His book *Sombra del paraíso* was a turning point in Spanish poetry.

Ámbito, 1928; *Espadas como labios*, 1932; *Pasión de la tierra*, 1935; *La destrucción o el amor*, 1935; *Sombra del paraíso*, 1944; *Mundo a solas*, 1950; *Nacimiento último*, 1953; *Historia del corazón*, 1954; *Poesías completas*, 1960; *En un vasto dominio*, 1962; *Retratos con nombre*, 1965; *Obras completas* and *Poemas de la consumación*, 1968.

CARLOS BOUSOÑO (1923–), critic as well as poet, comes from Boal in the province of Asturias. He received his Ph.D. in philology from the University of Madrid, where he teaches. He has turned from an earlier poetry of spiritual exile and religious concern, conventional in form, to a less conservative poetry of philosophical contemplation, an examination of conscience. Bousoño has lectured in the United States and Mexico. He has received important awards for his poems and his criticism.

Subida al amor, 1945; *Primavera de la muerte*, 1946; *Noche del sentido*, 1957; *Poesías completas*, 1960; *Invasión de la realidad*, 1962; *Oda en la ceniza*, 1967; and *Las monedas contra la losa*, 1973.

FRANCISCO BRINES (1932–   ) has a degree in law from the University at Salamanca and one in philosophy and letters from Madrid University. He has lectured at Oxford and has received important awards for his poetry and outstanding critical attention, although his output is spare. His poems are introspective, poems of "moral meditation," written in search of self-knowledge. In his poems he tries to relive experiences that reveal his strong attachment to life and time, whose passing he vividly regrets.

Las brasas, 1960; *El Santo Inocente*, 1965; *Palabras a la oscuridad*, 1966; and *Aún no*, 1971.

GABRIEL CELAYA (1911–   ) is a novelist, essayist and translator as well as poet, whose real name is Rafael Múgica. Pablo Neruda was an early influence, but Celaya soon found a social voice and a style of his own. His language is intentionally simple, verging on the prosaic, and the structure of his poems is often very loose. This style has made him the whipping boy for the youngest generation of poets in Spain, who stress the esthetic in their standards. Celaya has received various awards for his poetry, in Spain and abroad. He has translated Rimbaud's *A Season in Hell*.

Tranquilamente hablando, 1947; *Las cosas como son*, 1949; *Las cartas boca arriba*, 1951; *Paz y concierto*, 1953; *Cantos iberos*, 1955; *De claro en claro*, 1956; *Las resistencias de diamante*, 1957; *Episodios nacionales*, 1962; *Poesía 1934–1961*, 1962; *Dos cantatas*, 1964; *Los espejos transparentes*, 1968; *Lírica de cámara* and *Operaciones poéticas*, 1971.

LUIS CERNUDA (1902–1963) was born in Seville, where he studied literature under Pedro Salinas. He taught at the University of Toulouse in 1928-1929. During the Spanish Civil War he went to Great Britain, where he remained until 1947, teaching at Cranleigh School in Surrey, at the University of Glasgow, and at Cambridge. He came to the United States to teach at Mount Holyoke College, 1947-1951, and moved to Mexico in 1952. He translated Shakespeare's *Troilus and Cressida* and some of Hölderlin's and some of Yeats's poems. His acute literary sensibility makes him the most original critic of his generation. For the young poets beginning to write in the later 1950's, he was the poète maudit who shared their bitterness and their feeling of being spiritual misfits in postwar Spain. Others were attracted by the eroticism in his poetry. He never returned to Spain and died in Mexico in 1963.

Perfil del aire, 1927; *Donde habite el olvido*, 1934; *La realidad y el deseo*, 1936, 1940, 1958, 1964 and 1965. The latter is the over-all title Cernuda gave his poetry, incorporating new poems or entire books of poems into each new edition.

GERARDO DIEGO (1896–), pianist as well as poet, has given many concert readings. He founded and edited the literary re-view *Carmen*, which was primarily a vehicle for the generation of 1925 or 1927, which included Salinas, Guillén, Lorca, Alberti, Aleixandre, Prados and Diego himself. Comfortable in traditional forms as well as a daring innovator who cultivated ultraism, creationism, and even surrealism, he shifts back and forth between these styles. The main value of his traditional poems, which are perfectly shaped, is their music. They are generally unexciting in translation, while the striking images of his experimental writing preserve their grace and surprise in English.

Imagen, 1922; *Soria*, 1923; *Manual de espumas*, 1924; *Versos humanos*, 1925; *Fábula de Equis y Zeda* and *Poemas adrede*, 1932; *Ángeles de Compostela*, 1940 and 1961; *Alondra de verdad*, 1941; *Primera antología de sus versos* (1918-1941), 1941; *Biografía in-completa*, 1956; *La suerte o la muerte*, 1963; *Segunda antología de sus versos* (1941-1967) and *Cementerio civil*, 1972.

LEÓN FELIPE (1884–1968) gave up his profession as pharmacist to become a professional actor. He published his first book of poems, *Versos y oraciones de caminante*, at the age of thirty-six. He went to the United States in 1923 and the following year became professor of Spanish, first at Columbia University and then at Cornell, 1925–1928. Mexico was his home from 1930 to 1934, when he returned to Spain for two years, until he went to Panama to teach at the University there. He was back in Spain in 1937 but left in 1938, never to return. Most of the rest of his life was spent in Mexico where he died at the age of eighty-four. He was a rough-voiced poet, hungry and thirsty for justice, who is closer to Whitman and the prophets of the Bible than to the Spanish tradition.

Versos y oraciones de caminante, 1920; *Versos y oraciones de caminante. Libro II*, 1930; *El hacha (Elegía española)*, 1939; *Español del éxodo y del llanto*, 1939; *Llamadme publicano*, 1950; *El ciervo*, 1958; *Obras completas*, 1963; *¡Oh, este viejo y roto violín!*, 1965.

GLORIA FUERTES (1918–   ). The publication in 1962 of . . . *Que estás en la tierra*, a selection of her work put together by Jaime Gil de Biedma, drew attention to Gloria Fuertes as a poet of significance. She had started her literary career as a writer of children's stories and poems, and her later work often retains the playful qualities of the nursery rhyme, but behind the lighthearted surface of many of her poems there is a seriousness that sometimes comes through to the unwary only on a second or third reading. There is something of the clown in her work, with sadness and personal suffering underlying the irony or the sympathy she expresses for the oppression and suffering of others. She has taught at various universities in the United States but now makes her home in Madrid. Her frequent readings are very popular.

Isla ignorada, 1950; *Canciones para niños*, 1952; *Antología poética y Poemas del suburbio*, 1954; *Aconsejo beber hilo*, 1954; *Pirulí*, 1955; *Todo asusta*, 1958; . . . *Que estás en la tierra*, 1962; *Ni tiro, ni veneno, ni navaja*, 1966; *Poeta de guardia*, 1968; *Como atar los bigotes del tigre*, 1969; *Antología poética* (*1950–1969*) and *Sola en la sala*, 1973.

FEDERICO GARCÍA LORCA (1898–1936) was born in Fuente Vaqueros, near Granada. As a child, he showed deep interest in music, learned to play the piano, and later on composed and sang his own songs. He was also fascinated by the theater and made up little plays that he performed for the family and friends. He liked to paint, and his drawings are filled with aerial grace. His first published book, *Impresiones y paisajes*, 1918, was prose. In 1920 his first play, *El maleficio de la mariposa*, was staged in Madrid where he had gone to live in 1919. He and the composer Manuel de Falla organized the Fiesta del Cante Jondo in Granada in 1922, where he read some of the poems that would appear later in his book *Poema del cante jondo*. Lorca came to New York in June 1929 and stayed until the following April. There he wrote most of *Poeta en Nueva York*. He started a traveling theater group, "La Barraca," in 1931 and toured Spain with it in 1932–1933. Almost all of his important plays (*Mariana Pineda, La zapatera prodigiosa, Bodas de sangre, Yerma, Doña Rosita la soltera*, and *La casa de Bernarda Alba*) contain lovely lyrics. Moved by the fatal goring of the bullfighter Ignacio Sánchez Mejías in 1934, Lorca wrote his extraordinary *Lament* to the matador, who had been a close friend. He read his last play, *La casa de Bernarda Alba*, to a group of friends in Madrid a month before the Spanish Civil War broke out. Two months later he was arrested and shot to death by the Nationalists, while on a visit to Granada.

Libro de poemas, 1921; *Canciones*, 1927; *Romancero gitano*, 1928 and 1940, when it included *Poema del cante jondo* and *Llanto por Ignacio Sánchez Mejías; Seis poemas galegos*, 1936; *Obras completas*, 1938–1943, 8 volumes, ed. Losada; *Poeta en Nueva York*, 1940; and *Obras completas*, 1954, 1968, ed. Aguilar.

JAIME GIL DE BIEDMA (1929–) was born in Barcelona and has spent most of his life there, except for the Spanish Civil War years, when he lived in Nava de la Asunción, a small town in the province of Segovia. He is a noted critic and translator. He has traveled a great deal and, being fluent in English, has an extensive first-hand knowledge of English and American literature. His poetry is a deliberate account of his moral and intellectual development. There is always a personal awareness in his poems, whether their content be social criticism or erotic love, as in his later work, which has influenced some of the newest poets.

Según sentencia del tiempo, 1953; *Compañeros de viaje*, 1959; *Cuatro poemas morales*, 1961; *En favor de Venus*, 1965; *Moralidades*, 1966; *Poemas póstumos*, 1968; and *Las personas del verbo*, 1975.

ÁNGEL GONZÁLEZ (1925–   ) started out as a music critic and journalist. He has traveled to England, France and the United States, where he is now teaching. He published his first book of poems at the age of thirty-one, emerging with a personal style of his own. His work is haunted by the desolation that followed the Spanish Civil War, and there is much bitterness and disillusion under the irony and humor of his poetry.

Áspero mundo, 1956; *Sin esperanza, con convencimiento*, 1961; *Grado elemental*, 1962; *Palabra sobre palabra*, 1968; and *Breves acotaciones para una biografía*, 1971.

JORGE GUILLÉN (1893–   ), well known in the United States as poet and teacher, comes from Valladolid. He lived in Switzerland from 1909 to 1911, in Germany from 1913 to 1914, and taught at the Sorbonne from 1917 to 1923 and at Oxford, 1929–1931. He has also been a professor at McGill University in Canada, for a year, and at various universities in the United States, notably at Wellesley, 1940–1957. He was Charles Eliot Norton lecturer at Harvard in 1957–1958. In 1955 he was given the American Academy of Arts and Letters' Award of Merit and has received many other international prizes for his poetry. Selections of his work have appeared in English in *Cántico*, edited by Norman Thomas di Giovanni for Little, Brown and Co., in *Affirmation*, translations by Julian Palley published by the University of Oklahoma Press, and in many anthologies.

Cántico, 1928, 1936, 1945, 1950 (new poems incorporated into each successive edition); *Maremágnum*, 1957; *... Que van a dar a la mar*, 1960; *A la altura de las circunstancias*, 1963; *Homenaje*, 1967; *Aire nuestro: Cántico, Clamor, Homenaje*, 1968; *Guirnalda civil*, 1970.

MIGUEL HERNÁNDEZ (1910–1942) was a goatherd as a child, even before he started the little schooling he received. He studied for two or three years in his native Orihuela. He began reading books in the school library and, after he quit school to go back to herding his father's goats, he visited the public library regularly, reading indiscriminately at first, but his instinct and his genius quickly put him on to the trail of the poets of the Spanish Golden Age and, later, of the modern poets. He visited Madrid for the first time in 1931 and returned in 1934, when he met Neruda and Aleixandre, who helped him free himself from the tight structure of his earlier work. He was imprisoned at the end of the Spanish Civil War. More than two years in various prisons broke his health completely, and he died of tuberculosis in prison in Alicante, at the age of thirty-two.

Perito en lunas, 1933; *El rayo que no cesa*, 1936; *Viento de Pueblo*, 1937; *Sino sangriento y otros poemas*, 1939; *El hombre acecha*, 1939; *Seis poemas inéditos y nueve más*, 1951; *Cancionero y romancero de ausencias*, 1958; and *Obras completas*, 1960.

JOSÉ LUIS HIDALGO (1919–1947) was poet, painter, engraver, and essayist. His output of poetry was slim but his last book, *Los muertos (The Dead)*, proved him one of the most gifted poets of his generation. *Los muertos*, originally intended as a tribute to the Spanish Civil War dead and written, with the exception of two or

three poems, before he realized he was very ill, is filled with pre-
monitions and now seems a poem in memory of his own life and death.
He died of tuberculosis.

Raíz, 1944; *Los animales*, 1945; *Los muertos*, 1947; *Canciones para
niños*, 1951; and *Antología poética*, 1970.

JOSÉ HIERRO (1922–) was born in Madrid but spent
most of his childhood and adolescence in Santander, where the
Spanish Civil War caught him. Although too young to take an active
part in it, he was thrown into jail for political reasons while still an
adolescent. His second book, *Alegría*, won the Adonais poetry award,
the most coveted prize for young poets in Spain. His later books have
won other important awards. He is an art critic and teaches at
Madrid's Universidad Autónoma.

Tierra sin nosotros, 1947; *Alegría*, 1947; *Con las piedras, con el
viento*, 1950; *Quinta del 42*, 1953; *Antología poética*, 1953; *Estatuas
yacentes*, 1955; *Poesías completas*, 1962; and *Libro de las alucina-
ciones*, 1964.

JUAN RAMÓN JIMÉNEZ (1881–1958). When Juan Ramón
was a boy his father was a winegrower in the sleepy Andalusian town
of Moguer, and he grew up in a large house on the edge of town. After
flunking a history exam, he left law school, in Seville. He went to
Madrid for the first time in 1900 and met Rubén Darío there. In
1916 he visited New York and returned to Spain married to Zenobia
Camprubí Aymar, who was to be so important in his life. With her
he translated Tagore and John Synge into Spanish. He became the
center of literary life in Madrid, helping out younger poets, and yet
he was a recluse, neglecting everyday affairs, and an introspective
poet throughout his life. The books he published in Madrid between
1916 and 1923 were important in the formation of Guillén, Lorca,
Alberti and the other poets of that generation, and were a lasting
influence on Spanish poetry. In 1936 the Republican government

520

sent him as cultural attaché to the United States. He never returned
to Spain. Puerto Rico was his final home, and he received the Nobel
Prize there in 1956.

Almas de violeta, 1900; *Ninfeas*, 1900; *Rimas*, 1902; *Arias tristes*,
1903; *Jardines lejanos*, 1904; *Elejías puras*, 1908; *Elejías inter-
mediarias*, 1909; *Olvidanzas*, 1909; *Elejías lamentables*, 1910;
Baladas de primavera, 1910; *La soledad sonora*, 1911; *Pastorales*,
1911; *Poemas májicos y dolientes*, 1911; *Melancolía*, 1912;
Laberinto, 1913; *Estío*, 1916; *Sonetos espirituales*, 1917; *Diario de
un poeta recién casado*, 1917; *Eternidades*, 1918; *Piedra y cielo*,
1918; *Poesía (1917–1923)*, 1923; *Belleza*, 1923; *Canción*, 1936; *La
estación total con las canciones de la nueva luz*, 1946; *Romances de
Coral Gables*, 1948; *Animal de fondo*, 1949; *Libros de poesía*, 1959;
Primeros libros de poesía, 1959; *Libros inéditos de poesía*, 1964.

ANTONIO MACHADO (1875–1939). He was born in
Seville and moved to Madrid with his parents in 1883. His first
published writings were humorous articles. In 1889 he went to Paris
where he worked as translator. There he met Rubén Darío, to whom
he timidly showed his first poems. A few months later he was back
in Madrid, signing up as an actor with a theater company. In 1903
he published his first book of poems, *Soledades*. He settled in Soria
four years later, as a teacher of high school French. There he married
Leonor Izquierdo, his landlady's daughter; he was thirty-four and
she sixteen. She died of consumption two years later. Deeply affected,
he requested a transfer and was sent to Baeza, in Andalusia, far
from everything that reminded him of his dead wife. In 1919 he
once more requested a transfer and was assigned to Segovia, near
Madrid, which he could visit regularly and where he finally settled
in 1931. His most important writings from then on are the prose
commentaries on literature, philosophy, and politics that appear in
Juan de Mairena and the posthumous *Los complementarios*.
Machado's immersion in the language of the simple man, his awareness of the problems of his time, and his exemplary goodness attracted the first two generations of poets after the Spanish Civil War

as Jiménez, who had been so withdrawn from his times, did not. During the Civil War Machado was evacuated to Valencia. He died in Collioure in 1939, one month after crossing the French border with thousands of other refugees.

Soledades, 1903; *Soledades, galerías y otros poemas,* 1907; *Campos de Castilla,* 1912; *Poesías completas,* 1917, 1928, 1933, 1970; *Nuevas canciones,* 1924; *Obras. Poesía y prosa* (ed. by Aurora Albornoz and Guillermo de Torre), 1964.

BLAS DE OTERO (1916–   ) is generally considered the best poet to appear in Spain since the end of the Spanish Civil War. Although he is always placed side by side with Celaya as the most important of the social poets, Otero's work is never slack and careless, but rich and complex. Much of his work has appeared in mutilated form in Spain, where no new book was published between 1955 and 1964, when a badly chopped-up version of *Que trata de España* was published in Barcelona. (The book appeared whole in the Ruedo Ibérico edition in Paris the same year.) Since then he has published a book of new poems and his first book of prose, *Historias fingidas y verdaderas,* in 1970.

Cántico espiritual, 1942; *Ángel fieramente humano,* 1950; *Redoble de conciencia,* 1951; *Pido la paz y la palabra,* 1955; *Ancia,* 1958; *En castellano,* 1960; *Este no es un libro,* 1963; *Que trata de España,* 1964; and *Mientras,* 1970.

EMILIO PRADOS (1899–1962) was born in Malaga, where he attended grade school with Vicente Aleixandre. He studied natural sciences at the University of Madrid, where he met Lorca. In 1920 he fell ill with consumption and spent a year in Switzerland. He studied philosophy in Germany for a year. Back in Malaga, he and another young poet, Manuel Altolaguirre, started a private press to bring out the books of the best poets of their generation. At the same time, they published *Litoral,* an important literary review that carried the current work of the young poets. At the end of the Spanish Civil War he crossed the French border and later went into exile in Mexico, where he died on April 24, 1962.

Tiempo, 1925; *Canción del farero*, 1927; *Vuelta*, 1927; *El llanto subterraneo*, 1936; *Llanto en la sangre*, 1937; *Cancionero menor*, 1939; *Memoria del olvido*, 1940; *Mínima muerte*, 1942; *Jardín cerrado*, 1946; *Dormido en la yerba*, 1953; *Río natural*, 1957; *Circuncisión del sueño*, 1957; *La piedra escrita*, 1961; *Últimos poemas*, 1965.

CLAUDIO RODRÍGUEZ (1934–   ) is one of the outstanding poets of his generation. Although he is alive to his time and is critical of its moral disintegration, his poems move on the margin of the social poetry written in the fifties and sixties. The world around him is carefully taken in by his imagination and its objects retain their clear outlines, even when they turn into symbols to illustrate the poet's inner life and his moral judgments. He was lecturer in Spanish at Nottingham University from 1958 to 1960 and at Cambridge from 1960 to 1964.

Don de la ebriedad, 1953; *Conjuros*, 1958; *Alianza y condena*, 1965; and *Poesía* (*1953–1956*), 1971.

LUIS ROSALES (1910–   ). His first book, *Abril*, published in 1935, marked a new direction in Spanish poetry. Unfortunately, it led back to an old source, Garcilaso de la Vega, from whose poetry he and most of the other poets of his generation borrowed only its exterior elegance and formal perfection. It was escapist and generally religious in tone, and it seems outdated now. However, Rosales' later work is different, especially *La casa encendida*, which uses surrealism in a subtle and quiet, though insistent, manner. Rosales has also written plays and literary criticism.

Abril, 1935; *La casa encendida*, 1949, 1967; *Rimas*, 1951; *Segundo abril*, 1973.

CARLOS SAHAGÚN (1938–   ) wrote a slim book of poems, *Hombre naciente*, at the age of sixteen. His second and third books won important poetry awards. Dominant in these early books is the theme of growing up in the wake of the Spanish Civil War. In his last book, his concern turns from himself to others who also have to breathe the oppressive air of Franco's Spain. He taught at the University of Exeter in 1960–1961.

Profecías del agua, 1958; *Como si hubiera muerto un niño*, 1961; and *Estar contigo*, 1973.

PEDRO SALINAS (1891–1951) was born in Madrid where he carried out all his studies, receiving his Ph.D. in literature in 1916 at the University of Madrid. From 1914 to 1917 he was an instructor at the Sorbonne and he also taught at Cambridge University, in 1922–1923. In 1936 he went to the United States, where he taught at various colleges and universities, living in exile there—except for the period 1942–1945, when he was visiting professor at the University of Puerto Rico—until his death in Boston in 1951. He translated the works of Proust into Spanish. He himself was widely translated. His Turnbull Lectures on Poetry at John Hopkins University were published in book form as *Reality and the Poet in Spanish Poetry*. Selections of his poems appeared in *Lost Angel and Other Poems* and *Truth of Two*. His work has been included in many anthologies in Great Britain and the United States. In addition to poetry, he wrote important literary criticism, plays, and fiction.

Presagios, 1923; *Seguro azar*, 1929; *Fábula y signo*, 1933; *La voz a ti debida*, 1933; *Razón de amor*, 1936; *El contemplado*, 1946; *Todo más claro y otros poemas*, 1949; *Confianza*, 1955; *Poesías completas*, 1971.

MIGUEL DE UNAMUNO (1864–1936). At the age of fifteen Unamuno finished his preuniversity studies in his native Bilbao, and he received his Ph.D. from Madrid University in 1884.

In 1891 he moved to Salamanca to take over the chair of Greek at the university there. He became its rector in 1901 but was fired in 1914 for political reasons. However, he went on teaching at the university until February 1924, when he was exiled by the dictator Primo de Rivera to one of the Canary Islands, Fuerteventura. He escaped to France in June of that same year. Although he was granted pardon by the Spanish government, he refused to return to his country until the collapse of the dictatorship in 1930. He returned to Salamanca and, with the founding of the Republic, which he helped to build (he was appointed president of the Council of National Culture by the provisional government), he was once more made president of the university. In 1935 he was named Citizen of Honor of the Republic. He sided briefly with the Nationalists at the beginning of the Spanish Civil War but he declared himself against them in a speech he gave on Columbus Day (called in Spain *"el día de la Raza"*), 1936. He died suddenly on New Year's Eve of that year.

Known in the United States mainly for his philosophy and his fiction, Unamuno considered himself a poet first of all, although he did not publish his first book until 1907, when he was already famous for his prose. In spite of his unevenness, he is one of the most important twentieth-century Spanish poets.

Poesías, 1907; *Rosario de sonetos líricos,* 1911; *El Cristo de Velázquez,* 1920; *Andanzas y visiones españolas,* 1922; *Rimas de dentro,* 1923; *Teresa,* 1924; *De Fuerteventura a París,* 1925; *Romancero del destierro,* 1928; *Cancionero. Diario poético,* 1953; and *Obras completas,* vol. XIII, 1962, and vols. XIV, XV, 1963.

JOSÉ ÁNGEL VALENTE (1929–) began his university studies in Santiago de Compostela, in his native Galicia, but he graduated in philology from Madrid University. Although much of his poetry criticizes or openly attacks the dishonesty, hypocrisy, or indifference of those who have been running his country since the end of the Spanish Civil War, Valente has also always been a serious craftsman. His language is simple on the surface but complex in the context of the whole poem, not affectedly plain like the language of many poets of the generation immediately preceding his. He taught at Oxford from 1955 to 1958. He has been living in Geneva, Switzerland, since 1958. He is a noted critic as well as translator.

A modo de esperanza, 1955; *Poemas a Lázaro,* 1960; *Sobre el lugar del canto,* 1963; *La memoria y los signos,* 1966; *Siete representaciones,* 1967; *Breve son,* 1968; *Presentación y memorial para un monumento,* 1970; *El inocente* and *Punto cero,* 1973.

MANUEL VÁZQUEZ MONTALBÁN (1939–) is a prolific writer who has published novels, literary and sociological essays, and popular song lyrics. He has written a political column for a daily newspaper and is contributing editor for a weekly magazine, *Triunfo,* which has been frequently suppressed for its outspokenness. In 1962 he was sentenced to jail for taking part in the Barcelona student demonstrations supporting the mining strikes in Asturias. He served a year and a half of his sentence. In his poems as well as in his prose Vázquez Montalbán tries to destroy the valueless symbols of the culture of the twentieth century, especially the false myths built up around popular heroes (presidents, dictators, generals, movie actors, singers, celebrities, etc.) by the mass media. He makes frequent use of collage, borrowing from popular song lyrics, movies, ads, popular phrases and novels, and from older poets, sometimes parodying their style. But there is tenderness as well as irony and humor in his poems, which turn their sights on a world "where there is no room for fear or for courage."

Una educación sentimental, 1967; *Movimientos sin éxito,* 1969; *Coplas a la muerte de mi Tía Daniela* and *A la sombra de las muchachas sin flor,* 1973.

Index of Poets ❧

Index of Translators ❧

* Donald Hall thanks Larry Russ and Shelley Siegel for helping him with his translations.